God Thoughts

One Hundred Essays and Devotions

Ronnie Worsham

ISBN: 1985238381
ISBN 13: 9781985238381

To my faithful pastoral friends and ministry colleagues of the DFW Metro Family of Churches who exemplify to me daily true spirituality, stretching me in my experience of God and provoking within me deeper and richer thoughts about Him. Your friendship and partnership have made my past worthwhile and the future much brighter.

In Memory of

Ott Hollis, a country church Sunday-school teacher at the Ratliff City [Oklahoma] Church of Christ who six decades ago sparked a tiny, flickering flame inside of the heart of a little boy with a prayer that would ultimately become a fire in my heart:

"Father, give us the wisdom to use the knowledge that we have."

This prayer was the light and prayer that remained when all the other lights in me had seemingly died, and its yearning lies at the core of the thoughts herein.

And also the countless other oft-forgotten Sunday-school teachers who have undoubtedly done similarly in other young hearts in the church over its ages.

A Prayer

Lord, give my faith wings to fly,
Where the hearts of angels go,
Help my mind to dare imagine,
That which only faith can know.

Help me to believe in your love,
Know your immeasurable grace,
Let me share your banquet table,
Forever gaze upon your face.

Help my heart to be as your heart,
My desires to align with yours,
Give me eyes to see your presence,
Deep resolve that e'er endures.

God, you know my heart gets weary,
Lord, you know my faith grows weak,
But you see my deepest motives,
Know it's only you I seek.

I praise you with my being, Lord,
I laud you in my heart,
I bow before your presence,
To you all thankfulness impart!

Table of Contents

Introduction

I HAVE CALLED this book *God Thoughts* because it represents a collection of my thoughts about God, flowing generally from my daily quiet times with him. Although I do not see them as merely my thoughts alone, neither am I claiming they are wholly and divinely revealed thoughts received directly from God. I believe that they are a mixture of both. They are thoughts and insights that God has stirred within me over the decades as I have studied, prayed, and sought him. Those who know me well will see their application throughout my life, ministry, and communication.

Never have I felt myself a likely man of God. I am "too" in too many ways. I am too skeptical. My analytic mindset coupled with my early life experiences have made me naturally wary, making it difficult for me to believe the seemingly "unbelievable" things of life and God, and even worse, making it difficult for me to trust God, let alone others.

I am too worldly. I've often seen monasteries as an escape from the realities of the world, but I naturally spurn the austere and difficult. I like to feel good; I don't like to feel badly. I am by no means drawn to be an ascetic. Instinctively, I want what I want when I want it. I like comfort. I like my personal freedom where no one tells me what to do. I like my personal space where others cannot invade without my permission.

I am often melancholy. I am too emotional and feel too deeply. I get my feelings hurt too easily. I'm too sensitive.

I'm too complex. I can experience huge emotional swings in a short time. I am too temperamental. I am too conflicted on too many things.

Don't get me wrong; I don't simply yield to these overbearing inclinations of mine. I work daily at being self-controlled and spiritually sensible. I strive to keep my head in all circumstances. But I definitely hope to encourage those who feel similarly. And I know everyone does, at least sometimes.

But my ministry experiences with countless people tell me that I'm not alone. Thus, comes this compilation of my thoughts from over the years, drawing from scripture and a wide variety of life experiences. There is no particular order to these devotion thoughts, other than they appear alphabetically according to the title I gave each of them, and thus, the way my computer saved them. Each devotional essay is written fairly independently of all the others so that those who read and meditate on them can hopscotch around the various devotion thoughts without having missed something. Thus, there is much repetition of thoughts and explanations among them.

Scripture quotations are from the New International Version of the Bible, 2011, unless otherwise noted. I used other translations and paraphrases in certain instances, not because I was looking for a translation that said what I wanted, but because I wanted to use the translation that best worded the various scriptures as I personally understand them. Also, I added italics in certain scripture quotations for emphasis, and when I did, I noted it.

With all that said, my purpose in writing this is to draw people to God. I love God. I love the wisdom of God. I am a lifelong student of subjects secular and religious, but there's nothing I have ever seen like the insights scripture gives us on life. And as unbelievable as I often feel it all to be, I believe God is real and that he reveals himself every day and in every way. To me, the world reveals its creator everywhere one looks.

We have to, however, live reborn in order to "get it"—to see him—"No one can see the kingdom of God unless they are born again" (John 3:3). Therefore, we must pray and strive to have our heart's eyes opened so that we can see—have revealed to us by his Spirit—the unimaginable beauty that underlies both what appears to us now variously as the beautiful, the mundane, and sometimes the downright horrible. The hope (the very real expectation) that we have been given in Christ is simply incredible, and we can only understand it all through the power of the Holy Spirit. The scripture says, "No one has ever seen, no one has ever heard, no one has ever imagined what God has prepared for those who love him. But God has shown us these things through the Spirit" (1 Cor. 2:9–10). Those led by the Spirit of God will have opened to them the unimaginable by the one whose power is immeasurable.

So finally, Paul's prayer for all of us is my prayer for you, my readers—"And [I pray] that the eyes of your heart [the very center and core of your being] may be enlightened [flooded with light by the Holy Spirit], so that you will know *and* cherish the hope [the divine guarantee, the confident expectation] to which He has called you" (Eph. 1:18, Amplified Bible).

I pray that these, my own mind and heart thoughts, coupled with the Spirit's insights, may inspire the enrichment of your own experience of God.

1
Advice and Wise Counsel

In seeking wise counsel and advice from godly people, we find not bondage and control from others; rather we find incredible freedom from life's obstacles and consequences and the glorious blessings that come from good choices.

Wisdom is found in those who take advice
(Prov. 13:10).

WE SHOW OURSELVES to be fools when we fail to seek out, listen to, and take to heart godly wisdom. Claiming to be listening only to God while ignoring wise counsel from others is blatantly contradictory to the scripture.

When we come to see and know God, we instantly become much more humble. In following God we come to understand just how our limited, individual human capacity is to reason out righteousness within our self. Rather than resent wisdom and advice from others, we will embrace it—"The fear of the LORD is the beginning of knowledge, but fools despise wisdom and instruction" (Prov.

1:7). Despising wisdom and discipline means to fail to listen to or to take advice.

The modern mantra seems to be "follow your heart." That is as biblically ridiculous as it can possibly be—"The heart is deceitful above all things and beyond cure. Who can understand it?" (Jer. 17:9). The human *heart* that is not reined in by the rational mind is a corrupt, deceptive thing, because its reasoning is of the fleshly, the carnal, the worldly. The human *mind* that is not reined in by the word of God is even more corrupt, as it is finite, limited, worldly, and easily deceived. It ultimately finds itself opposing God. It can, as well, be cold, self-centered, and calculating.

But when the mind is guided by the word of God and the heart is guided by the mind filled with God's truth, wise living is the result—"Trust the Lord completely, and don't depend on your own knowledge. With every step you take, think about what he wants, and he will help you go the right way. Don't trust in your own wisdom, but fear and respect the Lord and stay away from evil" (Prov. 3:5–7, Easy-to-Read Version).

Listening to God's guidance makes our lifestyles as steady, even-keeled, and peaceful as is humanly possible in this world—"I am the Lord your God, who teaches you what is best for you, who directs you in the way you should go. If only you had paid attention to my commands, your peace would have been like a river, your well-being like the waves of the sea" (Isa. 48:17–18).

And God chooses to speak to us through people, especially those he has appointed—"So Christ himself gave the apostles, the prophets, the evangelists, the pastors and teachers, to equip his people for works of service, so that the body of Christ may be built up until we all reach unity in the faith and in the knowledge of the Son of God and become mature, attaining to the whole measure of the fullness of Christ. Then we will no longer be infants, tossed back and forth by the waves, and blown here and there by every wind of teaching and by the cunning and craftiness of people in their deceitful scheming" (Eph. 4:11). He calls, appoints, and directs godly leaders, and he has commanded them to carefully speak truth and wisdom into our lives—"Preach the word; be prepared in season and out of season; correct, rebuke and encourage—with great patience and careful instruction" (2 Tim. 4:2).

Not only that, he has commanded *all* Christians to be filled with his word and to share it with one another—"Let the message of Christ dwell among you richly as you teach and admonish one another with all wisdom through psalms, hymns, and songs from the Spirit, singing to God with gratitude in your hearts" (Col. 3:16). We are all to be bearers of God's word and wisdom to one another. And we are commanded, in respect of Christ, to listen to and follow, with humble, submissive spirits, the other members of his body—"Submit to one another out of reverence for Christ" (Eph. 5:21).

It is possible and in many cases probable that we, as humans, can be absolutely convinced that a thing or a way of life is good and right, and yet, be completely wrong—"There is a way that seems right to a man, but its end is the way to death" (Prov. 14:12). In fact, it is in our foolishness that we are often most defensive and defiant and most convinced we are right—"The way of fools seems right to them, but the wise listen to advice" (Prov. 12:15).

We should certainly first look prayerfully to God's word for answers that God has already given to us through scripture. Then, if the answers and applications of those scriptures are not clear, we should ask God himself for the wisdom to discern—"If any of you lacks wisdom, you should ask God, who gives generously to all without finding fault, and it will be given to you" (James 1:5). We should as well seek godly advice from those whose lives look like Jesus—"Consider the outcome of their way of life and imitate their faith" (Heb. 13:7).

However, far too many, out of carelessness and laziness, blindly and unwisely follow tradition and human-heart reasoning to determine their paths—"Those who trust in their own reasoning are fools, but those who walk in wisdom will be kept safe" (Prov. 28:26, Common English Bible), and "See to it that nobody enslaves you with philosophy and foolish deception, which conform to human traditions and the way the world thinks and acts rather than Christ" (Col. 2:8, Common English Bible). Rather the wise one seeks and listens to advice thus becoming even wiser, while the foolish one listens to other fools or listens not at all and becomes even more foolish!

God works in us through his scripture, the Holy Spirit, and prayer, as well as the body of Christ, the church, both individually and collectively. If we will be keen to listen to him speak however and whenever he does, we will become wiser—"Listen to advice and accept discipline, and at the end you will be counted among the wise. Many are the plans in a person's heart, but it is the Lord's purpose that prevails" (Prov. 19:20–21). It is through God-given wisdom that his will wins out in our lives!

Jesus's sheep will recognize and follow his voice however he may speak—"My sheep hear my voice, and I know them, and they follow me" (John 10:27). Because of the Holy Spirit in us, we can even recognize when it is *not* Jesus speaking to us—"But they will never follow a stranger; in fact, they will run away from him because they do not recognize a stranger's voice" (John 10:5). We listen and follow because we trust him.

God is forever communicating to us, and we would do well to listen up!

A Prayer:

> Give me a heart to seek truth, Lord,
> Give me the desire to seek you,
> Grant me a heart that is humble,
> And that always listens for you.

Help me to hear you in all ways,
Through the Spirit, the scripture, and others,
Teach me to seek out your wisdom,
Through advice from sisters and brothers.

Defeat within me my arrogance and blindness,
Forsake me not in my independent way,
Teach me to treat as valuable each moment,
To make the most of each and every day!

2
Anger

Anger left to its own device is vicious without limit.
It is a most lethal weapon.

Human anger does not produce the righteousness that God desires (James 1:20).

EVERYONE GETS ANGRY sometimes. Some get angry a lot of times. Anger is a part of our human experience. It is inevitable. But it must never be ignored. Ever. We either deal with it God's way and get the win or it will "deal on" us, and we will lose. And when we lose to our anger, so do all the others we affect.

There is a righteous anger, but still the Holy Spirit must be allowed to rein it in for us. Jesus displayed such anger on occasions—"He [Jesus] made a whip out of cords, and drove all from the temple courts, both sheep and cattle; he scattered the coins of the money changers and overturned their tables" (John 2:15). But evil still seeks opportunity even in righteous anger!

Reactive, spontaneous anger is an emotion seemingly designed to help the flesh survive. It is reactive to ongoing stimuli and occurrences. It stimulates our body and gets us going. It spurs us to act. But it is also impulsive and thoughtless. In fact, it actually suppresses logic. This kind of anger sends us strong warning signals that something is wrong, unjust, or threatening. As with fear, anger quickens our minds and bodies to be alert and ready. But when we get angry, sin is lurking nearby, and thus, we must handle our anger rightly—"*Why are you angry*? Why is your face downcast? If you do what is right, will you not be accepted? But *if you do not do what is right, sin is crouching at your door*; it desires to have you, but you must rule over it" (Gen. 4:6–7, italics added). When we do get angry, quickly asking ourselves why we are angry will stimulate logic, therefore suppressing the anger emotions, at least to some degree.

Reactive anger within itself is not a sin. But it can quickly turn into sin if we allow it to do so—"'In your anger do not sin': Do not let the sun go down while you are still angry, and do not give the devil a foothold" (Eph. 4:26–27; Psa. 4:4). Through anger, evil sees opportunity and seeks a foothold in our lives. Anger that gains a foothold will ultimately become a stronghold, if we idly let it happen. So, it is best that we not allow anger to gain a foothold inside of us, and we can do that by taking our "emotional thoughts" captive for Christ. The word of God will help us discern and eliminate the thoughts of the heart that are wrong—"The word of God is alive and active. Sharper than any double-edged sword, it penetrates even to dividing soul and spirit, joints and marrow; *it judges the thoughts and attitudes of the heart*" (Heb. 4:12, italics added). We must through the guidance of the word and the power of the Holy Spirit remove evil's foot from our heart's door by addressing and resolving our anger issues quickly.

On the other hand, anger that is not dealt with, and thus becomes pervasive and long-term within us, is an even bigger thing. It comes to seethe in us just below the surface and grow its roots into our hearts. It manifests itself in all kinds of ways—fits of rage, negativity, malice, grudges, vindictiveness, ill will, slander, division, and so forth. It may appear outwardly as only of the reactive kind, but in actuality it is not. Rather it originates from something far deeper and more malignant that resides in our heart. The underlying anger may begin at some point with a single anger reaction, but because right action was not taken, it settled in, and the foothold becomes a stronghold. Such strongholds can only be beaten through God's power and approaches—"The weapons we fight with are not the weapons of the world. On the contrary, they have divine power to demolish strongholds" (2 Cor. 10:4).

Jesus gave a serious warning about this kind of anger—"You have heard that it was said to the men of old, 'You shall not murder,' and 'Whoever murders shall be guilty before the court.' But I say to you that everyone who continues to be angry with his brother *or* harbors malice against him shall be guilty before the court; and whoever speaks [contemptuously and insultingly] to his brother, 'Raca (You empty-headed idiot)!' shall be guilty before the supreme court (Sanhedrin); and whoever says, 'You fool!' shall be in danger of the fiery hell" (Matt. 5:22–23, Amplified Bible). Such anger toward another is indeed inwardly murderous.

Losing our temper is a shortsighted and foolish way to handle anger—"A [shortsighted] fool always loses his temper *and* displays his anger, but a wise man [uses self-control and] holds it back" (Prov. 29:11, Amplified Bible). A short temper makes us do foolish things, and unresolved anger causes us to continue to behave aggressively or passive aggressively—"Short-tempered people make stupid mistakes, and schemers are hated" (Prov. 14:17, Common English Bible).

With foresight, by using the word of God and taking thoughts captive, anger can be contained and controlled—"Good sense *and* discretion make a man slow to anger. And it is his honor *and* glory to overlook a transgression *or* an offense [without seeking revenge and harboring resentment]" (Prov. 19:11, Amplified Bible). The world tells us to always resolve anger by expressing it. The word of God tells us to control what we say and do according to God's will—"Do not let any unwholesome talk come out of your mouths, but only what is helpful for building others up according to their needs, that it may benefit those who listen" (Eph. 4:29).

We must seek to control our anger by the thoughts we intentionally think. And if it seeps into our heart, we must arrest it quickly—"Refrain from anger and turn from wrath; do not fret—it leads only to evil. For those who are evil will be destroyed, but those who hope in the Lord will inherit the land" (Ps. 37:8–9). Through self-control and keeping our head, we must learn to be slow to become angry, because by doing so, we become spiritually and emotionally powerful—"He who is slow to anger is better *and* more honorable than the mighty [soldier]. And he who rules *and* controls his own spirit, than he who captures a city" (Prov. 16:32, Amplified Bible), and "Don't be too quick to get angry because anger lives in the fool's heart" (Eccles. 7:9).

Being easily angered is detrimental to both our own well-being and to that of others. Rather God calls us, as his children, to be peacemakers, not troublemakers. Hotheaded people can only cause trouble—"A hot-tempered person stirs up conflict, but the one who is patient calms a quarrel" (Prov. 15:18).

Rather God calls us to resist anger, deal with anger quickly, and to completely get rid of any anger lingering in our hearts—"But now rid yourselves [completely] of all these things: anger, rage, malice, slander, and obscene (abusive, filthy, vulgar) language from your mouth" (Col. 3:8, Amplified Bible). In doing so, peace will be ours—"You will go out in joy and be led forth in peace" (Isa. 55:12).

Deal with anger quickly lest it erode your sanity and become within you destructive and ruinous.

A Prayer:

Holy Spirit, rein in my heart and mind and conform them to yours.
Teach me to keep my head in all circumstances.
Grow me in self-control that I may be slow to anger and careful in expressing it.
Give me spiritual sanity that I may love you, and only you, with all my heart and mind.
Be Lord of my heart, O Jesus!
Amen.

3
Apostasy and Falling Away

Apostasy, or departing from truth and faithfulness, seems to be so far removed from most of us that we never consider it a pitfall for ourselves. But that is potentially a grave error on our part, both for us and those around us.

Be careful in your life and in your teaching. Continue to live and teach rightly. Then you will save yourself and those who listen to your teaching (1 Tim. 4:16, Easy-to-Read Version).

CREATION POINTS US to the reality of God—"For since the creation of the world God's invisible qualities—his eternal power and divine nature—have been clearly seen, being understood from what has been made, so that people are without excuse" (Rom. 1:20). And the Bible subsequently clearly points us to the reality of Jesus as the one Lord and Savior—"I am the way and the truth and the life. No one comes to the Father except through me" (John 14:6).

Christ never equivocated about who he was—"Anyone who has seen me has seen the Father" (John 14:9). Nor did his apostles equivocate about Christ's deity—"In the beginning was the Word, and the Word was with God, and the Word was God. He was with God in the beginning. Through him all things were made; without him nothing was made that has been made...The Word became flesh and made his dwelling among us. We have seen his glory, the glory of the one and only Son, who came from the Father, full of grace and truth" (John 1:1–3, 14).

It seems clear and logical, at least to most of us, that there are some things that are true and there are some things that aren't. There is truth, and there is untruth. There is the authentic and the inauthentic. And nothing is truer or more real than that Jesus is the Christ. All creation originated through him and was made for his purposes—"All things have been created through him and for him" (Col. 1:16).

Early on in human history, many rejected belief in God in favor of a human-centered existence—humanism. Many still do. They believed Satan's original lie and attempted to rewrite reality, writing God out of the script and humanity into its lead role—"They exchanged the truth about God for a lie, and worshiped and served created things rather than the Creator—who is forever praised" (Rom. 1:25). During his time on earth, many rejected Jesus as the Lord and Savior of the world—"He came to that which was his own, but his own did not receive him" (John 1:11).

But those who believed in and received him found truth and life—"To all who did receive him, to those who believed in his name, he gave the right to become children of God—children born not of natural descent, nor of human decision or a husband's will, but born of God" (John 1:12–13). It was no surprise, however, that while some would accept him, many would reject him. It had been clearly prophesied hundreds of years before he came—"He was despised and rejected by mankind, a man of suffering, and familiar with pain.

Like one from whom people hide their faces he was despised, and we held him in low esteem" (Isa. 53:3).

Although the majority of the world still accepts Jesus Christ as Lord, at least to some degree and in various ways, many have long "tripped over" believing in the reality of his deity—"But to those who do not believe, 'The stone the builders rejected has become the cornerstone,' and, 'A stone that causes people to stumble and a rock that makes them fall'" (1 Pet. 2:7–8, Ps. 118:22, Isa. 8:14). From his arrival and since his departure, Jesus has been the source of much strife, controversy, fighting, and war.

And just as it was prophesied that some would come to him and many would not, it was also prophesied that some, after coming to believe in and follow Jesus, would stop following him, falling so far as to listen to and follow demons—"The Spirit clearly says that in later times some will abandon the faith and follow deceiving spirits and things taught by demons" (1 Tim. 4:1). This is apostasy. This is falling away. It was inevitable.

Although inevitable, it certainly is not desirable—"If they have escaped the corruption of the world by knowing our Lord and Savior Jesus Christ and are again entangled in it and are overcome, they are worse off at the end than they were at the beginning. It would have been better for them not to have known the way of righteousness, than to have known it and then to turn their backs on the sacred command that was passed on to them" (2 Pet. 2:20–22).

Acceptance of Christ by faith is not such a complex thing, although accepting him as Lord will be challenging to those who want a savior without a Lord. But for those who stay firmly in the faith of Christ, there is great assurance—"I give them eternal life, and they shall never perish; no one will snatch them out of my hand" (John 10:28). But even for we believers, renouncing him or becoming complacent about him can still bring about an ultimate demise—"But we do not belong to those who shrink back and are destroyed" (Heb. 10:39), and "So, because you are lukewarm—neither hot nor cold—I am about to spit you out of my mouth" (Rev. 3:16).

Frighteningly, there is even such a rejection of Christ by a believer that brings such judgment from God that repentance and renewal is impossible—"It is impossible for those who have once been enlightened, who have tasted the heavenly gift, who have shared in the Holy Spirit, who have tasted the goodness of the word of God and the powers of the coming age and who have fallen away, to be brought back to repentance. To their loss they are crucifying the Son of God all over again and subjecting him to public disgrace" (Heb. 6:4–6). The bottom line is that God is not to be toyed with, even by his adopted children!

As believers we must make sure we do not fall prey to such an evil fate—"Therefore, my brothers and sisters, make every effort to confirm your calling and election. For if you do these things, you will never stumble, and you will receive a rich welcome into the eternal kingdom of our Lord and Savior Jesus Christ" (2 Pet. 1:10–11). We must make sure we are not the shallow soil on top of the rock that Jesus warned of—"Those on the rocky ground are the ones who receive the word with joy when they hear it, but they have no root. They believe for a while, but in the time of testing they fall away" (Luke 8:13). Nor do we want to be among those who allow the worldly to choke out the godly from us—"The seed that fell among thorns stands for those who hear, but as they go on their way they are choked by life's worries, riches and pleasures, and they do not mature" (Luke 8:14).

The warning of the apostle is still as clear as ever—"For the time will come when people will not put up with sound doctrine. Instead, to suit their own desires, they will gather around them a great number of teachers to say what their itching ears want to hear. They will turn their ears away from the truth and turn aside to myths" (2 Tim.

4:3–4). And we as believers must be ever alert and keep our faith squarely and firmly in Jesus—"Therefore, dear friends, since you have been forewarned, be on your guard so that you may not be carried away by the error of the lawless and fall from your secure position" (2 Pet. 3:17).

We must choose every day to firmly, boldly, and resolutely follow Jesus, and Jesus only, holding faithfully to him with all of our hearts, souls, and minds. And our fate is to be confident and not fearful as long as we remain faithful—"Such confidence we have through Christ before God" (2 Cor. 3:4).

A Prayer:

> Father, help my faith in you be resolute and my decision final.
> May I never be numbered among those who forsake you for a single moment.
> Jesus, be ever Lord of my every thought and action.
> May I always live for your glory and praise.
> Give me, toward you and your Spirit, an alert, eager mind and a soft, receptive heart.
> Keep me from falling back into unbelief or to be led astray from a pure and sincere devotion to Christ.
> Convict me, Lord, when my zeal withers and my commitment wanes.
> Save me, my loved ones, and all my descendants to the coming of Christ.
> Amen.

4
Approving of God

God does not need our justification or approval for who he is and what he does; we however desperately need his.

Oh, the depth of the riches of the wisdom and knowledge of God! How unsearchable his judgments, and his paths beyond tracing out! Who has known the mind of the Lord? Or who has been his counselor? Who has ever given to God, that God should repay them? For from him and through him and for him are all things. To him be the glory forever! Amen (Rom. 11:33–36).

IT IS ARROGANT and ignorant of ourselves to decide if we like or agree with someone(s) or something(s) before we decide whether we will believe in it (or them) or not. It is even more arrogant to figure ourselves to be the determiners of morality and righteousness in the first place—"But who are you, a human being, to talk back to God? Shall what is formed say to the one who formed it, 'Why did you make me like this?'" (Rom. 9:20).

As if to say, "I could never believe in a God who did such and such," when in fact, God's reality and sovereignty is in no way contingent or dependent on our ability to believe or agree with it all. When the wind blows from the north, it is useless to question whether it is blowing out of the north, because it is obvious. When it is a cold northerly, it does not help to decide not to believe in it because we do not like the cold air. Our belief changes reality in no way; however, it does cause us to lose touch with reality and live irrationally.

It is the same way with whether or not we believe in God. God is wholly independent of us, not the other way around. His first stated "name" in scripture is "I AM WHO I AM" (Exod. 3:14). He is the ever existent and unchanging one. If he exists and is who he says he is, then he does not need our belief nor does he need our approval to exist and do whatever it is he wants.

But we most definitely need his approval!

God has not only made his existence obvious; he has also clearly demonstrated his power and godly nature—"For since the creation of the world God's invisible qualities—his eternal power and divine nature—have been clearly seen, being understood from what has been made, so that people are without excuse" (Rom. 1:20). He ought to be obvious to us all. But those obsessed with themselves and intent on trying to control the world around them miss God mostly or altogether, seeing only themselves.

The reality is that the universe exists. And for many, perhaps even most, of us, the idea of an ever-existent or a self-creating universe is utterly ridiculous—"The fool says in his heart, 'There is no God'" (Ps. 14:1). God is the "Great I AM," not the "Great 'Who I Want Him to Be.'"

Because it denies the most basic reality, the result of unbelief is devastating—"They exchanged the truth about God for a lie, and worshiped and served created things rather than the Creator—who is forever praised" (Rom. 1:25), and "Furthermore, just as they did not think it worthwhile to retain the knowledge of God, so God gave them over to a depraved mind, so that they do what ought not to be done" (Rom. 1:28).

It should not be as Demosthenes, the Greek orator, is noted as having said centuries ago, "We believe what we want to believe." Rather it should be, "We believe what an honest, logical assessment suggests."

God has designed it so that only in total surrender to the reality that he is a good and merciful God will we be able to test and discern what his actual will for us even is—"With eyes wide open to the mercies of God, I beg you, my brothers, as an act of intelligent worship, to give him your bodies, as a living sacrifice, consecrated to him and acceptable by him. Don't let the world around you squeeze you into its own mould [sic], but let God re-mould your minds from within, so that you may prove in practice that the plan of God for you is good, meets all his demands and moves towards the goal of true maturity" (Rom. 12:1–2, J. B. Phillips New Testament).

When we feel the existence and nature of God is contingent on our approval, we commit a fatal error in logic and judgment. When we refuse to believe because we refuse to agree, we make an even greater mistake. God is who he is, and we best figure that out and conform ourselves to his reality. Those who know him can attest that the result of doing so is very positive indeed!

A Prayer:

> Lord, grant me an honest heart and mind to seek and see the reality of you.
> Help me not be counted among the fools who deny you—who you are and what you are.
> Give me wisdom to use the knowledge that I have to grow in a conscious faith.

Defeat within me the kind of arrogance that would assume that you and the world around me need my approval in order for you and it to be real or to be deemed good.
Give me a sound mind and help me to keep my head in all circumstances.
Amen.

5
Armor of God

God has for us an armor that is as real as anything humans can fashion. Although it is invisible to our present eyes, it is most visible to those forces that oppose us.

Put on the full armor of God, so that you can take your stand against the devil's schemes. For our struggle is not against flesh and blood, but against the rulers, against the authorities, against the powers of this dark world and against the spiritual forces of evil in the heavenly realms (Eph. 6:11–12).

WHEN WE COME to Christ, God puts his Holy Spirit in us to transform us and guide us—"He anointed us, set his seal of ownership on us, and put his Spirit in our hearts as a deposit, guaranteeing what is to come" (2 Cor. 1:21–22). Therefore, God doesn't just work *on* us from the outside, as we live our lives by faith in him, he works *from within* us to carry out his plan for us as his children—"Work out your salvation with fear and trembling, for *it is God who* *works in you* to will and to act in order to fulfill his good purpose" (Phil. 2:12–13, italics added).

By water and the Spirit we are borne out of living only for this world and are borne into God's kingdom—"Very truly I tell you, no one can see the kingdom of God unless they are born again...Very truly I tell you, no one can enter the kingdom of God unless they are born of water and the Spirit" (John 3:3, 5). It is through our faith in Christ and our baptism into him that we are literally engulfed by Christ into his body—"So in Christ Jesus you are all children of God through faith, for all of you who were baptized into Christ have clothed yourselves with Christ" (Gal. 3:26–27).

By faith in Christ, we are buried with him through baptism and we are raised by God's power to a new life in him—"Our whole self ruled by the flesh was put off when you were circumcised by Christ, having been buried with him in baptism, in which you were also raised with him through your faith in the working of God, who raised him from the dead" (Col. 2:11–12). When we are raised, we have a completely new, powerful life and an existence in the spiritual or heavenly realms—"God raised us up with Christ and seated us with him in the heavenly realms in Christ Jesus" (Eph. 2:6).

But it is in this new realm of existence that we find ourselves up against fierce evil forces that also operate there and that oppose us—"For our struggle is not against flesh and blood, but against the rulers, against the authorities, against the powers of this dark world and against the spiritual forces of evil in the heavenly realms" (Eph. 6:12). For this reason, God provides for us a spiritual armor that, although invisible to the human eyes, is real and quite formidable to those forces that would attack us. And only fully clad in the whole of this armor will we be properly protected from Satan's attacks—"Be strong in the Lord and in his mighty power. Put on the full armor of God, so that you can take your stand against the devil's schemes" (Eph. 6:10–11).

Days will always come when we find ourselves under attack; therefore, we must always be completely armored and prepared—"Put on the full armor of God, so that when the day of evil comes, you may be able to stand your ground, and after you have done everything, to stand" (Eph. 6:13). Each part of the armor is significant and vital to our survival and success.

There is first the "belt" of truth that holds the whole armor together at the waist—"Stand "firm then, with the belt of truth buckled around your waist, with the breastplate of righteousness in place" (Eph. 6:14). Jesus is the truth; therefore, his people will be people of truth. And through the scriptures, he has wholly provided us with the truths that we need to live for him—"All Scripture is God-breathed and is useful for teaching, rebuking, correcting and training in righteousness, so that the servant of God may be thoroughly equipped for every good work" (2 Tim. 3:16–17).

God provides us a "breastplate" of righteousness to cover our hearts—"Stand firm...with the breastplate of righteousness in place" (Eph. 6:14). There are three kinds of righteousness revealed in scripture: (1) self-righteousness, which must be achieved by complete adherence to the law, but is, in reality, completely unattainable by humans—"No one will be declared righteous in God's sight by the works of the law; rather, through the law we become conscious of our sin" (Rom. 3:20); (2) righteousness imputed to us by the grace of God through our faith in him—"In the gospel the righteousness of God is revealed—a righteousness that is by faith from first to last" (Rom. 1:17); and (3) a righteousness that comes not in order to try to *attain* a right relationship with God, but because he has already *atoned* for our sins so that we can live graceful and fully devoted lives for him—"I tell you that unless your righteousness surpasses that of the Pharisees and the teachers of the law, you will certainly not enter the kingdom of heaven" (Matt. 5:20).

There are also coverings for our all-important "feet" that give us the mobility we need as God's peacekeepers—"[Have] your feet fitted with the readiness that comes from the gospel of peace" (Eph. 6:15). Sore or damaged feet can incapacitate us, and thus, God gives us what we need to protect them.

And even the armor has some protection itself; God gives us a "shield" to protect even it—"In addition to all this, take up the shield of faith, with which you can extinguish all the flaming arrows of the evil one" (Eph. 6:16). Faith ultimately is our attachment to God, and it is what assures us victory over the enemy—"Every child of God is able to defeat the world. And we win the victory over the world by means of our faith" (1 John 5:4, Good News Translation).

We also must wear a protective helmet to protect our head. It is, of course, marked with God's insignia, identifying whose we are in this spiritual battle. The helmet protects our head and our brain, the seat of our mind (logic) and our heart (emotion). If we are to love God with our entire mind and heart, we must protect them from evil and allow it all to function properly in the mission God gives us.

Finally, we must arm ourselves in order, not to merely defend ourselves, but to take the fight to the enemy—"Take...[up] the sword of the Spirit, which is the word of God" (Eph. 6:17). The word of God powerful beyond human measure—"The word of God is alive and active, sharper than any double-edged sword" (Heb. 4:12). The Spirit uses the word within us to empower us to fight and ultimately win in the battle against the evil spiritual forces—"The grass withers and the flowers fall, but the word of our God endures forever" (Isa. 40:8).

Lastly, we must first concede the battle to God before we can fight the battle against evil on his behalf. We must cover all we do in prayers to him—"Pray in the Spirit on all occasions with all kinds of prayers and requests. With this in mind, be alert and always keep on praying for all the Lord's people" (Eph. 6:18). Prayer is a vital and powerful component of God's plan for us and through us. And praying in the Spirit is more than mere cursory prayers that can be prayed even by unbelievers. "Praying in the Spirit" can only be accomplished by those who are filled with the Spirit. The Holy Spirit is given to those who ask for him and who are obedient—"If you then, though you are evil, know how to give good gifts to your children, *how much more will your Father in heaven give the Holy Spirit to those who ask him*!" (Luke 11:13, italics added), and, "We are witnesses of these things, and *so is the Holy Spirit, whom God has given to those who obey him*" (Acts 5:32, italics added). Faithful, Spirit-filled prayers produce the most favorable outcomes for God's people and purposes because such prayers are inspired by God, they surrender us to him and his will rather than us fighting only with our own power, and they lead us to fight *for* God with his motives rather than just fighting *against* evil for our own.

To live successfully, the child of God must be armored, armed, and empowered by God. As God's servants and soldiers, we must be knowledgeable, intentional, purposeful, well trained, and ever-ready in this spiritual battle that has been brought to the doorsteps of our world by our most formidable enemy—the devil.

A Prayer:

> O Lord, without your armor I am defenseless in the heavenly realms against forces far stronger than I.
> Teach me and lead me to be obedient to you in fully armoring myself in my service to you.
> Strengthen my faith that I may have a shield against the arrows of doubt with which Satan intends to pierce my heart.
> Make my hands, mind, and heart deft in learning and wielding your word, O God.
> Amen.

6
Arrogance

Arrogance is a sure sign of a life not being lived out in the presence and direction of God.

Do nothing out of selfish ambition or vain conceit. Rather, in humility value others above yourselves (Phil. 2:3).

ARROGANCE IS GENERALLY defined as an outward display of overbearing pride, a sense of self-importance, and a misguided sense of superiority over others. It is always on display in various ways in those who possess it, which can be any of us at any time!

Arrogance causes us to talk much more about ourselves than others, and it drives us to try to impress others. Arrogance makes us haughty, snobbish, and elitist. It makes us blind to our own faults and acutely aware of others' issues. Arrogance gives us a sense of entitlement and makes us think we are worthy of certain "rights." It makes us feel and act as if we are privileged above others.

Arrogance is arguably as ugly as it gets to God—"To fear the Lord is to hate evil; I hate pride and arrogance" (Prov. 8:13). It is antithetical to who and what God is. He opposes it because it is not of him but rather is of evil. It brings us in opposition to God—"God opposes the proud but shows favor to the humble" (James 4:6, Prov. 3:34).

God calls those who would be first to be last, and he demands those who would be the master to be the servant of all—"Whoever wants to become great among you must be your servant" (Matt. 20:26), and "The last will be first, and the first will be last" (Matt. 20:26). Haughtiness among God's people and especially among leaders of God's people is particularly abhorrent to God. Jesus told a story to compare and contrast arrogance and humility—"To some who were confident of their own righteousness and looked down on everyone else, Jesus told this parable: 'Two men went up to the temple to pray, one a Pharisee and the other a tax collector.' The Pharisee stood by himself and prayed: "God, I thank you that I am not like other people—robbers, evildoers, adulterers—or even like this tax collector. I fast twice a week and give a tenth of all I get" ' " (Luke 18:9–12). An example of one so arrogant as to dare to boast even to God!'

Rather Jesus favors humility and never arrogance, using a most galling example to the self-righteous Jews, the tax collector, as his example—"But the tax collector stood at a distance. He would not even look up to heaven, but beat his breast and said, 'God, have mercy on me, a sinner.' I tell you that this man, rather than the other, went home justified before God. *For all those who exalt themselves will be humbled, and those who humble themselves will be exalted*" (Luke 18:9–14, italics added). God is humble, not haughty, and thus, he favors those who are humble. He hates arrogance, as should we.

As believers in Jesus, we are to be people of honesty and truth. Thus, we must see ourselves in light of truth and not through the deceived, evil eyes of self-aggrandizement—"Do not think of yourself more highly than you should. Instead, be modest in your thinking, and judge yourself according to the amount of faith that God has given you" (Rom. 12:3, Good News Translation). We are not intended to be *all about ourselves*, but instead, to be all about God and thus about others—"Do nothing out of selfish ambition or vain conceit. Rather, in humility value others above yourselves" (Phil. 2:3).

The kingdom of God then belongs not to those who are full of self but to those who are poor and empty of self—"Blessed are the poor in spirit, for theirs is the kingdom of heaven. Blessed are those who mourn, for they shall be comforted. Blessed are the meek, for they shall inherit the earth" (Matt. 5:3–5, English Standard Version). God's kingdom people imitate him and do as Jesus did, exalting others above self—"Be devoted to one another in love. Honor one another above yourselves" (Rom. 12:10).

The Bible warns of God's judgment on human arrogance—"Do not keep talking so proudly or let your mouth speak such arrogance, for the Lord is a God who knows, and by him deeds are weighed" (1 Sam. 2:3). Prideful arrogance may lead to a pretention of success, while in fact in the end bringing only failure—"Pride goes before destruction, a haughty spirit before a fall" (Prov. 16:18).

A good rule-of-thumb then is to "Never praise yourself. Let others do it" (Prov. 27:2, Easy-to-Read Version). If we are to follow Jesus, God's praise must weigh much more heavily than the praise of self or others—"Yet at the same time many even among the leaders believed in him. But because of the Pharisees they would not openly acknowledge their faith for fear they would be put out of the synagogue; for they loved human praise more than praise from God" (John 12:42–43).

A good, honest self-assessment should take place in us as we reflect on Jesus to be sure it is he who is living in us and not the spirit of this world—"Examine yourselves to see whether you are in the faith; test yourselves. Do you not realize that Christ Jesus is in you—unless, of course, you fail the test?" (2 Cor. 13:5).

A Prayer:

> Test me, O Lord, and see if arrogance exists in my heart.
> Defeat in me any spirit of pride and any sense of self-importance.
> May I live as a servant to all, as the least, the last, and the worst.
> Give me the heart of the humble tax collector not the arrogant Pharisee.
> Have mercy on me, Lord, and save me from the prideful cravings of the flesh.
> Amen.

7
Awe

The closer you get to God, the more in awe of him you will be. All roads that lead to God lead to indescribable awe.

Everyone was filled with awe (Acts 2:43).

OUR TENDENCY IS to reduce everything and everyone to our own lowest common denominator. That is, we relate it to our own selves. When we reduce "tree" to some definition that we have in mind rather than look at and behold a tree, the actual experience is lost. There is no awe in it. Such over-simplification allows us to feel we are in charge of things and can manage it all ourselves.

Humans have tried this with God through the ages, reducing God to lists of dos and don'ts, cold and intellectual theology, man-made idols, and created things. And the experience of God is lost. When we attempt to make God like us, we deter God from making us like him.

A real experience with God is awesome. It expands the mind and the heart. It opens us up to possibilities. It amazes us and fills us with wonder. It brings hope and confidence. True worship is both the cause of awe and the outcome of it.

Awe of God is both mental and emotional. It doesn't attempt to reduce God to our own size; rather, it leads us to see our own selves in the context of his size. Awe is the full-person recognition and experience of one that is, all at once, fearsome, enormous, amazing, and transformative. "Awesome" describes it in the positive; "awful" describes it in the negative. In Bible accounts, those who have encountered God have, depending on their conditions before him, experienced both. Those who were for him experienced awe and those who had wittingly or unwittingly opposed him experienced the awful realization of their foolishness.

Various words are translated as awe or other similar words from both Hebrew and Greek. Depending on the translation, there are several hundred references to such words and their variations—"awe," "reverence," "wonder," and "astonishment," along with related words like "fear," "afraid," and "tremble."

Awe, simply put, is deep reverence and respect. It is an experiential appreciation of magnitude and contrast. We most experience awe when God finally gets our undivided attention, as with the converts on Pentecost, when, as Luke tells us, "everyone was filled with awe..." (Acts 2:43). The outpouring of the Spirit, the conversion of 3000 people, and the many wonders and signs the apostles were performing had indeed gotten everyone's attention. Thus, awe.

In scripture, people who had direct encounters with God were shaken by the awe experience. Jacob experienced it when he had a dream of a stairway to heaven—"When Jacob awoke from his sleep, he thought, 'Surely the Lord is in this place, and I was not aware of it.' He was afraid and said, 'How *awesome* is this place! This is none other than the house of God; this is the gate of heaven'" (Gen. 28:16–17, italics added).

Similarly, when Jesus calmed a violent storm, the disciples were filled with "fear and amazement" (Luke 8:25). Also, the women who found Jesus's empty tomb after his resurrection were said to be "trembling and bewildered" (Mark 16:8).

As God's people we must be ever aware of his presence in and around us, thus we are commanded to "continue to work out your salvation with fear and trembling" (Phil. 2:12). And also to "worship God acceptably with reverence and awe" (Heb. 12:28).

Awe of God can begin experientially with our emotions, where an awesome reality of him suddenly hits us. But, we must embrace long-term such feelings of awe by realizing and contemplating their source and constantly remembering God's presence with us. Awe can also begin with a thought and produce within us the awe emotions of deep reverence and respect. We love God with all our hearts and all our minds when we allow ourselves to experience awe of him with both.

Awe is good when it reflects our acceptance of the reality of an awesome God. It is transformative; it transforms our perceptions of God within our hearts to a right sort of magnitude. It aligns the universe aright for us. And it transforms our perceptions of our own selves to the reality and experience of who we are before him. Comparatively speaking, a very big God loves a very little me. With him I am priceless; without him I am worthless.

Awe yields the glorious freedom and release derived from our surrender to the reality of who *is* God and who *is not* God.

A Prayer:

> I stand on the shore of eternity God,
> Agape in awe of you,
> The Designer, Creator, Magnificent One,
> That made this sky of blue.

I see beyond my vision,
Reach far beyond my scope,
To seek you, my God, my everything,
The only object of my hope.

Open the eyes of my heart to see your wonder,
Enable my mind to know clearly your grace,
Make my heart yours, pure and holy,
That I may forever gaze upon your face!

8
Baptism

Baptism was likely intended to be the simplest of rites, but some churches have seemed bent on making it impossibly complex and even void of the majestic.

Repent and be baptized, every one of you, in the name of Jesus Christ for the forgiveness of your sins. And you will receive the gift of the Holy Spirit. The promise is for you and your children and for all who are far off—for all whom the Lord our God will call (Acts 2:38–39).

HOW IS IT that God does the things he does? What clock or calendar does God use to determine *when* a thing will be done or was done? What mechanisms does God employ, and what dimensions does he work from? In his rebuke of Job, God asked his suffering servant some very challenging questions, which Job of course was incapable of answering—"Who is this that obscures my plans with words without knowledge? Brace yourself like a man; I will question you, and you shall answer me" (Job. 38:2-3). Perhaps we show our existential ignorance most when we dare question God's work, as if we are actually able to understand much at all of what he does and how he does it.

God is infinite in time—eternal. His existence is timeless—"I AM WHO I AM" (Exod. 3:14). Rather time is his brainchild and creation—"And there was evening, and there was morning—the first day" (Gen. 1:5). God exists outside of time—"I make known the end from the beginning, from ancient times, what is still to come" (Isa. 46:10). He doesn't experience time as we do—"With the Lord a day is like a thousand years, and a thousand years are like a day" (2 Pet. 3:8).

Also, God is infinite in his spatial presence—omnipresent. Indeed, God can and does manifest himself in time and space in a *present* way, as he did with Moses—"I will cause all my goodness to pass in front of you" (Exod. 33:19). And he will, in our own time and space, come near to us in some existential ways—"Seek the LORD while he may be found; call on him while he is near" (Isa. 55:6). But still, our overall experience of him will prove spatially limitless—"Where can I go from your Spirit? Where can I flee from your presence?" (Ps. 139:7).

Additionally, God is infinite in his power and capabilities—omnipotent. Nothing is beyond his capabilities—"With God all things are possible" (Matt. 19:26). He has done and can do all things—"You have made the heavens and the earth by your great power and outstretched arm. Nothing is too hard for you" (Jer. 32:17).

Finally, God is infinite in his knowledge and awareness—omniscient. He exists outside of and beyond our consciousness—"If our hearts condemn us, we know that God is greater than our hearts, and he knows everything" (1 John 3:20). All is revealed openly to him—"Nothing in all creation is hidden from God's sight. Everything is uncovered and laid bare before the eyes of him to whom we must give account" (Heb. 4:13).

If God is thus unlimited, how then can we, as mere mortal humans in our presently constrained existence, understand the activities and mechanisms used in and on our world and our individual selves by such an infinite being? How might we even begin to adequately conclude how God does what he does? Yet, we seemingly often can presume to do just that with our bold conjecture about and explanations of theology and doctrine.

We are so prone to speculate and dispute over what it is that God does, how he does it, and when it is to be done. We mentally and emotionally mistakenly try to reduce God to our own size and existence and then define him and his work as if were all our own doing. We mentally limit him to our own constraints. We thus can unwittingly produce within ourselves a mental idol of a thing we call God which is really not God at all.

God has made the finite out of the infinite. It is by faith in him that we extend our vision beyond this present, material existence out into the eternal, invisible one. By faith we stand on the shores of the finite and gaze in awe into the wonders of the infinite. Faith requires trusting God in those things we simply cannot understand about him because of what we are indeed capable of understanding about him.

Thus comes our battle at defining and understanding the sacrament—the rite—of such as baptismal rebirth, given to us by God himself—"Very truly I tell you, no one can see the kingdom of God unless they are born again" (John 3:3). "No way," we say, "Rebirth is physically impossible, given the restraints of our own mother's wombs!"—"Very truly I tell you, no one can enter the kingdom of God unless they are born of water and the Spirit" (John 3:5). Thus we contend with God's ability to do what he says he will do because our own faith constraints will not allow it—"I have spoken to you of earthly things and you do not believe; how then will you believe if I speak of heavenly things?" (John 3:12).

The rite of baptism is such a simple thing—"Then both Philip and the eunuch went down into the water and Philip baptized him" (Acts 8:38). A simple immersion in water by faith in God, it seems to have been intended, but with such supernaturally profound implications—"Repent and be baptized, every one of you, in the name of Jesus Christ for the forgiveness of your sins. And *you will receive the gift of the Holy Spirit*" (Acts 2:38, italics added).

Ours is to believe in the power of God's activities and capacities and not, in any way, in our own ability to unpack and control them—"So in Christ Jesus you are all children of God through faith, for all of you who were baptized into Christ have clothed yourselves with Christ" (Gal. 3:26–27). Baptism is a surrendering and not a conquering. It is done to us on the outside by another human being—"Philip baptized him" (Acts 8:38). It is by a lowly trust in others who are acting on God's behalf to assist us in our profession of faith in and acceptance of Christ—our complete and total surrender to God.

So in baptism what goes on outwardly happens to us through the actions of others. However, inwardly, it happens through the hand of God—"In him you were also circumcised with a circumcision not performed by human hands. Your whole self ruled by the flesh was put off when *you were circumcised by Christ,* having been buried with him in baptism, in which you were also *raised with him through your faith in the working of God*, who raised him from the dead" (Col. 2:11–12). It is Christ who performs his inner circumcision of our sinful nature. It is in the *working of God* that we are raised from the dead. Ours is but to believe it all—"Repent and believe the good news!" (Mark 1:15), and "We were all baptized by one Spirit so as to form one body—whether Jews or Gentiles, slave or free—and we were all given the one Spirit to drink" (1 Cor. 12:13).

To us is given this existential opportunity to be reborn by God's grace working through our faith in him! We can be transformed by the work of God from death to life, from unforgiven to forgiven, from Spiritless to Spirit-filled, from being separated from God to being joined to him, from temporal to eternal, and from lost to saved. We are transformed by him from pitiful to powerful because our images are made again to look like him—"And we all, who with unveiled faces contemplate the Lord's glory, are being transformed into his image with ever-increasing glory, which *comes from the Lord, who is the Spirit*" (2 Cor. 3:18, italics added).

God indeed can and does work above and beyond our understanding. Rather he responds to our trust. Our rebirth and regeneration are his work, and if we believe in him, he will work in us far beyond our ability to understand correctly—"God…gives life to the dead and calls into being things that were not" (Rom. 4:17).

Yes indeed! All our salvation and sanctification is from the Lord's Spirit and not reliant on our human strength with all our present constraints. He does not need us to understand a thing for him to do it. He does not even need us to be right about things. He needs us to trust in him, not in ourselves! For indeed we can always be wrong about something when we are right about most things. And we never know what we do not know.

But our faith *in* him gives our spirits wings to soar *with* him! We need only to believe in him and never in ourselves or others.

Ours is but to believe in God and his infinite powers! Such simple commands given to us, but with such eternally profound implications—"Repent and be baptized, every one of you, in the name of Jesus Christ for the forgiveness of your sins. And you will receive the gift of the Holy Spirit." A simple "amen" will suffice.

A Prayer:

> Give us faith to believe in your love, your goodness, and your limitless power and capabilities.
> Help us to see beyond ourselves that we can believe beyond ourselves.
> Give us the simplicity in Christ that we can trust in the complexity of your wonders.
> Make your infinite overflow into our finite.
> Rebirth us into your glory and goodness.
> We believe, Lord, help us with our unbelief, that you might be manifested in and glorified through us.
> Amen!

9
Beatitudes

Arguably, the beatitudes are the nine most profound statements ever uttered about human morality, character, and ethics. Together, they define what it means to live gracefully in this present world.

Now when Jesus saw the crowds, he went up on a mountainside and sat down. His disciples came to him, and he began to teach them. He said: "Blessed are the…" (Matt. 5:1–10).

EVERY COMMAND OR example that calls us to be like God offers with it the opportunity to exist as he exists and to experience life as he knows it. It affords us the opportunity to live in the presence of his glorious goodness and perfection and to experience the inner blessedness of life in him. The sacrifices we make for him in this temporal existence yield infinitely greater blessings for us in the eternal one—"I have told you this so that my joy may be in you and that your joy may be complete" (John 15:11).

“Blessedness” (*makarios*, Greek) had generally been seen as out of the reach of the common people and to be the purview only of the “gods” or the dead who had gone to the realm of the gods. Or to be the privilege of the socially elite and wealthy or those super righteous individuals in society who had been granted all the earthly material things. Jesus’s pronouncements of states of blessedness in the Sermon on the Mount echo a completely different sentiment. He pronounces blessings on the poor (in spirit or otherwise), the mourners, the humble and lowly, the hungry and thirsty, and the persecuted, all seen in Jesus himself, as God in the flesh.

In this life, we have all been offered by God the opportunity *to choose to be different* from God (opposite, really) *so that we can choose whether to be like him* or not—“But if serving the LORD seems undesirable to you, then choose for yourselves this day whom you will serve” (Josh. 24:15). God is wholly the opposite of all that is worldly or carnal. He is a giver—“graceful.” And he wants us to be like him. Therefore, he wants us to be glad and cheerful givers of all good things, as he is—“Each of you should give what you have decided in your heart to give, not reluctantly or under compulsion, for God loves a cheerful giver” (2 Cor. 9:7). In doing as God does and being as God is, all of us can experience life as God knows it—blessed.

Thus, it is by and to his own character that he invites us—“His divine power has given us everything we need for a godly life through our knowledge of him *who called us by his own glory and goodness*. Through these he has given us his very great and precious promises, so that through them *you may participate in the divine nature*, having escaped the corruption in the world caused by evil desires” (2 Pet. 1:3–4, italics added). According to his foreordination and grace, he calls, he elects, he sustains in Christ, and he rewards those he chooses—“Those he predestined, he also called; those he called, he also justified; those he justified, he also glorified” (Rom. 8:30).

And it is through our surrendering to his call to participate in his character that we find inclusion in his kingdom—"Blessed are the poor in spirit, for *theirs is the kingdom of heaven*" (Matt. 5:3). Rather than being full of himself, God in and through Christ chose to empty himself—"Let this mind be in you all, which was also in Christ Jesus, who, being in the form of God, did not consider equality with God something to be grasped. But He emptied Himself, taking upon Himself the form of a servant, and was made in the likeness of men" (Phil. 2:5–7). Rather than being *full of himself*, as is the worldly human tendency, God is *empty of himself*—"I am meek and lowly in heart" (Matt. 11:29, Modern English Version). He calls us to the same.

And those empty of self are those who can mourn and care for others—"Blessed are those who mourn, for they will be comforted" (Matt. 5:4). Rather than being insensitive souls who choose to ignore the travails of the world in order to be *happy*, God calls us to feel the hurts of the world and to care about those pains—"You had the kind of sorrow God wanted you to have. Now see what that sorrow has brought you: It has made you very serious. It made you want to prove that you were not wrong. It made you angry and afraid. It made you want to see me. *It made you care.* It made you want the right thing to be done" (2 Cor. 7:11, Easy-to-Read Version).

Also, in God's kingdom it is not the proud, the wealthy, and the elite who will be the greatest heirs; it will be the humble and lowly—"Blessed are the meek, for they will inherit the earth" (Matt. 5:5). It is the meek that will inherit, and perhaps rule over, the whole earth.

Rather than it being those who feast and drink sumptuously who find happiness and joy, it will be those who are starving and thirsty to the brink of death who will do so—"Blessed are those who hunger and thirst for righteousness, for they will be filled" (Matt. 5:6).

Unlike the typical politicized world where the *haves* pull strings and get off the hook when they err, in God's kingdom, those who actually show mercy to others are the ones who will actually receive mercy from God—"Blessed are the merciful, for they will be shown mercy" (Matt. 5:7).

And contrary to conventional thinking, it will not be the worldly-wise, the decadent, and the privileged who will receive an audience with God; it is those who are pure and sincere in a heart before him that will actually see him—"Blessed are the pure in heart, for they will see God" (Matt. 5:8).

It will also not be the powerful conquerors and enforcers who will be God's coveted children; it will be those who bring peace between humanity and its God and within humanity itself—"Blessed are the peacemakers, for they will be called children of God" (Matt. 5:9).

Finally, those lauded, loved, and adored by the world are not the ones who will be blessed with inclusion in God's kingdom; it is those who endure social rejection and persecution for the sake of doing and being righteous like God—"Blessed are those who are persecuted because of righteousness, for theirs is the kingdom of heaven" (Matt. 5:9).

The gospel itself expresses and extends the grace of God to humanity. Then, the ethics and virtues of the Sermon on the Mount, and more specifically the beatitudes, show how we, as God's people, are to express this glorious grace to others. And in doing so we will be most blessed by God.

A Prayer:

> Lord, may I find my inner joy, happiness, and blessedness
>   by being and doing as you.
> Let my ethics and my virtues be as yours.
> Teach me to know that blessedness is a result of surrender and not of conquest.

Help me believe that right results follow right behaviors
that are done without expectation of reward.
May my imitation of you be reward enough for me.
And let me never shrink back from the threats of the world
in my pursuit of your glory and goodness.
Amen.

10
Bible Inspiration

That God merely divinely dictated the Bible scriptures to writers may at first seem an honorable and righteous view of inspiration, but it belies what is a much loftier reality.

For prophecy never had its origin in the human will, but prophets, though human, spoke from God as they were carried along by the Holy Spirit (2 Pet. 1:21).

THE SCRIPTURES—THE BIBLE texts—were given to us by God through certain writers to provide us the knowledge we need to live for and with him—"All Scripture is God-breathed [inspired] and is useful for teaching, rebuking, correcting and training in righteousness, so that the servant of God may be thoroughly equipped for every good work" (2 Tim. 3:16–17). Understanding this, from the biblical perspective, is a paramount reality—"Above all, you must understand that no prophecy of Scripture came about by the prophet's own interpretation of things. For prophecy never had its origin in the human will, but prophets, though human, spoke from God as they were carried along by the Holy Spirit" (2 Pet. 1:20–21).

Prophets were God's spokespersons. When such as these were speaking or writing from God, they were said to be prophesying. Their works are thus called prophecy. Their job and purpose was to speak God's words to the people. Moses was one of the first recognized prophets. It was his job to speak the words of God to the people of Israel—"Then the Lord said to Moses, 'See, I have made you like God to Pharaoh, and your brother Aaron will be your prophet. You are to say everything I command you, and your brother Aaron is to tell Pharaoh to let the Israelites go out of his country'" (Exod. 7:1–2). It was also his job to write down the words of God for the people—"Then the Lord said to Moses, 'Write down these words, for in accordance with these words I have made a covenant with you and with Israel'" (Exod. 34:27). His words, spoken and written, are then no less *inspired* today than they were when first spoken.

Although prophecy came to be associated with predicting the future because of the divine ability prophets exhibited when delivering God's messages, prophecy was never primarily about prediction. Rather it has always been, first and foremost, about revealing God's messages—revealing God—to humanity.

God wants and desires to communicate and reveal himself to us. He wants us to know him!

God is the *Great I Am.* He is the ever-existent one. Unlike humans, he is not to be defined by what he does. What he does and what he says only reveal who he is—"In the beginning was the Word, and the Word was with God, and the Word was God" (John 1:1). He revealed himself first through the creation—"the Spirit of God was hovering over the waters" (Gen. 1:2). The creation remains still the great revelation of God—"Since the creation of the world God's invisible qualities…have been clearly seen, being understood from what has been made" (Rom. 1:20). Then, he reveals himself further through the scripture, the Bible—"All scripture is God-breathed…" The Holy Spirit is the agent of both creation and scripture, and prophets are agents of the Holy Spirit—"prophets...spoke from God as they were carried along by the Holy Spirit."

But the Spirit's agency does not end with the initial delivery of scripture to humanity; he continues daily his work in delivering God's messages to each believer—"However, as it is written: 'What no eye has seen, what no ear has heard, and what no human mind has conceived'—the things God has prepared for those who love him—these are *the things God has revealed to us by his Spirit*. The Spirit searches all things, even the deep things of God" (1 Cor. 2:9–10, italics added).

The Spirit enables each believer to understand God's revelation and gifts to us—"What we have received is not the spirit of the world, but the Spirit who is from God, so that we may understand what God has freely given us. This is what we speak, not in words taught us by human wisdom but in words taught by the Spirit, explaining spiritual realities with Spirit-taught words" (1 Cor. 2:12–13). God gifts believers with the Holy Spirit so that we might have within us the spiritual sensibility to follow and stay in Christ, and not stray by following other voices—"But you have an anointing from the Holy One, and all of you know the truth...As for you, the anointing you received from him remains in you, and you do not need anyone to teach you. But as his anointing teaches you about all things and as that anointing is real, not counterfeit—just as it has taught you, remain in him" (1 John 2:20, 27).

So, the ever-existent one has revealed himself by his Spirit through creation and through scripture, and he seals that revelation within believers through the continued action of the Holy Spirit within us. Through the work of his Spirit, each may hear and recognize Christ's voice—"The gatekeeper opens the gate for him, and the sheep listen to his voice. He calls his own sheep by name and leads them out. When he has brought out all his own, he goes on ahead of them, and his sheep follow him because they know his voice. But they will never follow a stranger; in fact, they will run away from him because they do not recognize a stranger's voice" (John 10:3–5).

It is by our hearing and following Christ through the Spirit that our status as children of God is sealed and demonstrated—"For those who are led by the Spirit of God are the children of God" (Rom. 8:14). The creation is at the forefront of revealing God to us, but now the creation itself awaits the revealing of God's children—"For the creation waits in eager expectation for the children of God to be revealed" (Rom. 8:19).

An interim work of God in transmitting the scriptures was accomplished in earlier times through the scribes who copied and recopied the scripture, lest the sacred writings be lost through the decay or destruction of the originals. History records and verifies their care and accuracy in recording the original writings. Also, God has similarly used editors who compiled the writings, as well as the church and its leaders that carefully selected which of those writings were indeed inspired by God and were to be included in the Bible.

God wants to be known by humanity, and he has made the whole creation, in which we live and at which we marvel, a revelation of himself. He has given us the Bible to further explain and document his identity and his purpose in us. And he wants us, as his children, to be a final revelation in this age.

In the end, God will fully reveal himself to us and reveal us to ourselves—"For now we see only a reflection as in a mirror; then we shall see face to face. Now I know in part; then I shall know fully, even as I am fully known" (1 Cor. 13:12). And all humanity will finally see and admit that God is real and that Jesus is Lord—"Therefore God exalted him to the highest place and gave him the name that is above every name, that at the name of Jesus every knee should bow, in heaven and on earth and under the earth, and every tongue acknowledge that Jesus Christ is Lord, to the glory of God the Father" (Phil. 2:9–11).

Amen!

A Prayer:

Lord, fill me with your Spirit that I might see and know you.
Thank you for the revelation of creation and for the revelation of the sacred writings, the Bible.
Thank you for all those whom you used to transmit your words to us so lovingly and carefully.
Renew your anointing in me that I can hear clearly and follow carefully the voice of my Lord and Savior Jesus Christ.
Help me to understand better and better the revelation of the Bible.
Make my faith genuine and my confession true.
Reveal yourself in me, your child, that through me you can also reveal yourself to others.
Jesus is Lord.

11
Brokenness

Brokenness before God is the most painful fate of all, but it also yields a most glorious aroma to God.

The L*ORD is close to the brokenhearted and saves those who are crushed in spirit* (Ps. 34:18).

WE, IN OUR fleshly state, prefer to serve God in at least some self-perception of wholeness and personal respectability. We want to look together and in control. In fact, it is not "safe" among most others to look broken and weak. So we come to God to "get it together" and to "get things under control." We expect him to fix everything according to the human patterns laid out for us. We cherry pick all his promises in such a way to fit into our personal self-help constructs, carefully crafted to build up and reinforce these unreal and unholy expectations of ours.

Yet in doing all this, we only propagate the destructiveness of the toxic fruit of that deadly tree, the Tree of the Knowledge of Good and Evil, with its false promise of making us "like God."

When attempt to make it about us, we choose the wrong tree—the wrong path. In doing so, we choose death. When we make it about God, we choose life—"For whoever wants to save their life will lose it, but whoever loses their life for me will save it" (Luke 9:23).

How can one look at the life of Jesus and come out with such foolish expectations and designs?—"It was the LORD's will to crush him and cause him to suffer" (Isa. 53:10). Somehow in the origin of sin comes this idea that this life is about making us happy. Somewhere in our own quests to be "gods" came this notion of present-day idealism—that God intends to make our present lives heavenly. This is unfortunate. One of the greatest sources of our unhappiness is our unmet expectations, albeit unreal expectations. This is true in every facet of our lives.

The reality is that in our fallen state, present in our flesh from our conception, we are not useful to God or to ourselves. In this unregenerate, dead condition, we can only be made useful by God's regeneration. He must transform us in order to use us. But we must be broken from this sinful state in order to be remade and to become useful to God.

Humanity, however, confuses spiritual brokenness with emotional decrepit-ness or inner dilapidation and thus rejects any possibility of good being derived from any kind of brokenness. Because in the realization of our spiritual bankruptcy apart from God, humanity's only answer is to try to fill ourselves up with more of what breaks us in the first place—self and sin—"They did not think it worthwhile to retain the knowledge of God, so God gave them over to a depraved mind" (Rom. 1:28).

There are and always were only two choices—two trees representing life and death, two ways leading to blessings or curses, two roads leading to either life or destruction. But because of the fall, all humans are broken by the world from the start, with no choice to be otherwise. And we attempt to put ourselves back together in a warped, deformed, disjointed way that becomes the norm and thus is not seen as the "monsterfication" of our humanness that it really is. When gross disfigurement is the norm, what should be abhorrent to us and what is detestable to God, because of what has happened to us, becomes acceptable to us and somehow looks right to us—"Woe to those who call evil good and good evil" (Isa. 5:20). In our unbelief, it is cool to us to be total freaks. We come to expect it and to celebrate it. We parade our disfigurements—our selfishness, our greed, our arrogance, our self-centeredness, our hatred, our gross immorality, and our spiritual malignancy—as if they are desirable rather than detestable. Experiencing and causing pain is the norm.

But when we come to God, he must first break us in order to remake us.

There is a moving story from Luke's account of Jesus's ministry in the northern town of Capernaum (Luke 7:36–50). Jesus was having dinner with a seemingly well-put-together Jewish man named Simon, a Pharisee, in fact. During the meal, Luke reports that a sinful woman came, apparently uninvited, into the room where they were dining, broke open an alabaster jar of perfume she carried with her, and anointed Jesus's feet with it. She kissed his feet and wiped them with her hair. Jesus allowed it to go on uncontested. The upright host was a bit indignant at the scene, noting that if Jesus were a true prophet then he would know the woman was a "sinner" and thus clearly would not allow such a display from this kind of person.

However, as in so many encounters with Jesus, the one assumed to be fixed and put together proved to be the broken one and the one who was broken was the one was who was being fixed!

Alabaster jars were made from a precious stone that came from Alabastron in Egypt, thus the stone's name. Jars were fashioned from this stone, and expensive perfumes and ointments were sealed in them to protect the perfume from spoiling and to keep the scent in until it was used. The top was broken off when used and thus it could be used only once. Her display was then not only audacious, given her intrusion into the meal, but it was extravagant, considering this could easily have been her most precious possession. Perhaps her bravery is just one more clue the gospel writers give as to the state of women. They were the ones who supported Jesus (Luke 8:1–3), and they were the ones who remained near him after the male apostles had fled in fear (Matt. 27:55–56). It was women who first witnessed and proclaimed the good news of Jesus's resurrection (Luke 24:1–10). These women, who represented some that had been most broken under the oppression of the curse, were the ones first and most put back together by Jesus!

But it was only when her jar had been broken that the aroma could be experienced and thus it would be known for sure that her audacity was accompanied by such extravagant worship and appreciation of Jesus—"But thanks be to God, who always leads us as captives in Christ's triumphal procession and *uses us to spread the aroma of the knowledge of him everywhere*" (2 Cor. 2:14, italics added). And although the aroma was to Jesus pleasing, touching, and most meaningful, it was to the self-righteous Pharisee repugnant and shameful—"For we are to God the pleasing aroma of Christ among those who are being saved and those who are perishing. To the one we are an aroma that brings death; to the other, an aroma that brings life" (2 Cor. 2:15–16).

Brokenness is then to be seen as our realization of the devastating effects of sin on us. It is not something we *do to* ourselves; it is something we *realize about* ourselves—sin completely breaks us all! And when we allow this reality to sink in, we feel deeply and agonizingly all its implications about us—our worthlessness apart from God, our depravity, and our wretchedness. When we believe strongly enough to turn to God in the reality of our brokenness, we find the same sweet reception this woman found. Jesus explained to his host the contrast of the woman's heart to Simon's,

> Do you see this woman? I came into your house. You did not give me any water for my feet, but she wet my feet with her tears and wiped them with her hair. You did not give me a kiss, but this woman, from the time I entered, has not stopped kissing my feet. You did not put oil on my head, but she has poured perfume on my feet. Therefore, I tell you, her many sins have been forgiven—as her great love has shown. But whoever has been forgiven little loves little (Luke 7:44–47).

The Psalmist recognized the blessed state of the broken one before God—"My sacrifice, O God, is a broken spirit; a broken and contrite heart you, God, will not despise" (Ps. 51:17). Isaiah wrote, "For this is what the high and exalted One says—he who lives forever, whose name is holy: 'I live in a high and holy place, but also with the one who is contrite and lowly in spirit, to revive the spirit of the lowly and to revive the heart of the contrite'" (Isa. 57:15). In his human state, Jesus's was an exemplary, broken, lowly spirit—"I am gentle and humble in heart" (Matt. 11:29). Again, Isaiah quotes God as saying, "These are the ones I look on with favor: those who are humble and contrite in spirit, and who tremble at my word" (Isa. 66:2).

When we realize our disfigured, sinful, broken condition under the curse, apart from God, and we bring the reality to God rather than looking for human healing, we find healing and life—"He heals the brokenhearted and binds up their wounds" (Ps. 147:3). It is only when we break open before God our most precious possessions—the hearts God has given us—that his aroma will flow from us and healing comes to us.

A Prayer:

I break the seal of my heart before you God,
That you might enjoy the scent,
Of the image of you inside me,
Of my ultimate purpose and my intent.

I lay at your feet before you,
Anoint them with all the contents here inside,
Seeking out your love and healing,
You magnificent love, so deep and wide.

I have nothing else to give you,
But this broken one that is me,
Please heal me and fill me with your Spirit,
That I may dare look up now, and your face see!

12
Choice and Change

What I may presently be has little to do with what I can or should be.

We are now God's children, but it is not yet clear what we shall become. But we know that when Christ appears, we shall be like him (1 John 3:2, Good News Translation).

HUMANISTIC PSYCHOLOGY TRIES to persuade us of a kind of organic fatalism—that there are certain programmed-in behavioral traits that are inevitable and that for us to try to resist them is to deny who we "really are." Apart from God, this might generally be true. But through God, it is not true at all. The existential, spiritual reality is that what we currently are or where we started our life is not what is to ultimately define us, but it is where we are going and what we will become that define us!

Because of God's breath of life breathed into us, we as humans can choose to live above and beyond mere animal instinct. We not only can change but also can be transformed—"We…are being transformed into his image with ever-increasing glory" (2 Cor. 3:18).

In Christ, we are transformed as from a larva to a butterfly (*metamorphoo*, Greek, same root as metamorphosis).

As in metamorphosis, our underlying DNA remains relatively unchanged, but by the very design of our genetics, total transformation of our being can be triggered from within, empowered by the Spirit of God himself—"This comes from the Lord who is the Spirit" (2 Cor. 3:18, English Standard Version).

This transformation capability is hardwired into each one of us by the germ of God. It is triggered by our call through the gospel of Christ, and it presents, then, a conscious, mental choice each called one must make—"And do not be conformed to this world [any longer with its superficial values and customs], but be transformed *and* progressively changed [as you mature spiritually] by the renewing of your mind [focusing on godly values and ethical attitudes], so that you may prove [for yourselves] what the will of God is, that which is good and acceptable and perfect [in His plan and purpose for you]" (Rom. 12:2, Amplified Bible).

That one has the propensity to lie does not fate that person to be a liar. That one has the propensity to steal does not fate that person to be a thief. That one has the propensity to murder or molest children does not within itself make that person a murderer or a pedophile. That is absurd. Possibility does not define probability. While perhaps from a humanistic perspective, we are defined by our fleshly desires, spiritually we are defined not by what we desire but by what we choose. And we need not ever merely yield to whatever we might desire, for desire is of the flesh but in our spirit there is choice.

Nor are we defined by our intermittent weaknesses and failures. An exception does not create a new rule or pattern; it only proves the original rule or pattern. Believers have within us not only the seed of the flesh but also the seed of the Spirit of God, and the overall of who we are is determined by what is ultimately germinated through the ultimate choice we make—"Or do you not know that the unrighteous will not inherit the kingdom of God? Do not be deceived: neither the sexually immoral, nor idolaters, nor adulterers, nor men who practice homosexuality, nor thieves, nor the greedy, nor drunkards, nor revilers, nor swindlers will inherit the kingdom of God. And *such were some of you. But you were washed, you were sanctified, you were justified in the name of the Lord Jesus Christ and by the Spirit of our God*" (1 Cor. 6:9–11, English Standard Version, italics added).

Therefore, we need not allow ourselves to be defined by the flesh. We can change our minds ("renew our mind"; "repent"). It is true that in this world we are indeed fated by the flesh to a battle of opposing forces—"I do not understand what I do. For what I want to do I do not do, but what I hate I do" (Rom. 7:15). But through the Spirit of God, we can become fated only to God—"Therefore, if anyone is in Christ, the new creation has come: The old has gone, the new is here!" (2 Cor. 5:17).

For the one receiving Christ, the pathos of the fleshly condition is fully addressed by Christ—"What a wretched man I am! Who will rescue me from this body that is subject to death? Thanks be to God, who delivers me through Jesus Christ our Lord!" (Rom. 7:24–25). Yes, the underlying flesh will desire what it will desire. It has an appetite for pleasure, leisure, and indulgence, but we must resist it in favor of what we *choose* to be rather than what has chosen us. Fleshly desire never ceases but should daily remind us of the curse that has fallen on creation and manifests itself in us, and that we therefore must resist in favor of choosing to be like God.

We find life not through yielding to what seemingly chooses us by the flesh; we find life in what we choose through the Spirit—"For if you live according to the flesh, you will die; but if by the Spirit you put to death the misdeeds of the body, you will live" (Rom. 8:13). Those nagging and perhaps constant pangs of evil desire that we have chosen against and have put away should only remind of the far greater pleasures, glory, and joy to come.

A Prayer:

Oh Transforming Spirit, fill me with the vision of all that you have fated me for in Christ Jesus.
Make my vision of myself not that which the flesh seemingly fates me for, but rather, that which the Spirit shows me.
Help me never to yield to the baser instincts of my evil fleshly desires, but help me to yield to the holy and spiritual yearnings imbued by your Holy Spirit.
I thirst for you, O God, so fill me now with the desire to only be like you, my Father.
Bind me not to the ravages of my fleshly DNA, but rather, enable and empower me through your DNA, and enlivened by your Holy Spirit.
I was made in your image; renew me to again look more and more like you.

13
Choice

Choice is arguably the most exquisite blessing God has given us. It spells freedom. It defines us as individual beings. It allows us to love as God loves. Choice grants to each of us incredible power. But with it come responsibilities and rewards, temporal and eternal, as well as consequences. Each choice we make affects everything that follows it.

Today I am giving you a choice of two ways. And I ask heaven and earth to be witnesses of your choice. You can choose life or death. The first choice will bring a blessing. The other choice will bring a curse. So choose life! Then you and your children will live (Deut. 30:19, Easy-to-Read Version).

CHOICE. IT IS a manifestation of freedom. It is a most exquisite blessing of the elite and privileged, thus it is granted to every human being! We all are indeed privileged!

There is a paradigm in Christianity of a kind of spiritual fatalism, seemingly suggesting that not only does God not give each of us a choice in whether we will come to him or not but also that ultimately every choice we make somehow has already been made by him. While often focusing on the indisputable sovereignty of God, its implications bear greatly on all subsequent views of God and man. It argues in a compelling fashion that many were predestined from creation for destruction. As an ideology, it bleeds into all sorts of macro-ideas and views, not only concerning the salvation of each individual but also it bears heavily on micro-perspectives of daily life.

But God gave humanity the ultimate choice from the beginning—the Tree of Life, trust in God, or the Tree of the Knowledge of Good and Evil, trust in self (Gen. 2 & 3). Original humanity's choice. Needless to say, they chose badly. The Bible demonstrates over and over that God has called various people and people groups to make a choice, both the ultimate choice of whether or not to follow God as well as countless other choices involved in living for him—"But if serving the LORD seems undesirable to you, then choose for yourselves this day whom you will serve" (Josh. 24:15).

Humanity, from our very beginning, seems prone to choose badly. We are drawn, individually and collectively, to overreactions, overcorrections, and over-rotations, all too often to the extreme. This is demonstrated in the Bible and by history, theologically, and doctrinally. It is just as true academically, socially, and politically. Extremism seems somehow to create an illusion of safety for us. Extremism of all kinds seems to conjure variously, within adherents to it, senses of uniqueness, originality, self-righteousness, power, exclusivity, and so on. Frankly, extremism sells well! Oh, how we can love to feel special, above and beyond most others.

Extremes in all regards seem to be strong magnets, drawing to their poles the unsuspecting that might otherwise venture too closely to them. However, there is to be a balance and temperance in the person of God, a mental and emotional steadiness—"But you, keep your head in all situations" (2 Tim. 4:5). This steadiness keeps one from falling prey to the wanton lure of extremes and excesses—"Whoever fears God will avoid all extremes" (Eccles. 7:18).

One such extreme is seen in giving God credit for personally causing every single good and bad thing that happens every minute of every day for every single person. It is spiritual fatalism. The opposite extreme, of course, is that God made creation and then personally withdrew from it, leaving its outcomes to the devices of its designed-in processes and random happenstance. This is called deism. Both spiritual fatalism and deism are extremes; neither holds up well under thorough scriptural scrutiny.

Scripture indicates that God certainly fates *some* things, both in regard to the overall and in regard to the specific. He is well within his sovereign right to do so—"Things that are made don't have the power to question the one who makes them" (Isa. 45:9, Easy-to-Read Version), and "I [God] will have mercy on whom I have mercy, and I will have compassion on whom I have compassion" (Rom. 9:15, Exod. 33:19).

That humans, both in general and in particular, have been given the ultimate opportunity of choice—that of choosing whether or not to follow God—neither negates God's sovereignty nor elevates humanity above our standing as in absolute subservience to our God. God gave humanity, in general, the choice, and as he wills, he gives individuals the choice—"No one can come to me unless the Father who sent me draws them" (John 6:44). And God's calling on any one individual may not result in their actually being chosen (elected or selected)—"For many are called (invited, summoned), but few are chosen" (Matt. 22:14).

God made humanity like him—"God created mankind in his own image, in the image of God he created them; male and female he created them" (Gen. 1:27). And, in Christ, he is conforming a new humanity back to his original design—"His purpose was to create in himself one new humanity" (Eph. 2:15), and "We...are being transformed into his image" (2 Cor. 3:18).

God had and still has the freedom of choice—"In your relationships with one another, have the same mindset as Christ Jesus: Who, being in very nature God, did not consider equality with God something to be used to his own advantage" (Phil. 2:5–6). God's love (*agape*, Greek) requires a will and a choice to even exist. God, who is himself love (1 John 4:8), in Jesus, had a choice of whether to descend to the earthly realm to show himself to humanity and to sacrifice himself for our sin—"The Father loves me because I give my life. I give my life so that I can get it back again. No one takes my life away from me. I give my own life freely. I have the right to give my life, and I have the right to get it back again. This is what the Father told me" (John 10:17–18), Easy-to-Read Version). It is this same mind-set or attitude that God calls us to. He wants us to choose him. He will not force himself on us.

God seemingly gives us the choice to not choose him in order to give us the choice to choose him. We cannot have one choice without the other. Humanity would not have the choice to choose God unless God had given it to us. Neither does any one of us have the choice to choose him unless God grants it to us out of his grace and divine purpose.

And that is exactly what he has done—"That [Christ] was the true light which shines upon every man as he comes into the world. He came into the world—the world he had created—and the world failed to recognize [sic] him. He came into his own creation, and his own people would not accept him. Yet wherever men did accept him he gave them the power to become sons of God. These were the men who truly believed in him, and their birth depended not on the course of nature nor on any impulse or plan of man, but on God" (John 1:9–13, J. B. Phillips New Testament).

When God grants us, by an act of his grace, a choice, large or small, we must choose him and his way and will every time. We must seek to know him and offer ourselves as living sacrifices to him. Then we will be able to "test and approve what God's will is" (Rom. 12:1–2). Only in rightly understanding what God's will is can we have assurance that God is approving of the choices we make—"This is the confidence we have in approaching God: that if we ask anything according to his will, he hears us" (1 John 5:14).

A Prayer:

> Lord, give me wisdom to use the knowledge that I have.
> Help me to discern wisely and to choose wisely.
> Let my will be perfectly aligned to your will.
> Lead me by your Holy Spirit that my choices are the ones you want for me.
> I choose you, O God; have mercy on me and choose me.
> Amen.

14
Christ

Christ is the human revelation of the divine and the summation and personification of all that is good, beautiful, and excellent.

The Word became flesh and made his dwelling among us. We have seen his glory, the glory of the one and only Son, who came from the Father, full of grace and truth (John 1:14).

"JESUS" MEANS "YAHWEH saves." Christ (Greek) and Messiah (Hebrew) mean "the anointed one" or "king." He is called by many names. Among many others, he is referred to as Son of God, Son of Man, Bread of Life, Wonderful Counselor, Prince of Peace, Lamb of God, Lord, Savior, the Word, the Light, the Life, the Way, the Gate, and so forth. It took time for the disciples to finally reckon with who Jesus ultimately was, although Jesus had told them—"Anyone who has seen me has seen the Father" (John 14:9). After he calmed a raging storm while they were in a boat on the Sea of Galilee, Mark tells us, "They were terrified and asked each other, 'Who is this? Even the wind and the waves obey him!'"

(Mark 4:41). Thomas serves as the one struggling with the most doubt even after the resurrection, yet when he encounters the risen Christ in bodily form, he exclaimed to Jesus, "My Lord and my God!" (John 20:28).

Although the true oneness of Yahweh is a divine mystery and impossible for humans to fully grasp, God has indeed manifested himself to humanity. Yahweh first revealed himself directly through the creation and various interactions. Then, he revealed himself in human form in Jesus. Lastly, he is revealing himself through the Holy Spirit whom Jesus sent back to us after his ascension from heaven and who fills baptized believers (Acts 2:38–39). Thus, "For those who are led by the Spirit of God are the children of God" (Rom. 8:14). Because to be led by the Spirit is to be led by Jesus and to be led by Jesus is to be led by Yahweh. The Father, the Son, and the Holy Spirit are one.

The people who witnessed Jesus's life on earth were notably amazed and astonished by him. For example: "When Jesus had finished saying these things, *the crowds were amazed* at his teaching, because he taught as one who had authority, and not as their teachers of the law" (Matt. 7:28–29), and "Coming to his hometown, he began teaching the people in their synagogue, and *they were amazed*. 'Where did this man get this wisdom and these miraculous powers?' they asked" (Matt. 13:54). Even the Roman leader, Pilate, was amazed because Jesus was not intimidated even at the threat of execution, refusing to defend himself. Mark simply tells us, "Pilate was amazed" (Mark 15:5).

Plainly and simply put, Jesus was and is other-humanly. He was God personified. But he was also fully human. But because of his human perfection, due to his godliness, he was "out of this world." The people testified to this variously in their amazement at his words, teachings, miracles, power, interactions, self-control, love, concern, purposefulness, endurance, fearlessness, wisdom, insight, authority, and so forth. Thus, the apostle John testifies about him,

"We beheld his glory..." (John 1:14, King James Version). Later John said, concerning those who witnessed Jesus on earth, "We proclaim to you what we have seen and heard..." (1 John 1:3). The apostle Peter said, "We were eyewitnesses of his majesty" (2 Pet. 1:16). They saw him. They testified about him. And they died holding true to what they knew to be the truth—Jesus was and is indeed Lord of the universe!

It was this same Jesus who came to life on earth that had created the world in the first place—"Through him all things were made; without him nothing was made that has been made" (John 1:3). It was and is he who sustains the creation still to this day—"The Son is the radiance of God's glory and the exact representation of his being, sustaining all things by his powerful word" (Heb. 1:3). His glory pervades the universe—"The heavens declare the glory of God; the skies proclaim the work of his hands" (Ps. 19:1). Yet, "He was in the world, and though the world was made through him, the world did not recognize him" (John 1:10). Perhaps because when many of us as unbelievers look for God, when we do not already know him, we are in fact looking for an image made in our own likeness—the only god we've ever really known and served.

Thus the Revelation depicts one hundred million angels in heaven singing the praises of Christ, "Worthy is the Lamb, who was slain, to receive power and wealth and wisdom and strength and honor and glory and praise!" (Rev. 5:12).

We must come to that reality now, or it will be forced on us later. Declaring "Jesus is Lord" is an inevitability for each of us—"Therefore God exalted him to the highest place and gave him the name that is above every name, that at the name of Jesus every knee should bow, in heaven and on earth and under the earth, and every tongue acknowledge that Jesus Christ is Lord, to the glory of God the Father" (Phil. 2:9–11).

It is a good idea to truly and firmly *get* it now than to suddenly have to *get* it later.

A Prayer (Phil 3:7–11):

> "But whatever were gains to me I now consider loss for the sake of Christ. What is more, I consider everything a loss because of the surpassing worth of knowing Christ Jesus my Lord, for whose sake I have lost all things. I consider them garbage, that I may gain Christ and be found in him, not having a righteousness of my own that comes from the law, but that which is through faith in Christ—the righteousness that comes from God on the basis of faith. I want to know Christ—yes, to know the power of his resurrection and participation in his sufferings, becoming like him in his death, and so, somehow, attaining to the resurrection from the dead."

15
Christian Atrocities and Sins

Christians' failures through the ages in no way subvert the gospel message; on the contrary, they validate it.

Here is a trustworthy saying that deserves full acceptance: Christ Jesus came into the world to save sinners—of whom I am the worst (1 Tim. 1:15).

THE FAILURES OF the church and the sins of Christians are not in fact a refutation of the gospel; they are in actuality a demonstration of it. Humanity chose to go against God early on, as depicted in Adam and Eve in the Garden of Eden (Gen. 3). And after our sin dilemma was fully demonstrated through both the Old and the New Testament, the apostle Paul summarized it for us, "All have sinned and fall short of the glory of God" (Rom. 3:23).

The Bible never pulls punches about human sinfulness, beginning with the story of Cain killing his brother Abel over God accepting Abel's offering and rejecting Cain's. Killing over religion is nothing new; it started almost from the beginning.

Noah is chosen as the deliverer of humanity as well as much of the animal kingdom but then plants a vineyard, makes wine, gets drunk, and ends up cursing his son Ham. Abraham was the father of our faith but still was deceptive and manipulative, as was his grandson, Jacob, who became Israel, the father of the nation.

The first king of Israel, Saul, was rejected as king over his disobedience to God. The second king, David, suffered for a lifetime because of an adulterous affair with Bathsheba and the arranged killing of her soldier husband in battle. Solomon became not only very wealthy but also extremely wise; however, he still forsook God in many ways.

The story of Israel is a story of infidelity to God, failing to obey the covenant, and ultimately, rejecting and affecting the execution of the very Messiah that God had sent to deliver them. The Corinthian church is the one church that is revealed to have had special gifts from the Holy Spirit, yet because of serious sin among them individually and collectively, Paul said he could not address them as spiritual people but only as worldly ones. Paul prophesied in a number of ways of the falling away that would occur in the church in the ages following his.

The Law of Moses was a manifestation of the fruit of the Tree of the Knowledge of Good and Evil, the fruit tree that God told Adam and Eve would kill them. Humanity's propensity to go against God through sin is God's way of revealing himself in stark contrast. But our desire to do and be good reveals him just as much.

When God is discounted or minimized because of human sin and atrocities, those who do so merely show their limitations, misunderstandings, and their desperate need of the God they doubt. This is our God who through our own ineptitude not only reveals to us our need for him but also offers himself to us! God also reveals our propensity to good, as we are made in his image, through our similar propensity to not trust him and not do what is right. He calls us out of the sinful dilemma by his own glory and goodness and empowers us to participate in his own divine nature (2 Pet. 1:3–4).

Christian atrocities and sins do not nullify the covenant of Christ; they demonstrate his power to save us at our worst. Neither does Christ's mercy on us justify the wrongs we have committed; rather his mercy showered on us only validates the fact that we misbehaved badly in the first place.

A Prayer:

God, help me see through your eyes and not through the eyes and perspectives of other people.
Help me to see beyond humanity's definitions and to see those definitions that are rooted in you and that are therefore the truth.
Help me to seek to understand you in trust, not to try to judge through human understanding.
Lead me to never be turned away from your majestic name because of what any others might do in your name.
Help me to be saved by my trust in your goodness and never to fall into the trap of thinking I might otherwise be saved by my own goodness or the goodness of others.
Amen.

16
Communicating Carefully and Thoughtfully

One can always say more louder later, but one can never take back what has already been said.

Do not let any unwholesome talk come out of your mouths, but only what is helpful for building others up according to their needs, that it may benefit those who listen (Eph. 4:29).

"**STICKS AND STONES** may break my bones, but words can never harm me." Perhaps a harmless childhood deflection, but it is untrue nonetheless. The reality is that words can break a heart. Words can in fact alter the course of a life or a nation. Words matter—"The tongue has the power of life and death, and those who love it will eat its fruit" (Prov. 18:21). And, "The soothing tongue is a tree of life, but a perverse tongue crushes the spirit" (Prov. 15:4). Yes indeed, what one says matters a whole, whole lot.

"Everyone should be quick to listen, slow to speak and slow to become angry" (James 1:19). The children of God—the peacemakers—choose the words they speak very carefully, because words can heal and bring peace or words can harm and divide. James warns, "No human being can tame the tongue. It is a restless evil, full of deadly poison" (James 3:8). It is such a serious problem that James also concludes that, "Those who consider themselves religious and yet do not keep a tight rein on their tongues deceive themselves, and their religion is worthless" (James 1:26). The tradeoff is not worth it.

Jesus said, "What goes into someone's mouth does not defile them, but what comes out of their mouth, that is what defiles them" (Matt. 15:11). Serious business, this mouth of ours. Because it is the gateway to the heart, where real danger resides—"A good man brings good things out of the good stored up in his heart, and an evil man brings evil things out of the evil stored up in his heart. For the mouth speaks what the heart is full of" (Luke 6:45).

We must first of all, by the power of the word of God and the Spirit of God, be purged inwardly: "First clean the inside of the cup and dish, and then the outside also will be clean" (Matt. 23:26); "You are already clean because of the word I have spoken to you" (John 15:3); and "And we all, who with unveiled faces contemplate the Lord's glory, are being transformed into his image with ever-increasing glory, which comes from the Lord, who is the Spirit" (2 Cor. 3:18).

Then we must tap into our Spirit-given self-control (2 Tim. 1:7) to carefully choose what we say and how we say it—"If anyone speaks, they should do so as one who speaks the very words of God" (1 Pet. 4:11). Jesus must first be Lord of our heart, and then he will be Lord of our manner of speech.

If it proves necessary, we can always say more to another at a later time. We can always speak more forcefully to another at a later date. But we can never really take back what we have already spoken or the way in which we spoke it. Rashness can be deadly when it comes to the words we speak to others, thus we should be "slow to speak."

On the contrary, if we choose our words carefully, our spoken words can bring great blessings to others. “Let your conversation be always full of grace, seasoned with salt…” (Col. 4:6).

Jesus’s grave warning about our words should suffice to get the point across to us—“But I tell you that everyone will have to give account on the Day of Judgment for every empty word they have spoken” (Matt. 12:36).

So, we must heed what the children’s song cautions: “So, Be Careful Little Lips What You Say…”

A Prayer:

> Lord, help me to be careful in all I say,
> To avoid idle and useless words,
> To be efficient in all that I say.
>
> Give me discernment to know what to say that is beneficial to others,
> To bless and not curse in the words I speak,
> To make my words count for good and not bad.
>
> Grant me self-control to contain myself and not say too much to others, especially in confrontation,
> To be kind and gentle, not unnecessarily harsh and rough,
> To speak to heal and not to hurt.
>
> Help me to see my words as a window through which I can see into my heart,
> And to allow your word and your Spirit to cleanse me from the inside out,
> So that, because what is inside is of you, what comes out of my mouth will be of you.

17
Communication and Life

Our communication is more than simply what we say; it is the sum of all we are, every word we speak, and everything we do in life.

Let your conversation be always full of grace, seasoned with salt (Col. 4:5–6).

IT IS IMPOSSIBLE not to communicate. To not say anything is to say something. To withdraw or completely disappear, says something to those who know us. Our whole life makes an ultimate statement to the world. Each thing we say or do, or even don't say or do, makes a statement. The sum of all our communication determines the ultimate impact our lives are to have; therefore, it is paramount that we exercise careful control over it.

What we communicate and how we communicate are at the basis of human society. To communicate something is to make that information "common" to another or to others. Communication is what we do as community. It is a part of all communions. Yet most communicate fairly haphazardly. God wants us to be purposeful and helpful with what we say and do.

Both how and what we communicate matter greatly. So much of what we say, is said nonverbally through gestures, body postures, facial expressions, and so forth. We can easily find ourselves saying one thing with our words but another with our bodies. Countless relationships are damaged, some seemingly irreparably, through unwise, harsh, hurtful words and manners. Loved ones are the most common targets—spouses, children, parents, in-laws, and friends—"The tongue also is a fire, a world of evil among the parts of the body. It corrupts the whole body, sets the whole course of one's life on fire, and is itself set on fire by hell" (James 3:6).

What we communicate to others and what others communicate to us matter and can affect us greatly—"Death and life are in the power of the tongue" (Prov. 18:21, Common English Bible). Communication is a life and death matter.

To communicate effectively to others, we must learn to receive communication effectively—to listen. We must listen well, both with our ears and our eyes. And our interpretation of what is communicated to us needs to be heard patiently. We must learn to be careful, objective, and reasonable in our hearing of others. Otherwise, we are like television sets or stereos, set only to project but never to listen. Although all too common, a fixation on "hearing oneself talk" is utterly foolish and counterproductive—"Fools find no pleasure in understanding but delight in airing their own opinions" (Prov. 18:2).

Because words are so powerful, our tongue is a powerful weapon—"The tongue also is a fire, a world of evil among the parts of the body. It corrupts the whole body, sets the whole course of one's life on fire, and is itself set on fire by hell" (James 3:6). The tongue can be the most deadly of all weapons—"It is a restless evil, full of deadly poison" (James 3:8).

As with handling a dangerous weapon, we must exercise caution with our words and actions toward others—"Everyone should be quick to listen, slow to speak and slow to become angry" (James

1:19). An unleashed tongue is as an unsheathed sword or an unholstered gun, and thus it must be carefully contained and very carefully and thoughtfully engaged—"Set a guard over my mouth, LORD; keep watch over the door of my lips" (Ps. 141:3). Like weapons, our words and actions must not be thoughtlessly played around with—"With lots of words comes wrongdoing, but the wise restrain their lips" (Prov. 10:19, Common English Version).

But as communication can be used for death and destruction, so also it can be used for health and healing—"The words of the reckless pierce like swords, but *the tongue of the wise brings healing*" (Prov. 12:18, italics added). Tact, diplomacy, and civility flow directly from biblical principles and can produce peace and harmony out of division and chaos. Used as a wisely administered surgical scalpel, communication can be used for help and healing; used as a sword, it can be used for anything but.

And not all weapons are equal. Some are much more destructive than others, just as some ammunition is much more destructive than others. The type of weapon being used certainly determines destructive force, but what the weapon is armed with is of equal consideration. The helpfulness or deadliness of what comes out of us is determined by what is inside of us—"*What people say with their mouths comes from what fills their hearts.* Those who are good have good things saved in their hearts. That's why they say good things. But *those who are evil have hearts full of evil, and that's why they say things that are evil*" (Matt. 12:34–35, Easy-to-Read Version, italics added).

Our ability to impact others through communication is a sacred trust from God. We are like him; therefore, we have similar abilities to his, although not in degree, in kind. God is a communicator. And Jesus *is* the communication of God to us. For that reason, among possible others, he is called "the Word"—"In the beginning was the Word, and the Word was with God, and the Word was God" (John 1:1). He is the human expression of God. He is the human communication of God's person and essence to us—"The Son is the radiance of God's glory and the exact representation of his being" (Heb. 1:3).

Just as more people are *physically* wounded in homes than about anywhere else, so it is that more people are wounded *emotionally and spiritually* by words and actions in homes than anywhere else as well. Churches, too, as spiritual families, can be hotbeds of abusive verbal exchanges, subtle and not so subtle. We have more intimate and open access to one another in such places. Those who are children or who are weaker are often subjected to verbal and physical cruelty that leave lifelong damage. Verbal abuse can be every bit as damaging as physical abuse, and often even more so. Even if it was not intended to be damaging.

God wants us to be the salt of the earth, seasoning and preserving (protecting from rot) the world around us—"You are the salt of the earth. But if the salt loses its saltiness, how can it be made salty again? It is no longer good for anything, except to be thrown out and trampled underfoot" (Matt. 5:13). Therefore, he wants our words and actions to be consistent with this purpose—"*Be wise in the way you act toward outsiders*; make the most of every opportunity. *Let your conversation be always full of grace, seasoned with salt*, so that you may know how to answer everyone" (Col. 4:5–6, italics added).

Failure to contain our tongues reflects disingenuousness and insincerity—"Those who consider themselves religious and yet *do not keep a tight rein on their tongues deceive themselves*, and their religion is worthless" (James 1:26, italics added). As light and salt in the world, we, as believers, must in everything exercise care in all our human interactions—"*Do everything without complaining or arguing* so that you will be blameless and pure, children of God without any fault. But you are living with evil people all around you, who have lost their sense of what is right. *Among those people you shine like lights in a dark world, and you offer them the teaching that gives life*" (Phil. 2:14–16, Easy-to-Read Version, italics added).

Therefore our prayer should be as the psalm, "May my words and thoughts please you" (Ps. 19:14, Easy-to-Read Version). And our careful commitment in all our communication should thus be exemplary to those who hear and observe us—"Don't let anyone treat you as if you are not important. Be an example to show the believers how they should live. Show them by what you say, by the way you live, by your love, by your faith, and by your pure life" (1 Tim. 4:12, Easy-to-Read Version).

All in all, be an example in reflecting whose you are—God's—in everything you are.

A Prayer:

Purify my heart, O Lord, and make my mouth and my life
a fountain of the goodness of your sweet Holy Spirit.
Teach me to guard my words and my ways.
Pour into me your goodness, crowding out the corruption
of the flesh that abides in me, so that what comes out
of me is helpful and can bless, rather than curse, those
around me.
Make my life salt and light for you, Dear God.
Amen.

18
Complaining and Grumbling

Complaining lips reflect a proud, thankless heart.

Do everything without grumbling or arguing, so that you may become blameless and pure, "children of God without fault in a warped and crooked generation" (Phil. 2:14–15).

DISCONTENTMENT IS AN inner disease of the heart and mind. Grumbling, complaining, murmuring, arguing, and criticizing are its outcomes. And they are corrosive, destructive, and malignant. They are, as well, contagious! Complaining and arguing are against the very nature and will of God—"Do Everything without grumbling or arguing, so that you may become blameless and pure, 'children of God without fault…'" (Phil. 2:14–15).

There is indeed something that may seem like complaining and criticizing that is actually helpful and proper. Called "constructive criticism," its intent and outcome are much different because it comes from a different heart. Constructive criticism seeks only improvement while trusting and accepting whatever is to come. It is always thankful. It seeks not control but only surrender. It comes from a humble, indebted heart not from the prideful heart of one who feels entitled and privileged. Thus it is "constructive" and not destructive. Grumbling, on the other hand, is prideful and arrogant. It is destructive. Its source seeks to esteem itself by denigrating others, and by inference, either intended or unintended, denigrating God.

Rather than complain when we face discomfort, hardship, frustration, and such, God would have us trust him through it, and therefore experience joy in the midst of it. For it is, in fact, through trial that we grow the most—"Consider it pure joy, my brothers and sisters, whenever you face trials of many kinds, because you know that the testing of your faith produces perseverance. Let perseverance finish its work so that you may be mature and complete, not lacking anything" (James 1:2–4). Grumbling against either God or others will in actuality not only *not* help us but also backfire, bringing God's judgment on us—"*Don't grumble against one another*, brothers and sisters, *or you will be judged*. The Judge is standing at the door!" (James 5:9, italics added).

Instead, God wants us to be thankful no matter what happens—"Give thanks in all circumstances; for this is God's will for you in Christ Jesus" (1 Thess. 5:18). He wants us to do the things he teaches us without complaint—"Offer hospitality to one another without grumbling" (1 Pet. 4:9). As believers, we have given ourselves to him; we are his—"You are not your own; you were bought at a price. Therefore honor God with your bodies" (1 Cor. 6:19–20). Since we have given ourselves to him, we should humbly, trustingly, and thankfully submit to his bidding.

Job is the ultimate example of one who might be considered as worthy of having a "beef" with God, losing pretty much all that he had in a single afternoon. Yet, his righteousness and faith glowed in his moment of testing—"At this, Job got up and tore his robe and shaved his head. Then he fell to the ground in worship and said: 'Naked I came from my mother's womb, and naked I will depart. The Lord gave and the Lord has taken away; may the name of the Lord be praised.' In all this, Job did not sin by charging God with wrongdoing" (Job. 1:20–22). Rather than grumble, he trusted. Rather than complain, he praised. And rather than curse, he mourned and lamented. And in the end God rewarded with more than he had had before. Job's story can be our story, if we will imitate him.

The Israelites, the most blessed nation on the earth, quickly became a complaining lot—"In the desert the whole community grumbled against Moses and Aaron." The Israelites said to them, "If only we had died by the LORD's hand in Egypt! There we sat around pots of meat and ate all the food we wanted, but you have brought us out into this desert to starve this entire assembly to death" (Exod. 16:2–3). While their grumbling was ostensibly against Moses and Aaron, their God-given leaders, it was indirectly at God—"[Moses said to the people,] 'Who are we? You are not grumbling against us, but against the LORD'" (Exod. 16:8).

We, as believers in Christ, are warned of this egregious behavior toward the Lord—"Now these things occurred as examples to keep us from setting our hearts on evil things as they did…*do not grumble, as some of them did—and were killed by the destroying angel*. These things happened to them as examples and were written down as warnings for us, on whom the culmination of the ages has come. So, if you think you are standing firm, be careful that you don't fall!" (1 Cor. 10:6, 10–12, italics added). Grumbling and arguing are to be considered most serious offenses before God and not merely a mild, normal symptom of human discontent!

And many of our hardships are, in the first place, not caused by God or by others anyway but rather are caused by our own sin and misbehavior—"Do not be deceived: God cannot be mocked. A man reaps what he sows. Whoever sows to please their flesh, from the flesh will reap destruction; whoever sows to please the Spirit, from the Spirit will reap eternal life" (Gal. 6:7–8). So much of what we complain about is our own doing and thus often is to be remedied not by God or others but by *our own* right or corrective behavior. What then is our complaint against God or others for our own failings—"Why should the living complain when punished for their sins?" (Lam. 3:39).

There is a real difference between constructive criticism and complaining criticism. The former is helpful; the latter is harmful. Moses own father-in-law, Jethro, Priest of Midian, gave Moses constructive criticism when he saw the inefficiency in his process of leading and judging Israel—"What you are doing is not good. You and these people who come to you will only wear yourselves out. The work is too heavy for you; you cannot handle it alone. Listen now to me and I will give you some advice, and may God be with you" (Exod. 18:17–19). Moses implemented Jethro's constructive suggestion to the benefit of both himself and the people!

There is also indeed a difference between complaining and lamenting. There is even an inspired book of laments in our Bible, Lamentations! The faithful sufferer, Job, gave vent to his own laments over his dire condition—"I loathe my very life; therefore I will give free rein to my complaint and speak out in the bitterness of my soul" (Job 10:1).

There is, as well, a difference between *asking questions* of God or others and *questioning* them. Job certainly lamented and posed questions to God, but when his questions to God became a questioning *of* God, he brought God's wrath down upon himself—"Then the Lord spoke to Job from a whirlwind and said, 'Who is this ignorant person saying these foolish things? Prepare yourself for an attack! Get ready to answer the questions I will ask you'" (Job. 38, Easy-to-Read Version). God's rebuke of Job got even worse before it got better.

In a last challenging question from God, Job finally got the message, and thus repented before God—"The Lord said to Job: 'Will the one who contends with the Almighty correct him? Let him who accuses God answer him!' Then Job answered the Lord: 'I am unworthy—how can I reply to you? I put my hand over my mouth. I spoke once, but I have no answer—twice, but I will say no more'" (Job. 40:1–5).

Even those original Jews who first heard Jesus grumbled and complained, alleging misbehavior on his part—"Now all the tax collectors and sinners [including nonobservant Jews] were coming near Jesus to listen to Him. Both the Pharisees and the scribes began muttering and complaining, saying, 'This man accepts and welcomes sinners and eats with them'" (Luke 15:1–2, Amplified Bible). At the conclusion of his difficult-to-hear "bread of life" sermon, many listening to him complained—"At this the Jews there began to grumble about him because he said, 'I am the bread that came down from heaven.' They said, 'Is this not Jesus, the son of Joseph, whose father and mother we know? How can he now say, 'I came down from heaven?' 'Stop grumbling among yourselves,' Jesus answered" (John 6:41–43).

Argumentative, disputing attitudes flow directly from a complaining spirit and are equally undesirable—"What causes fights and quarrels among you? Don't they come from your desires that battle within you? You desire but do not have, so you kill. You covet but you cannot get what you want, so you quarrel and fight. You do not have because you do not ask God. When you ask, you do not receive, because you ask with wrong motives, that you may spend what you get on your pleasures" (James 4:1–3). Jealousy and arguing among us reflects worldliness and never what some may feel to be a kind of spiritual elitism somehow worthy to criticize others—"You are still worldly [controlled by ordinary impulses, the sinful capacity]. For as long as there is jealousy and strife *and* discord among you, are you not unspiritual, and are you not walking like ordinary men [unchanged by faith]?" (1 Cor. 3:1–3, Amplified Bible).

In reality, if our focus is right, what flows in and out of us will be right as well—"Finally, brothers and sisters, whatever is true, whatever is noble, whatever is right, whatever is pure, whatever is lovely, whatever is admirable—if anything is excellent or praiseworthy—think about such things" (Phil. 4:8).

A Prayer:

> Father, help mine never to be grumbling, complaining spirit.
> May I never bring such shame on you, the body of Christ, or myself by a critical, questioning, malignant, and unappreciative spirit.
> Let my mind always be aware of your goodness and blessings, and from my heart flow the fruit of thankfulness.
> Make me one who ever builds up and never tears down.
> Amen.

19
Covetousness

Our greatest fear is often not that God will fail to give us what we need; it is that he will fail to give us what we want.

When you ask, you do not receive, because you ask with wrong motives, that you may spend what you get on your pleasures (James 4:3).

TRUSTING GOD IS not about believing that he will give you all you want or even what *you* believe you need. It is believing that his work in you is good and right regardless of the circumstances and outcomes. Trusting God is to be satisfied with what you have because you believe you have all you actually need, and it is accepting it fully and joyfully.

We have needs, and we have wants. We may need things we don't want. And, we surely often want things we don't need. Only God knows for sure which is which.

Our faith must not seek to align God with us; it must align us with God. We discover and adjust ourselves to the Great I Am, the

Ever-Existent One, because we have come to believe he is the standard of right, of truth, and of good. We believe it because we trust in him and his supremacy. He is who he is, and he does not change. He does not need to change. The creation came into existence by his design and for his purpose. He construed its parameters—its dimensions, its morality, its laws, its purpose, and so forth. He designed us in his image and breathed his life into us. We must seek out and find him as he is and discover his designs as they are, rather than seeking to attempt to impose our own will on who and what already is.

One of the original Ten Commandments is "Thou shalt not covet..." (Exod. 20:17, King James Version). To covet means to lust after. To lust after is to crave and set intentions on that which is not ours, whether it is a thing or it is a person. When we covet, we breach faith with God, failing to trust him. "But seek first his kingdom and his righteousness, and all these things will be given to you as well" (Matt. 6:33). We must put his kingdom first, and then we must trust that we have been and will be given what we truly need.

And when we covet, we not only breach faith with God concerning our own life and existence but also breach faith with God concerning others' lives and existences. We assume to take the role of "God" in others' lives for ourselves. Perhaps we dare take from others that which is not ours to take or to give to them that which they do not need and which might otherwise prove harmful to them. We are completely incompetent in the role of God in others' lives or our own life.

To surrender to God requires us to give up covetousness. Covetousness runs counter to surrender. Rather covetousness seeks to conquer, not to surrender—"Those who want to get rich fall into temptation and a trap and into many foolish and harmful desires that plunge people into ruin and destruction" (1 Tim. 6:9). We fall into much grief when we covet, because we seek to play God, and we will always fail miserably at it. We fall into an eternally destructive trap when we try to have more than we need—"It is easier for a camel to go through the eye of a needle than for someone who is rich to enter the kingdom of God" (Matt. 19:24).

To covet is, in perhaps seeking freedom as the world sees it, to be enslaved to the worst master of all—our own sinful human heart. To surrender to Christ is to be enslaved to the only one who can finally free us from such bondage—"So if the Son sets you free, you will be free indeed" (John 8:36).

Total freedom requires complete surrender. Complete surrender requires whole-hearted trust. Whole-hearted trust requires faithful conviction. Faithful conviction requires honest seeking. Covetousness finally melts away under the glare of the truth that is discovered through complete surrender to Christ.

A Prayer:

Help me, O Lord, to see that all that exists belongs to you, and ultimately not to me or anyone else.
Show me how to be thankful for what I have, not resentful for what I do not have.
Free me from the lust of things and grow me in a thirst for you.
Remind me that I can receive nothing good that is not from you, and that I cannot give to another what has not first been given to me.
Help me to see myself as a trustee of the things you assign to my care and not an owner of anything, including my very self or of those I love.
May I never ever covet that which is not mine or those things that are not meant to be mine.
Help me to be content with what I have, and ready to give up anything in my present possession in order to please you.

20
Creation

If there is indeed a Mother Nature, she most assuredly has an all-powerful Heavenly Father.

In the beginning God created the heavens and the earth (Gen. 1:1).

THERE IS TO believers a seeming lunacy in unbelief. And it is just such lunacy that makes unbelief scoff at honest belief. Humanity's continued attempt to "be like God" (read here, "be God") has exposed itself over and over as foolish and futile. Yet, humanity at large continues its hot pursuit of divinity through its self-worshiping religion of humanism.

"Although they claimed to be wise, they became fools and exchanged the glory of the immortal God for images made to look like a mortal human being and birds and animals and reptiles" (Rom. 1:22–23). Yes indeed, in the original sin, we tried to act as though we were gods! And this base, ridiculous desire continues still to be the prime motive and mother of all sins.

A universe with a beginning, even by the admission of science's own "discovery," shows itself to have a source. This source of energy is said by science to be pure energy, and it became matter. This matter exploded in a "Big Bang" and developed over eons into our present world. Amazing as it is, some scientists speculate our universe may only be one of an infinitesimal number of other such events.

A pure energy source of unknown existence or origin exploded into matter. Unbelievers would have us believe this matter spontaneously, by chance, arranged itself into a world of being, balance, and wonder. Higher beings, such as humankind, came into existence over eons of time purely by chance through mutations that occurred over and over throughout millennia and against incredible odds. Really? It is simply utterly impossible!

And yet, science scoffs at the faith of believers!

Simply put, there is no greater or blinder faith that can be found than that of "unbelief." Some dare to call our planet "Mother Earth." A giant rock, albeit because of its creator an amazing one, is said to be our "mother," huh? And the cool intellectualism that blinds and brainwashes the masses scoffs at the idea of a Heavenly Father.

Stated simply, "The fool has said in his heart there is no God" (Ps. 14:1).

It is true there is much imbalanced and often ignorant speculation from believers about creation. There are many conclusions and supposed "truths" that are posited that are simply and seemingly untenable, and many are likely harmful. Some, if not many, of Christians' claims surely are patently untrue. However, the core truth that "In the beginning God created the heavens and the earth" explains with consistency and cogency what we observe in and around ourselves—intelligent design. Forethought. Intentionality. Utter brilliance.

None of us can explain all the nuances of existence or fully understand all the underlying purposes of creation—"Oh, the depth of the riches of the wisdom and knowledge of God! How unsearchable his judgments, and his paths beyond tracing out! Who has known the mind of the Lord? Or who has been his counselor?" (Rom. 11:33–34). But one thing is clear to those who believe—there is a creator behind all that we see and experience. The evidence as we see it and believe it is that Yahweh is the creator's name and that the book we call the Bible explains to us what we need to know to live in harmony with him and his purposes in this creation he has placed us in.

Yes, if our planet might dare be called our "Mother Earth," she sure has an intelligent and all-powerful Heavenly Father!

A Prayer:

You are the Creator,
It is clear to see,
You made all that is,
And you made even me.

That you are is obvious,
Your eternal power clear,
In unbelief I'm frightened,
In belief I need not fear.

Open my eyes to see you,
Touch my heart that I may know,
Your beauty and your goodness,
Through the wonders creation shows.

21
Critical Thinking

Critical thinking is to critical as day is to night.

The person with the Spirit makes judgments about all things, but such a person is not subject to merely human judgments, for, "Who has known the mind of the Lord so as to instruct him?" But we have the mind of Christ (1 Cor. 2:15-16, Isa. 40:13).

WHEN WE ARE critical at heart, we are dark and likely walking in darkness. To be critical is to be judgmental and condemning, and such judgment is against the Spirit of grace—"Speak and act as those who are going to be judged by the law that gives freedom, because judgment without mercy will be shown to anyone who has not been merciful. Mercy triumphs over judgment" (James 2:12–13). Mercy triumphs over judgment as light triumphs over darkness, as good triumphs over evil, and as God triumphs over Satan.

God is rich in mercy (Eph. 2:4–5) and full of grace (John 1:14). God indeed judges those of us who presume to be judges of others—"Do not judge, or you too will be judged. For in the same way you judge others, you will be judged, and with the measure you use, it will be measured to you" (Matt. 7:1–2).

There is, however, a type of judgment or spiritual discernment that is actually required of us as the people of God—"What business is it of mine to judge those outside the church? Are you not to judge those inside? God will judge those outside" (1 Cor. 5:12–13). It is not seeking to destroy but to restore. It seeks not condemnation but restoration. Through it we make godly, Spirit-guided decisions regarding ourselves as well as those for whom and to whom we are responsible. Any criticism that comes is constructive rather than destructive. It elevates and believes in others. To think critically as God would have us do, we must think reasonably, responsibly, and soberly rather than in the way of the world—"For by the grace given me I say to every one of you: Do not think of yourself more highly than you ought, but rather think of yourself with sober judgment, in accordance with the faith God has distributed to each of you" (Rom. 12:3). Spiritual discernment requires humility, clear thinking, and sober judgment.

Spiritual discernment is critical thinking. It is logic. It is sober—unclouded by the haze that clouds our minds when we are full of ourselves. Spiritual discernment is godly reason and logic. It is accepting the responsibility of the decision-making and kingdom work that God has given to us as his servants. But such "judgment" is discernment in carrying out *God's will*, not judgment in carrying out *our own desires*.

God engages our spiritual discernment as we carry out his will—"I will give you the keys of the kingdom of heaven; whatever you bind on earth will be bound in heaven, and whatever you loose on earth will be loosed in heaven" (Matt. 16:19). But there are limits on the level of delegation for each of us from the greatest to the least, and we must each honestly seek to understand the responsibility that we are given in our roles and situations and think soberly—with positive critical thinking—as we carry out God's will. Whether as parents with our children (Eph. 6:4) or leaders in our church communities (Heb. 13:17), we must carry out God's will and purposes, as best we can in accordance with the wisdom and the responsibility given to us by God. But we must never presume to play God.

Because even our critical thinking will not always be right—"My conscience is clear, but that does not make me innocent. It is the Lord who judges me. Therefore judge nothing before the appointed time; wait until the Lord comes. He will bring to light what is hidden in darkness and will expose the motives of the heart. At that time each will receive their praise from God" (1 Cor. 4:4–5). God will search our hearts and our minds in order to judge our behavior—"I the Lord search the heart and examine the mind, to reward each person according to their conduct, according to what their deeds deserve" (Jer. 17:10). Because God alone can know the deepest and truest thoughts and motives of the human heart—"The heart is deceitful above all things and beyond cure" (Jer. 17:9), and "The Lord searches every heart and understands every desire and every thought" (1 Chron. 28:9).

Ours is to be a judgment of discernment flowing from sound, Spirit-led thinking as we carry out the will of God. Spiritual discernment is sound critical thinking rather than the judgment of condemnation. It seeks to build up, not to tear down. Spiritual discernment is good spiritual logic and reason. Condemnation on the other hand is a kind of thinking and judgment that is critical in nature. It is condemning and belittling of others, including ourselves.

Critical thinking is of the light. Being critical is of darkness.

A Prayer:

> Lord, help me discern between critical thinking and being critical;
> To know the difference between asking questions of you and questioning you.

Help me to love you with my mind—to think your way and to think your thoughts.

Show me how to take captive my every thought to make it obedient to you.

Let me never stoop to be a negative critic of a world in the painful grip of sin;

To never judge another for being like me, one in desperate need of help.

Let my thoughts and my expressions be bright, hopeful, and healing, even those of correction and rebuke.

May I own the reality that, through your Spirit, I, along with all believers, have the mind of Christ.

22
Devoted Hearts

Most of all, God desires from us hearts of faith that are fully committed to him.

The eyes of the Lord range throughout the earth to strengthen those whose hearts are fully committed to him (2 Chr. 16:9).

GOD SEES US heart level. He sees the thoughts of both our minds and our hearts as actual behavior—"I the Lord search the heart and examine the mind, to reward each person according to their conduct, according to what their deeds deserve" (Jer. 17:9). The love of God (*agape*, Greek) is a fixed love based on truth and right. God is said to, in fact, be this kind of love (1 John 4:8).

The apostle Paul described love this way: "Love is patient, love is kind. It does not envy, it does not boast, it is not proud. It does not dishonor others, it is not self-seeking, it is not easily angered, it keeps no record of wrongs. Love does not delight in evil but rejoices with the truth. It always protects, always trusts, always hopes, always perseveres" (1 Cor. 13:4–7). It is this kind of love that is enduring and never ends, because it is of God.

Agape is eternal and supersedes all situations; it is not a momentary and situational love. It is unconditional love; it is not conditional. It is a love of the will, not a love of the want. It is proactive based on truth, justice, mercy, right, and what is best, rather than reactive to personal interests and desires. It is based on who we are before God, not who another is before us. It is observant, active, pursuing, and passionate, not dull, passive, self-absorbed, and apathetic—"For God so loved the world that he gave…" (John 3:16).

The "Great Commandment" of Jesus calls us to love God in this way—"Love the Lord your God with all your heart and with all your soul and with all your mind" (Matt. 22:37). This command requires something of us. In fact, it requires everything of us—"Love the Lord your God with *all*…" Every bit of it. Every bit of you! And God sees where our minds and our hearts are going.

We are not to be victims of our subjective, meandering thoughts of mind and heart. The heart is deceptive because its thoughts, left alone, are based on animal instinct and feeling—"The heart is deceitful above all things and beyond cure. Who can understand it?" (Jer. 17:9). The word of God will judge these heart thoughts however—"For the word of God is alive and active. Sharper than any double-edged sword, it penetrates even to dividing soul and spirit, joints and marrow; *it judges the thoughts and attitudes of the heart*" (Heb. 4:12, italics added). Thus we must recognize and capture what our heart and mind thoughts are and bring them into obedience to Christ—"We take captive every thought to make it obedient to Christ" (2 Cor. 10:5).

And our all-surpassing mind and heart thoughts are to be focused in on loving God—to will and to do what is right and best in his regard. To love God is to be wholly devoted to him—"For Christ's love compels us…" (2 Cor. 5:14). It is to love him with our minds—to think his thoughts, to take on his right and good attitudes, and to regard every bit of his creation as he regards it. It is to love him with our hearts—to assume his devotions, to regard his passions, and to live for his purposes—"So from now on we regard no one from a worldly point of view" (2 Cor. 5:16).

God looks at our hearts, because he only need look there to predict what our outward behaviors will be—"For the mouth speaks what the heart is full of" (Luke 6:45). God examines our minds because the mind is what controls the heart—it controls what goes into the heart and thus ultimately what comes out—"Be transformed by the renewing of your mind…" (Rom. 12:2).

Also, God commands us to love him with all our souls. Our soul is our core identity—our personality. It is at the core of who we are—how we see our self in relation to God, how we see and relate to our own self, and how we see and relate to others. It is the summation of all our perceptions of God, self, and others. Our soul is who we are at present and thus determines who we are becoming. And God wants us to completely identify with him.

God knows each of us as what our mind thinks, our heart feels, and by our souls' identity. It is at this level that he connects with us, and thus it is at this level that we either find salvation in him or that our hearts condemn us as insincere before him—"The Spirit himself testifies with our spirit that we are God's children" (Rom. 8:16).

A Prayer:

> Grant me a heart, O Lord, devoted,
> A heart that's pure and true,
> Let my every thought and motive,
> Be sanctified by you.
>
> Let my heart not turn away from you,
> To sinful lusts that would distract,
> Help my heart to be a pure one,
> That nothing in me from you detract.

I devote myself to you now fully,
I surrender here and now all to you,
Make my life a testimony of you,
In everything I say and do!

23
Discouragement, Perseverance, and Salvation

We cannot promise Christ that we will not fall or err in living our life for him. Falling and making mistakes is a part of learning to walk and live. What we can promise him, however, is that we will always get right back up and that we will never give up or quit.

Let us not become weary in doing good, for at the proper time we will reap a harvest if we do not give up (Gal. 6:9).

SALVATION BY FAITH infers the totality of faith, from beginning to end, and not just one's faith in initially coming to Christ in rebirth—"For I am not ashamed of the gospel, because it is the power of God that brings salvation to everyone who believes: first to the Jew, then to the Gentile. For in the gospel the righteousness of God is revealed—*a righteousness that is by faith from first to last*, just as it is written: 'The righteous *will live by* faith'" (Rom. 1:16–17,

Hab. 2:4, italics added). Being saved by faith means *both* coming to faith *and* living by faith.

The apostle Paul who seemingly was inspired above all others to fully explain salvation by faith in Christ Jesus, wrote of himself as he neared his own end, "I have fought the good fight, I have finished the race, *I have kept the faith*" (2 Tim. 4:7, italics added). Faith is something to be *kept*; it is not just a mental ascent to a truth and a subsequent casual admission to it when convenient. The Lord was faithful to God from beginning to end. The apostle Paul was faithful from the beginning of coming to faith to end of his life. And the Lord similarly calls us to be faithful from our reception of Christ by faith until our death in him—"Be faithful until death, and I will give you the crown of life" (Rev. 2:10, New King James Version).

Faith is not an event. Faith is not a thing. Faith is a covenant relationship in which one comes to trust another. Thus one *en*trusts something to the other. And ours is a lifelong covenant with him to remain faithful to him. God is always faithful. The only question is, will we be?

In salvation, God calls us to entrust ourselves to him by dying to self and living for him—"*I have been crucified with Christ and I no longer live*, but *Christ lives in me*. The life I now live in the body, I live by faith in the Son of God, who loved me and gave himself for me" (Gal. 2:20, italics added). He died for us so that we could see and understand what it means to die to a self-willed life and live a life of sacrifice and service for him—"And he died for all, that those who live should no longer live for themselves but for him who died for them and was raised again" (2 Cor. 5:15).

God promises to those who accept him in faith the gift of himself, the Holy Spirit. He promises that if we will trust him and commit ourselves to him, he will entrust himself to us as a gift and come to live inside of us—"Repent and be baptized, every one of you, in the name of Jesus Christ for the forgiveness of your sins. And *you will receive the gift of the Holy Spirit*. The *promise is for you and your children and for all who are far off—for all whom the Lord our God will call*" (Acts 2:38–39, italics added).

But at our death to self and rebirth to God, our faith "work" doesn't end. The only work God requires of us for salvation is to believe in Jesus Christ—"The people asked Jesus, 'What does God want us to do?' Jesus answered, 'The work God wants you to do is this: to believe in the one he sent'" (John 6:28–29, Easy-to-Read Version). God's love is unconditional and it is his very essence—"So we know the love that God has for us, and we trust that love. *God is love*. Everyone who lives in love lives in God, and God lives in them" (1 John 4:16, Easy-to-Read Version, italics added).

Although his grace is immeasurable and readily lavished on us, it is not unconditional, from the beginning of our coming to faith to the end of our life on earth (Eph. 1:4–8). God's grace, shown to us in his mercy given to us in Christ Jesus, is first contingent upon our coming to trust God's righteousness and goodness and never our own—"It is by grace you have been saved, through faith—and this is not from yourselves, it is the gift of God—not by works, so that no one can boast. For we are God's handiwork, created in Christ Jesus to do good works, which God prepared in advance for us to do" (Eph. 2:8–10).

God's grace toward us is, secondly, conditional on our generously showing grace and mercy to others in our service to God and men—"*If* you forgive others their sins, your heavenly Father will also forgive you. But *if you don't* forgive others, neither will your Father forgive your sins" (Matt. 6:14–15, Common English Bible, italics added). Jesus himself made this quite clear in his parable about the "unmerciful servant" who was forgiven much by his master but was unwilling to forgive another even just a little—"[The master said to the unmerciful servant,] 'Shouldn't you also have mercy on your fellow servant, just as I had mercy on you?' His master was furious and handed him over to the guard responsible for punishing prisoners, until he had paid the whole debt. [Jesus explained,] '*My heavenly Father will also do the same to you if you don't forgive your brother or sister from your heart'*" (Matt. 18:32–35, Common English Bible, italics added).

Jesus made clear that unless we, even as Christians, forgive others their sins against us, God will restore our own sin debt to him back to our account. God is sovereign, and he can certainly do as he pleases in regard to his mercy—"I will have mercy on whom I have mercy, and I will have compassion on whom I have compassion" (Rom. 9:15, Exodus 33:19). God is incredibly graceful to us, lavishing his mercy and compassion on us, and he expects us to do likewise toward others.

God's grace is, thirdly, contingent upon our not becoming discouraged, and thus, quitting—"*You need to persevere so that when you have done the will of God*, you will receive what he has promised. For, 'In just a little while, he who is coming will come and will not delay.' And, 'But my righteous one will live by faith. And *I take no pleasure in the one who shrinks back*.' But *we do not belong to those who shrink back and are destroyed, but to those who have faith and are saved*" (Heb. 10:36–39, italics added).

Our complete reception of the gospel and living by faith in Christ is a threefold continuum, as Paul pointed out—"I want to remind you of the gospel I preached to you, which *you received* and *on which you have taken your stand*. By this gospel you are saved, if you *hold firmly to the word* I preached to you. *Otherwise, you have believed in vain*" (1 Cor. 15:1–2, italics added). Living by faith requires, first, an acceptance of the truth of Jesus as Lord and Savior ("you received"), second, a faithful surrender to the reality of it ("on which you have taken your stand"), and, third, living a life of surrender to it ("hold firmly to the word").

Therefore, the one commitment we must make from the very beginning is that we will never quit. We should have the same spirit the apostles had when after the particularly tough "bread of life" sermon had caused many to leave, and Jesus asked them if they wanted to leave as well. Their answer, spoken by the apostle Peter, was simple and resolute—"Lord, to whom shall we go? You have the words of eternal life. We have come to believe and to know that you are the Holy One of God" (John 6:68–69).

Resolve to never quit.

A Prayer:

> Lord, I commit to you to never, never, never quit in my pursuit of you.
> I cannot promise you that I will not err or fall; because you know I get weak.
> What I do promise is that I will never just lay there, but that I will quickly get back up when falls happen.
> I trust you. I trust your goodness and grace. My faith in you is resolute.
> Jesus is Lord.
> Amen.

24
Doubt

Doubt is the water faith walks on.

Then Peter got down out of the boat, walked on the water and came toward Jesus (Matt. 14:29).

DOUBT IS THE water faith walks on and the sea it sails on, and the Holy Spirit is what keeps faith afloat and is himself the wind in its sails. Doubt does not defy faith; it validates it. There can be no faith without doubt—"For we live by faith, not by sight" (2 Cor. 5:7).

To live by faith means to base what we believe about what we cannot see on what we believe about what we can see. That we presently cannot see something does not mean it does not exist. Such thinking is utterly ridiculous. To see the invisible as somehow less real than what we call the visible is foolish indeed—"So we fix our eyes not on what is seen, but on what is unseen, since what is seen is temporary, but what is unseen is eternal" (2 Cor. 4:18).

The majority of the human experience is reliant on the invisible—"The coming of the kingdom of God is not something that can be observed, nor will people say, 'Here it is,' or 'There it is,' because the kingdom of God is in your midst" (Luke 17:20–21). What is presently invisible can however be "seen" to a degree through what is visible; the eternal can be accessed through the temporal; the Creator can be known through the created—"For since the creation of the world God's invisible qualities—his eternal power and divine nature—have been clearly seen, being understood from what has been made, so that people are without excuse" (Rom. 1:20).

To live by doubt means to see the visible as somehow more real than the invisible. Thomas encountered much doubt about that which he saw as unbelievable and impossible—the resurrection of the body of a brutally tortured and executed Jesus. To the apostles who had first seen the resurrected Christ, when Thomas was not present, Thomas said, "Unless I see the nail marks in his hands and put my finger where the nails were, and put my hand into his side, I will not believe" (John 20:25). Upon his personal witness of Jesus's resurrected body, Thomas exclaims, "My Lord and my God!" (John 20:28). The sudden appearance of the invisible yet quite real, resurrected Christ changed forever not only Thomas's reality but also changed reality for all of us!

Jesus pronounced a blessing on the honest, sincere ones who believe in the existent realities they cannot see—"Blessed are those who have not seen and yet have believed" (John 20:29). The honest soul recognizes the essential coexistence of faith and doubt—"I do believe; help me overcome my unbelief!" (Mark 9:24).

Jesus—the Ever-Existent One—beckons us to, "Stop doubting and believe" (John 20:27). Belief must not be based on mere conjecture, tradition, culture, or human desire but based on the evidence of what is seen—a creation, the testimony of eyewitnesses, obviously inspired scriptures, an empty tomb of the resurrected Christ, and the fingerprints of God all around us.

Jesus calls us out of the relative safety of this present boat in which we exist out into the ocean of abundant, eternal existence. "Shortly before dawn Jesus went out to them, walking on the lake.

When the disciples saw him walking on the lake, they were terrified. 'It's a ghost,' they said, and cried out in fear. But Jesus immediately said to them: 'Take courage! It is I. Don't be afraid.' 'Lord, if it's you,' Peter replied, 'tell me to come to you on the water.' 'Come,' he said. Then Peter got down out of the boat, walked on the water and came toward Jesus. But when he saw the wind, he was afraid and, beginning to sink, cried out, 'Lord, save me!' Immediately Jesus reached out his hand and caught him. 'You of little faith,' he said, 'why did you doubt?'" (Matt. 14:25–31).

When faith takes us beyond the realities that we can see into the deeper realities that we cannot presently see, we extend ourselves into the eternal. There the impossible becomes possible, the unthinkable becomes reality, and the unimaginable becomes existential. In such faith, we find God.

But in this present existence, we must in faith get out of the boat and walk on the waters of doubt produced by what is presently unseen.

A Prayer:

Call me out of the boat, Lord, to walk on water,
To transcend doubt and come to you,
Give me faith and the brave acts that follow,
To know the power that you imbue.

Show me how to believe your word, God,
To own and act on your every word,
Make my life a testimony to your reality,
That others may see in me you, Lord!

25
Emotions, Part 1

Emotions are real but they are not necessarily connected to reality; they are indeed real but they are not trustworthy.

The heart is deceitful above all things and beyond cure. Who can understand it? (Jer. 17:9).

JUST FOLLOW YOUR heart goes a modern mantra. It is not a new human idea but finds a comfortable home in modern humanism, existentialism, modernism, and postmodernism, pervasive philosophies of more recent times. They are, however, the fruit of the wrong tree—the Tree of the Knowledge of Good and Evil. Satan lied to the first humans, telling them that if they would eat the forbidden fruit of reliance on human knowledge, "you will be like God, knowing good and evil" (Gen. 3:5). Rooting our purpose and existence in mere feelings of our hearts can only lead to disaster.

When differentiated from the mind, the heart represents the seat of emotions. Its activities are contrasted with the facts and logic of our mind. The heart, as spoken of in this regard is not the internal circulatory organ; rather it is a part of the brain where attitudes, preferences, intuition, and such are processed. It is the repository where our "life formulas" are developed and stored. It is the seat of emotions, desires, wants, and the ambiguous.

While the mind controls what goes into the heart, the heart ultimately controls behavior, because it is where information, observations, beliefs, perceptions, data, and so forth are processed to determine what actions or behaviors are merited—"Above all else, guard your heart, for everything you do flows from it" (Prov. 4:23).

But emotions are chemically produced by the flesh and thus are not to be the guiding force in our life—"In your anger do not sin": Do not let the sun go down while you are still angry, and do not give the devil a foothold" (Eph. 4:26–27). Emotions can indeed become a primary entry for Satan into our lives. Momentary anger seethes and become full of bitterness, malice, and hate. Our emotions often can run quite counter to the will of God—"Because human anger does not produce the righteousness that God desires" (James 1:20).

The human heart and emotions must not be seen as bad things though. They are necessary things, God-given things. But they must not be what rule us. To effectively serve God, the heart, along with its emotions, must be under the control of a mind that is under the control of God. Or else, there will be a perception, a misperception in fact, of human control, which only leads to insanity and chaos.

Self-control for the Christian begins with controlling the head, particularly the mind—"For God did not give us a spirit of timidity *or* cowardice *or* fear, but [He has given us a spirit] of power and of love and of sound judgment *and* personal discipline [abilities that result in a calm, well-balanced mind and self-control]" (2 Tim. 1:7, Amplified Bible). Biblical self-discipline is less about controlling the calendar and more about controlling one's head—our inner mind and heart thoughts.

A Prayer:

> Jesus, help me to make you wholly Lord of my heart,
> And to never confuse my emotions with your will.
>
> May your word be written on my heart Lord that I won't sin against you,
> And that it will be your word that will judge my heart's thoughts and attitudes, rather than mere human principles and traditions.

26
Emotions, Part 2

The heart may control behavior, but it is the mind that controls the heart.

We demolish arguments and every pretension that sets itself up against the knowledge of God, and we take captive every thought to make it obedient to Christ (2 Cor. 10:5).

GOD TEACHES US to steer our lives by first controlling our minds, not by following first our hearts. Our faith decision to follow Christ begins with a change of mind. To repent, the decision step of faith, literally means to "change one's mind" or "to change the inner man." Thus, we must not be steered or even swayed by the moods and emotions, either our own or those of others—"But you, keep your head in all situations..." (2 Tim. 4:5). Rather we must use our heads—our minds.

It is with this inner transformation of the mind produced by the Spirit and the word of God that we are then able to discern what God's will is—"Do not conform to the pattern of this world, but be transformed by the renewing of your mind. Then you will be able to test and approve what God's will is—his good, pleasing and perfect will" (Rom. 12:2). Emotions however, if left to their own device, cloud our judgment, create self-centeredness and subjectivity, and otherwise rob us of the ability to think clearly and cogently.

A sound mind and a head clear of emotional fog allows us to stay focused on the real and the important—"The end *and* culmination of all things is near. Therefore, be sound-minded and self-controlled for the purpose of prayer [staying balanced and focused on the things of God so that your communication will be clear, reasonable, specific and pleasing to Him.]" (1 Pet. 4:7, Amplified Bible). But such a sound mind and clear head requires spirituality, intentionality, obedience, and determination.

It is this intentionality of mental focus on God's will and control that allows our whole minds and hearts to be safely guarded in him—"Rejoice in the Lord always. I will say it again: Rejoice! Let your gentleness be evident to all. The Lord is near. Do not be anxious about anything, but in every situation, by prayer and petition, with thanksgiving, present your requests to God. And the peace of God, which transcends all understanding, will guard your hearts and your minds in Christ Jesus" (Phil. 4:4–7). It is under God's sentry of sanity that we then can focus on the right and true things—"Finally, brothers and sisters, whatever is true, whatever is noble, whatever is right, whatever is pure, whatever is lovely, whatever is admirable—if anything is excellent or praiseworthy—think about such things" (Phil. 4:8).

It is with the right attitude of mind that we are thus enabled to be recreated to be like God—"You were taught, with regard to your former way of life, to put off your old self, which is being corrupted by its deceitful desires; to be made new in the attitude of your minds; and to put on the new self, created to be like God in true righteousness and holiness" (Eph. 4:22–24).

Therefore, we must heed the command of the apostle, "Set your minds on things above, not on earthly things" (Col. 3:2). Because to have a heart for Christ, we must first have the mind of Christ, a gift given us through the power of the Holy Spirit—"The person with the Spirit makes judgments about all things, but such a person is not subject to merely human judgments, for, 'Who has known the mind of the Lord so as to instruct him?' But we have the mind of Christ" (1 Cor. 2:15–16).

Indeed, we have the mind of Christ. However, it is our responsibility to be in the Spirit and therefore of a sound mind. Is it not then odd that many believe that to be in the Spirit means to be given over to the momentary emotions—to follow one's heart? Rather, when we are first acting with the mind of Christ, we can safely be intoxicated with the inner joys and workings of the Holy Spirit within us—"Do not get drunk on wine, which leads to debauchery. Instead, be filled with the Spirit…" (Eph. 5:18).

And then, in such a godly context of inner being, emotions are not a bad thing but a very good thing.

A Prayer:

> Lord, consecrate my inner emotions that they be of you and not of me.
> Give me a heart that is resolute in its devotion to you and not drawn by the world.
> Let me not be guided by my heart in its deceitfulness, but help me, through the transforming power of your Spirit and word, to allow it command only in its conformity to your will.

27
Evil's Purpose

In the grace of God, evil finds its purpose.

But Scripture has locked up everything under the control of sin, so that what was promised, being given through faith in Jesus Christ, might be given to those who believe (Gal. 3:22).

GOD IS A God of grace—"In him we have redemption through his blood, the forgiveness of sins, in accordance with the riches of God's grace" (Eph. 1:7). His rich mercy flows out of his immeasurable grace—"Because of his great love for us, God, who is rich in mercy, made us alive with Christ even when we were dead in transgressions—it is by grace you have been saved" (Eph. 2:4–5).

Yet it is he who created all things, even Satan—"Through him all things were made; without him nothing was made that has been made" (John 1:3), and, "For in him all things were created: things in heaven and on earth, visible and invisible, whether thrones or powers or rulers or authorities; all things have been created through him and for him" (Col. 1:16). Thus, all things, including those powers of darkness who champion evil, were created by his foreknowledge.

Everything concerning God is intentional and purposeful. Even evil—"The Lord works out everything to its proper end—even the wicked for a day of disaster" (Prov. 16:4). There is an ultimate good purpose for sin's entry into the world.

God hates evil, yet he is recorded multiple times as having somehow willed it. Concerning Jesus, Peter says in his Pentecost sermon, "This man [Jesus] was handed over to you by God's deliberate plan and foreknowledge; and you, with the help of wicked men, put him to death by nailing him to the cross" (Acts 2:23). God hates murder (Prov. 6:16–19), yet willed it to happen to his own son—to himself!

In another case, God says, "See, it is I who created the blacksmith who fans the coals into flame and forges a weapon fit for its work. And it is I who have created the destroyer to wreak havoc; no weapon forged against you will prevail, and you will refute every tongue that accuses you. This is the heritage of the servants of the Lord, and this is their vindication from me" (Isa. 54:16–17). In other words, God created the blacksmith who forged the weapons and the destroying armies who used them against his people. Yes indeed, God wills evil for good purposes and promises that in him evil will not prevail but that its havoc will be vindicated.

Again, in his righteous judgment, God sent the king of Assyria and his armies to punish Israel for their gross and persistent evil—"Woe to the Assyrian, the rod of my anger, in whose hand is the club of my wrath! I send him against a godless nation, I dispatch him against a people who anger me, to seize loot and snatch plunder, and to trample them down like mud in the streets" (Isa. 10:5–6). Yet after sending the Assyrians, who had their own evil motives, to punish his people, God says, "When the Lord has finished all his work against Mount Zion and Jerusalem, he will say, 'I will punish the king of Assyria for the willful pride of his heart and the haughty look in his eyes'" (Isa. 10:12). He called Assyria to bring destruction, and then he punished Assyria for their deed.

No one can even begin to understand such mysteries of God's purposes. However, God shows himself to be good and kind, meek and lowly, and just and merciful. His utter wisdom, beauty, and ingenuity are revealed by creation—"God saw all that he had made, and it was very good" (Gen. 1:31), and "God's invisible qualities—his eternal power and divine nature—have been clearly seen, being understood from what has been made..." (Rom. 1:20).

While God's creation is presently corrupted by sin, beneath the dingy corrosion lies a pristine and ultimately good creation awaiting its final restoration and redemption back to its foreordained glory—"For the creation was subjected to frustration, not by its own choice, but by the will of the one who subjected it, in hope [expectation] that the creation itself will be liberated from its bondage to decay and brought into the freedom and glory of the children of God" (Rom. 8:20–21). God's plan for it all will finally prevail—"It is the Lord's purpose that prevails" (Prov. 19:21).

And it will all be well worth it for those who believe. Paul, the apostle, wrote, "For our light and momentary troubles are achieving for us an eternal glory that far outweighs them all. So we fix our eyes not on what is seen, but on what is unseen, since what is seen is temporary, but what is unseen is eternal" (2 Cor. 4:17–18). The present things that seem so big, so atrocious, and so painful will seem incidental, light, and momentary, and their achieved purposes will finally be lauded.

In unbelief, one might dare to think that our potential reward in the next life is not worth the pain of this one. But every great achievement or improved state of being has come with a corresponding great price. And when the great thing is achieved or the new state is arrived at, one seldom questions the cost.

A Prayer:

> Lord, I trust you, even though I often don't comprehend or understand you.
> I even find my naïve and unsuspecting will in conflict with you.
> I dare inwardly to move beyond asking questions of you to questioning you.
> Help me to find your grace through my sin, to find your goodness through my lack of it, to find your power in my weakness, and to receive your mercy through the extension of mercy.
> Let me see through your matchless grace evil's purpose in your creation.

28
Extremes, Part 1

Moderation is a godly virtue; only in a few things is the extreme the standard.

Whoever fears God will avoid all extremes (Eccles. 7:18).

EXTREMISM IS USUALLY not a good thing—religious or secular. Certainly trying to simply blend into the crowd, wherever the crowd may go, is not a good thing either. But the way of God is not typically one of extremes; rather it is one of control.

The virtue that causes the child of God to avoid extremes and excesses of all kinds is *temperance*. Temperance—self-control—is about keeping one's head in all circumstances. It is staying level. Extremism comes about through our passions, when we become inflamed in lust, greed, anger, hate, blind love, and so forth. We "lose our heads," and it causes us to do things in extremes and excesses.

In the flesh we are ultimately motivated by one of two things: fear of losing something or fear of not getting something. When those fears light the flames of other passions, such as hate or lust, extreme behaviors will result. When those fears are irrational, even though they may lead us down a path that seems right, they lead us away from God, not toward God—"There is a way that appears to be right, but in the end it leads to death" (Prov. 14:12).

Religious extremism, asceticism, and excess religiosity may at first appear particular pious and righteous, but in reality lack any value in relating to God, rather they prove counterproductive.

> Since you died with Christ to the elemental spiritual forces of this world, why, as though you still belonged to the world, do you submit to its rules: "Do not handle! Do not taste! Do not touch!"? These rules, which have to do with things that are all destined to perish with use, are based on merely human commands and teachings. Such regulations indeed have an appearance of wisdom, with their self-imposed worship, their false humility and their harsh treatment of the body, but they lack any value in restraining sensual indulgence (Col. 2:20–23).

When we fear only God, we need not fear losing or failing to gain something—"Seek first his kingdom" (Matt. 6:33). We need not engage in such fear at all, for "perfect love drives out fear" (1 John 4:18).

In the flesh we are generally reactive to stimuli—we hit, hurt, or hate, or we help, relieve, and love, because we feel others have hit us, hurt us, and hated us or because they help and love us. We only barter affections; we actually give nothing. We love if others love us; we hate if they hate us. When we are reactive, we will be controlled by external forces. When we are controlled by such forces, we take control from God.

But Jesus has taught us not to be controlled by external forces but only by him—"Rather than striking back at one who hurts you, turn the other cheek; if another would sue you for one thing, give additionally rather than resist; go the extra mile with one who would use unjust laws to force you to do an unfair thing; and give to the those who ask from you, even unjustly" (Matt. 5:38–42). And don't just love those who love you. If you want to be like God—self-controlled, not others controlled—don't just love those who love you, love even those who may hate you and be an enemy (Matt. 5:43–46).

Jesus was not controlled by other humans but only by God. He "reacted" only to God and "pro-acted" with everyone else—"I do as the Father has commanded me, so that the world may know that I love the Father" (John 14:31, English Standard Version). He reacted in favor neither to the zealots who were Jewish political extremists, the Pharisees who were Jewish religious extremists, nor to the poor who were in extreme need. He was reactive neither to the Jewish leadership who sought excessive control in their own country nor the Roman authorities who sought control in excess over the whole world—"You would have no authority over me at all unless it had been given you from above" (John 19:11).

Jesus feared (revered) only God and thus reacted to his call and command, not to the calls and commands of others who would ignite our more base passions and self-interests. He teaches us to only revere God—"And do not fear those who kill the body but cannot kill the soul. Rather fear him who can destroy both soul and body in hell" (Matt. 10:28).

Paradoxically, extremism is wrought not out of confidence or secure faith; rather it is a product of human insecurity, lack of faith, and fear. It is the result of one loving or fearing something or someone more than God.

A Prayer:

Teach me temperance, Lord, that I can avoid unnecessary extremes.
Help me never to need the attention that extremism often draws.
Give me strength not to be drawn out by human reactions that are of the flesh.
Grant me self-control that I may live a life surrendered to you and not to those of myself or others.
Be the controller of my destiny, Lord, that no other may ever be at the helm!

29
Extremes, Part 2

Moderation is a godly virtue; only in a few things is the extreme the standard. Extreme zealotry is seldom good.

"I am allowed to do anything," you say. My answer to this is that not all things are good. Even if it is true that "I am allowed to do anything," I will not let anything control me like a slave. (1 Cor. 6:12, Easy-to-Read Version).

NATIONALISM, SOME PATRIOTISM, political parties, ideologies, political agendas, social agendas, some religions and religious views, and so forth, often foster extremism—arrogance, narrow-mindedness, irrationality, hate, resentment, malice, division, and worse. All which are opposed to the purposes of God. But Jesus was completely zealous only for God, not some ideology or "position" in regard to God. Jesus was temperate; Jesus was balanced. He was controlled by nothing or no one but God—"I love the Father and do exactly what my Father has commanded me" (John 14:31).

The ancient Greeks sought a sort of "golden mean" in defining their words, which, by definition, avoided extremes and excess. Temperance, moderation, and self-control are all words we use to describe our golden mean in regard to God. These are words he gave to the writers of scripture—"This is what we speak, not in words taught us by human wisdom but in words taught by the Spirit, explaining spiritual realities with Spirit-taught words" (1 Cor. 2:13). Such words matter, and their interpretation shows us the sweet spot for our thoughts, feelings, and behavior—the golden mean. The golden mean that avoids human extremes and excesses.

Solomon pursued and tried excesses in most human regards—projects, accomplishments, pleasures, and wealth. He also sought out things that were otherwise considered good, such as wisdom and hard work. But seeking those things instead of seeking God is, as Solomon concluded, "meaningless" (Book of Ecclesiastes).

On the other hand, Jesus did not seek worldly power, wealth, control, approval, pleasures, or accomplishments, but only to carry out the mission he came for. He came and lived only to accomplish God's will and work—"Behold, I have come to do your will" (Heb. 10:9). And oddly, his moderation, temperance, and avoidance of excesses appeared in excess to a world horribly imbalanced by its own sinful extremes. They attributed his devotion to and power from God as demonic (Matt. 12:24). They attributed his loving association to the poor and marginalized as gluttony and drunkenness (Luke 7:34).

They sneered at Jesus because of their own issues, extremes, and sins, but Jesus responded, "You are the ones who justify yourselves in the eyes of others, but God knows your hearts. What people value highly is detestable in God's sight" (Luke 16:14–15).

He loved his mother and his siblings, and he provided for his mother's care after his death. However, he loved God and his kingdom people more—"Whoever does the will of God, he is my brother and sister and mother" (Mark 3:35). And he calls us to similar devotion—"Whoever loves father or mother more than me is not worthy of me, and whoever loves son or daughter more than me is not worthy of me" (Matt. 10:37).

But temperance, moderation, and self-control by definition are the similar virtues that lead us to have spiritual control over the stronger passions that drive us to human extremes. As children of God, we are given the spiritual vision that allows objectivity and the freedom from the fear of what others will think of us—"The person with the Spirit makes judgments about all things, but such a person is not subject to merely human judgments" (1 Cor. 2:15).

The only extreme of the children of God is to be their devotion to God. The Spirit-led, word-guided children of God will refuse to be swayed and inflamed by the traps of the evil one working through fearful extremists—politically, socially, morally, doctrinally, or religiously. When we love God to the extreme he tells us to, there is no room for extremism in other regards—"Love the Lord your God with *all* your heart and with *all* your soul and with *all* your strength and with *all* your mind" (Luke 10:27, Deut. 6:5, italics added).

Human extremism masquerading somehow as devotion to God is historically and geographically universal and is one of Satan's ultimate traps for the one serving Christ. The worst who have lived among us have often committed their horrendous crimes under some alleged or supposed banner of their god(s). We however must take care to never err in this regard.

The true child of God will indeed "grasp the one and not let go of the other" in all regards and thus will avoid the extremes of either (Eccles. 7:18).

But fearing God will deter the true child of God from falling into the trap and enable us to find the self-control granted to us in order to give God control.

A Prayer:

> Lord, if I must be out on the fringes—in the extremes—in
> any way, please let me be led there only by your Spirit.
> Show me, Jesus, how to be radical, where it is necessary,
> in the right ways and never in the wrong ways.
> Transform me and conform me to your glorious image.

30
Faith

Faith is a straining of the heart growing out of a conviction of the mind.

And without faith it is impossible to please God, because anyone who comes to him must believe that he exists and that he rewards those who earnestly seek him (Heb. 11:6).

FAITH IS THE ability to perceive what we cannot see. It is the ability to understand what we cannot explain. Faith is the capability of experiencing what we cannot fully comprehend. It is the present's connection to the eternal. Through faith we find the path to overcoming doubt, fear, and anxiety. In faith we find the reason to resist hate, malice, resentment, anger, and division. In faith we find the embracing of real love, true peace, and legitimate power. By faith we become true winners in life—"This is the victory that has overcome the world, even our faith" (1 John 5:4).

Faith is not however a standalone virtue. Faith is a connection. Faith is a trust in someone or something. Our faith trusts in someone or something other than ourselves. It is a deep belief in the reality, power, and goodness of Yahweh, God, as revealed in the Lord Jesus Christ—"Anyone who has seen me has seen the Father" (John 14:9).

Such authentic faith is a full-person experience—mind, heart, spirit, soul, and body—"If you declare with your mouth, 'Jesus is Lord,' and believe in your heart that God raised him from the dead, you will be saved. For it is with your heart that you believe and are justified, and it is with your mouth that you profess your faith and are saved" (Rom. 10:9–10). Faith is much more than any ritual, rite, prayer, or words can encapsulate. It is a reality that captures the heart and mind and lifts us to a different plane—"God raised us up with Christ and seated us with him in the heavenly realms in Christ Jesus" (Eph. 2:6).

Such faith is not a mere mental assent to a belief; it is a way of thinking, feeling, and acting, from beginning to end—"You need to persevere so that when you have done the will of God, you will receive what he has promised. For, 'In just a little while, he who is coming will come and will not delay.' And, 'But my righteous one will live by faith. And I take no pleasure in the one who shrinks back.' But we do not belong to those who shrink back and are destroyed, but to those who have faith and are saved" (Heb. 10:36–39). Faith is a life of reaching out from what is seen into what is unseen—"So we fix our eyes not on what is seen, but on what is unseen" (2 Cor. 4:18).

Salvation too is much more than a momentary act of grace on God's part to bring us into a relationship with him—it is eternal for God, and for us it is a lifelong, beginning to end, creation to glory, act of grace on God's part, bringing us into and maintaining us in Christ—"I am not ashamed of the gospel, because it is the power of God that brings salvation to everyone who believes: first to the Jew, then to the Gentile. For in the gospel the righteousness of God is revealed—a righteousness that is by faith from first to last, just as it is written: 'The righteous will live by faith'" (Rom. 1:16–17). Salvation saves us not just from the salvation-threatening consequence of our sins but also from the devastation of sin itself.

It is our faith that connects us to the eternal and divine. It allows us to extrapolate from what we can see and reason out to that which we cannot see and reason out. It gives a real reason to sacrifice, the purpose for giving generously, a basis for true unity, and the power to love unconditionally. Because our faith connects us to God, the ultimate source for everything good.

Yes, inauthentic and illegitimately-placed faith often gives genuine faith a bad name. Such causes unbelievers to understandably doubt the value of faith. But genuine faith is the most precious commodity one can possess—it is worth more than all material blessings (1 Pet. 1:7).

But to find such precious faith, we must strain, not haphazardly and with little effort, hoping it just swoops upon us; we must believe that God rewards those who earnestly seek him, and therefore, we must earnestly seek him!

A Prayer:

> Lord, I believe, help me in my unbelief.
> God, I trust you, but relieve my inner doubt.
> Jesus, I need you, defeat my fleshly nature.
> Spirit, cleanse me wholly from the inside out!

31
Faith is Not a Mere Emotion, Part 1

Faith is not a feeling one is subject to, but a decision one makes based on evidence and reason.

Now faith is confidence in what we hope for and assurance about what we do not see (Heb. 11:1).

BECAUSE THE HUMAN heart is deceptive, human emotions are deceptive—"The heart is deceitful above all things" (Jer. 17:9). We can feel many things that may have no grounding in reality. We can be fearful when nothing fearful is present. We can feel unloved when in fact we are very loved. We are often said to be "conflicted" when our emotions variously even run in polar opposite directions over the same thing.

The very definitions of feelings and emotions are debated. Are they even the same thing? For the human experience, outside the psychology lab, they are experienced, interpreted, categorized, and handled according to our own life situations and influences. Early on, we learn to manipulate our feelings and emotions, stimulating or subduing them in various ways. Often dangerously so.

For the common person, emotions and feelings are generally defined as the same thing. At a higher level, perhaps it might be said that emotions are the basic human reactions that are primarily physiologically and chemically produced. Feelings then are defined as our mental reactions to these emotional experiences, and they, within themselves, produce additional emotions. The study and understanding of emotions and feelings change constantly as science continues to probe the brain and the human emotional and mental experience.

At ground level, where we all live, no matter how you see and understand the human heart, apart from objective rational mental analysis, emotions and feelings are very subjective. That is, the heart left to its own device is reactive primarily to personal emotional responses to life stimuli as well as to our own inner interpretations of and momentary responses to them. Our interpretation of truth, therefore, becomes very self-centered and thus self-serving.

Even the mind can be sucked in, when we allow ourselves to see our emotions and feelings as objective truth. Or worse yet, we begin to believe that there is no objective truth and that truth therefore is relative to and dependent on our own existential experiences. At the natural end of this illogic is the practical conclusion that, "I am actually the god of my own world." Thus, I should adhere slavishly to the modern humanistic mantra—"just follow your heart."

Such a flawed mentality is, of course, the fruit of the deadly Tree of the Knowledge of Good and Evil, cultivated by the Evil One himself—"'You will not certainly die,' the serpent said [lied] to the woman. 'For God knows that when you eat from it your eyes will be opened, and you will be like God, knowing good and evil'" (Gen. 3:4–5).

It may be true that I might be deeply fearful of a thing, but equally true that there is in actuality no real basis for the fear. Mental illness feeds on these inner mechanisms of disconnect and illogic. Similarly, I may feel there is no God. Or I may feel that he is not present. Or that if he is present, he has no regard for me. When, in fact, the truth is just the opposite. And for the unbeliever, this is exactly what is going on.

Unbelief is merely an evil thought that comes directly from the heart—"For out of the heart come evil thoughts…" (Matt. 15:19). Unbelief is an evil thought. The greatest moral truth is that God is—Yahweh, "I AM WHO I AM" (Exod. 3:14). Unbelief is not based on rationality or truth; rather it is based on the inner workings of a heart unmoored in reality—"The fool says in his heart, 'There is no God'" (Ps. 14:1). Unbelief is a mental impression and feeling in reaction to an emotion. It is based on illogic, not logic.

Because I cannot experience God with the most basic human senses of seeing, hearing, touching, tasting, and smelling—those things within us that trigger our emotions—I wrongly conclude that God therefore does not exist. When in fact there are countless things that cannot be sensed in any of these ways yet are fully existent, such as the countless people who exist in the world that we have never met. Yet, they are just as real as I am. Some of the most basic realities of all cannot be perceived by human senses but only reasoned out from what can be sensed.

The world of unbelief maintains its own deceptive sense of control and freedom through its manipulated, mood altering, psychological, and intellectual maneuverings, masquerading somehow as higher-level thinking and learning—"…the world through its wisdom did not know him [God]…" (Cor. 1:21). Yet, it is only through the most objective reality of all—the truth of God—that real freedom and control is gained in our lives—"If you hold to my teaching, you are really my disciples. Then you will know the truth, and the truth will set you free" (John 8:31–32).

A Prayer:

> Help me not to define faith as an emotion that I am merely subject to,
> But help me to see faith as what I believe based on experience and learning.
> Give me wisdom to discern, intellect to interpret and learn, and the desire needed to do the work that faith requires.

32
Faith is Not a Mere Emotion, Part 2

Unbelief happens when a human heart is left to wallow in its own illogic.

The fool says in his heart, "There is no God" (Ps. 14:1).

UNBELIEF COMES ABOUT when a hardened, self-serving heart causes flawed thinking—"So I tell you this, and insist on it in the Lord, that you must no longer live as the Gentiles do, in the futility of their thinking" (Eph. 4:17). The heart wants to do what feels good in the present. Good thinking prohibits such futile and dangerous illogic.

So, the heart hardens itself against objective reality in order to continue to manipulate its moods with its own selfish and delectable pleasures—"They are darkened in their understanding and separated from the life of God because of the ignorance that is in them due to the hardening of their hearts" (Eph. 4:18).

The result is disastrous individually and collectively—"They have become callous and have given themselves up to sensuality, greedy to practice every kind of impurity" (Eph. 4:19, English Standard Version). Sounds familiar, does it not?

For the sensible believer, however, such is not so—"That, however, is not the way of life you learned when you heard about Christ and were taught in him in accordance with the truth that is in Jesus" (Eph. 4:20–21). The most objective reality and truth of the universe is its eternal Creator, Jesus Christ—"Through him all things were made; without him nothing was made that has been made" (John 1:3).

Yes, indeed, there is a sort of "faith" in religion at large, including Christianity itself, which is subjective and often blind and superstitious. This sort of sad substitute for faith often drives away sensible people, many of whom assume such misrepresentations to be valid representations of faith. When, in fact, nothing could be further from the truth!

As artists and architects make themselves known through their work, the ultimate designer himself, God, makes himself very known through the incomparable creation in which we live and are a part of—"What may be known about God is plain to them, because God has made it plain to them" (Rom. 1:19). The invisible nature of God can be perceived by us through those things that are visible and open to sensory experience—"For since the creation of the world God's invisible qualities—his eternal power and divine nature—have been clearly seen, being understood from what has been made, so that people are without excuse" (Rom. 1:20).

However, humanity loves the deadly, self-serving fruit based on its own knowledge and interpretations of right and wrong. How much disastrous social and historical data will be needed for us to ever learn? But in our own desire for some illusion of freedom and control, we fall into the most deadly trap of all—"For although they knew God, they neither glorified him as God nor gave thanks to him, but their thinking became futile and their foolish hearts were darkened" (Rom. 1:21).

Foolish minds and darkened hearts produce most deadly results—"Although they claimed to be wise, they became fools and exchanged the glory of the immortal God for images made to look like a mortal human being and birds and animals and reptiles" (Rom. 1:22–23). Such foolishness leads us from belief to unbelief and causes us to exchange the priceless for the worthless and instead of serving the Creator to serve the created—"They exchanged the truth about God for a lie, and worshiped and served created things rather than the Creator—who is forever praised" (Rom. 1:25).

The degradation that can occur due to unbelief, or seriously flawed beliefs based only on contrived notions of reality, are simply unbelievable, and when they happen, all of us stand with our mouths agape—"Furthermore, just as they did not think it worthwhile to retain the knowledge of God, so God gave them over to a depraved mind, so that they do what ought not to be done" (Rom. 1:28). The very sad individual and collective examples in history are now countless.

Genuine faith is not an emotion or a feeling based on emotion. Genuine faith is based on the most basic realities and truths of all—those of creation itself. Science and reason in their most objective forms are the greatest friends of faith! The Creator can be understood through what has been made. Unbelief is therefore inexcusable.

Those who would rely on their inner emotional stirrings to find faith live their lives in futility. Those who would examine the universe objectively will find the Creator. The scriptures and the Holy Spirit can then lead the way down the right path.

Subsequently, the results of good thinking are marvelous—"You were taught, with regard to your former way of life, to put off your old self, which is being corrupted by its deceitful desires; to be made new in the attitude of your minds; and to put on the new self, created to be like God in true righteousness and holiness" (Eph. 4:22–24).

A Prayer:

> Lord, don't abandon me to the illogic of humanistic thinking.
> By your Spirit lift my logic above that which is merely human to that which is purely of you.
> Help me to think with the mind of Christ and for my thoughts to be captivated by him.
> May I never subscribe to the driveling notions of the "follow-your-heart" foolishness.

33
False Prophets, Part 1

False prophets lead you to them; true prophets lead you to Him.

Watch out for false prophets. They come to you in sheep's clothing, but inwardly they are ferocious wolves (Matt. 7:15).

EVEN AS CHRISTIANS, when we consume a steady diet of the fruit of the Tree of the Knowledge of Good and Evil, we become puffed up, proud, and egotistical, and, in regard to God, hard. We trust in our own *rightness* rather than in God's. We are often led there by preachers or others who themselves take pride in their own personal and corporate "rightness." Therefore, we drift farther away from God and he from us—"God opposes the proud..." (James 4:6).

On the other hand, when we eat from the eternal, life-giving Tree of Life, Jesus Christ, we become humble and malleable before God—"...but [God] shows favor to the humble" (James 4:6). We trust in God's goodness and rightness rather than our own or anyone else's—"Let God be true, and every human being a liar" (Rom. 3:4). The ones who believe they are most *right*, that their denominations are the most right, d so forth are already most wrong at the heart level.

Our *theology* is the substance of our belief in and about God. It is how we perceive him, understand him, and present him to others. If we get God wrong, we have everything wrong—"They exchanged the truth about God for a lie, and worshiped and served created things rather than the Creator—who is forever praised" (Rom. 1:25). If we serve a lie about God rather than the truth of God, our worship and service will prove commensurably futile.

Jesus came to show us who God really is and teach us how critical it is to our life, both here and in the hereafter, that we get the existence and essence of God right—"...if you do not believe that I am he, you will indeed die in your sins" (John 8:24). God is good beyond compare, he loves beyond comprehension, he is utterly graceful, he is good and just, he is righteous, and he is all-powerful. And he loves us beyond human imagination—"I am the Lord your God, who teaches you what is best for you, who directs you in the way you should go. If only you had paid attention to my commands, your peace would have been like a river, your well-being like the waves of the sea" (Isa. 48:17–18).

Our *doctrine* is what we do with our theology; that is, how we apply our belief about God to our life individually and to church and society collectively—"Watch your life and doctrine closely. Persevere in them, because if you do, you will save both yourself and your hearers" (1 Tim. 4:16). All false teaching has at its roots a misbelief about God. If our theology is bad, our doctrine will be bad. We cannot have good doctrine and yet hold to bad theology—"...a bad tree cannot bear good fruit" (Matt. 7:18). Nor can we have good theology and yet bad doctrine—"A good tree cannot bear bad fruit" (Matt. 7:18). When we place our trust primarily in the correctness of our doctrine rather than in the correctness of our theology—our simple trust in the God revealed in Jesus Christ—we are eating from the deadly fruit of the Tree of the Knowledge of Good and Evil. We place our trust in the goodness and rightness of other humans and in ourselves rather than in the goodness and rightness of God.

The trap of deceptive theology is first set by and for the false prophets, opening the door for all the bad doctrines to follow.

A Prayer:

> Help my heart not be lead astray, Lord, by the allure of deceiving spirits.
> Give me an ear for your voice, Jesus, that I may listen to and follow only you.
> Grant me the discernment I need to hear and follow only those who hear and follow only you.

34
False Prophets, Part 2

A true prophet and preacher of Christ will serve as a one-way sign pointing straight to Jesus.

I resolved to know nothing while I was with you except Jesus Christ and him crucified (1 Cor. 2:2).

CONTRARY TO WHAT some might thoughtlessly assume, good theology doesn't make us less concerned about doctrine; it makes us appropriately concerned for doctrine—"Watch your life and doctrine closely" (1 Tim. 4:16). However, a right belief in God keeps us from inappropriately placing our trust in our correctness of doctrine and frees us to place our trust in God. Good doctrine keeps us focused on God rather than on ourselves or on others—"The Spirit himself testifies with our spirit that we are God's children" (Rom. 8:16).

Israel, as a whole, made such a deadly mistake in focusing on their rightness of doctrine concerning the Law of Moses, yet they missed the God of that Law—Immanuel (meaning, "God with us")—when he came. They studied the scripture but missed the author of it—"You study the Scriptures diligently because you think that in them you have eternal life. These are the very Scriptures that testify about me, yet you refuse to come to me to have life" (John 5:39–40). Although the Creator is clearly visible through the creation, the created did not recognize its Creator when he came into the world he had made—"He was in the world, and though the world was made through him, the world did not recognize him" (John 1:10).

Why did the creation not recognize God? It is because humankind becomes self-focused rather than God-focused. Then, when God doesn't look like us, we don't recognize him—"He was in the world, and though the world was made through him, the world did not recognize him" (John 1:10).

Prophets are men and women who speak directly from and for God. The first and primary prophets are selected by God and speak from direct divine revelation—"Christ himself gave the apostles, the prophets, the evangelists, the pastors and teachers" (Eph. 4:11). Preachers and teachers, when they deliver these divine revelations, are acting secondarily as prophets.

Beware of the preacher who amasses large crowds of adoring ones who do little but listen. Beware of the leader who seems enamored with the glamour afforded them by their adoring fans. Good leaders lead leaders; bad leaders lead only followers. If policing our evil associations is critical, policing whom we listen to and follow is even much more important—"Do not be misled: 'Bad company corrupts good character'" (1 Cor. 15:33). Beware of the "popular" ones—"Woe to you when everyone speaks well of you, for that is how their ancestors treated the false prophets" (Luke 6:26).

Yet, be sure that false prophets do not present themselves as vicious wolves but rather as harmless sheep—"They come to you in sheep's clothing, but inwardly they are ferocious wolves" (Matt. 7:15). A wool suit and fine-sounding sermons no more make one a true prophet than a sheepskin draped over a wolf makes a sheep.

Such people are likely deceived themselves and thus can only deceive. It is only by their fruit that the true and the false prophets can be fully recognized—"Remember your leaders, who spoke the word of God to you. Consider the outcome of their way of life and imitate their faith" (Heb. 13:7). Yes indeed, consider the outcome of their way of life—observe the fruit of their lives.

After giving us the warning to watch out for false prophets, Jesus gives us a description of their fruit to watch out for. The fruit that false Christian prophets produce is Christian religiosity and activity devoid of sincere identification with Jesus—"Not everyone who says to me, 'Lord, Lord,' will enter the kingdom of heaven, but only the one who does the will of my Father who is in heaven" (Matt. 7:21). Their followers will claim at judgment: "Lord, Lord, did we not prophesy in your name and in your name drive out demons and in your name perform many miracles?" (Matt. 7:22). Tragically, Jesus's necessary response will be: "I never knew you. Away from me, you evildoers!" (Matt. 7:23).

False prophets will inevitably draw you to themselves, their organizations, their ways, their doctrinal opinions, and their personalities. You will feel compelled to listen to them and follow their ways in order to feel close to Jesus. The true prophets will lead you simply to Jesus.

Watch out for the false prophets. And before it is too late, make sure you aren't found to be one.

A Prayer:

> Lord, let me be wary without being judgmental,
> Lead me to think critically without being critical,
> Help me see clearly who is of you, God,
> Make me honest and completely apolitical.

Help me not to be drawn by what is human,
Attune my soul to only you, my Lord,
Defeat within me my own inner false prophet,
Sanctify me, dear Savior, by your word!

35
Fear

Fear is both an attitude and an emotion. It is not necessarily good or bad. But in it lies the power of our salvation or the power of our undoing.

The fear of the L*ORD* *is the beginning of knowledge, but fools despise wisdom and instruction* (Prov. 1:7).

FOR MANY, BEING a Christian means to live in perpetual fear of erring, of making mistakes. Those who are fearful often see God simply as a commander—even an oppressive one. Although the grace of God should free us from such crippling fear, it doesn't free us to gratify our sinful natures—"What shall we say, then? Shall we go on sinning so that grace may increase? By no means! We are those who have died to sin; how can we live in it any longer?" (Rom. 6:1–2).

We are not merely slaves meant only to serve some practical purposes of God; rather we are his children meant to live in a perpetual relationship to him as his children—"The Spirit you received does not make you slaves, so that you live in fear again; rather, the Spirit you received brought about your adoption to sonship" (Rom.

8:15). As God's children, we are heirs of God's possessions—"I pray that the eyes of your heart may be enlightened in order that you may know the hope to which he has called you, *the riches of his glorious inheritance in his holy people*, and his incomparably great power for us who believe" (Eph. 1:18–19).

We are not merely employees in the kingdom of God—glorified kingdom civil servants. Worse yet, we are not slaves. Rather we are God's partners and coworkers—"For we are co-workers in God's service; you are God's field, God's building" (1 Cor. 3:9). Ours is a position of honor and esteem.

There are revealed two kinds of fear in the scripture—one healthy and the other unhealthy. The healthy kind is reverence and respect. It grows out of knowing who God really is, not who Satan deceives us into thinking God is. In discovering the meek and lowly, faithful, righteous, graceful, loving, kind, and good Creator, we come to trust him fully and completely.

The second fear is one of intimidation, dread, and terror. It grows out of not knowing the real God and therefore *not* trusting him. Many things happen in this life that may seem at least unfortunate if not disastrous. Understanding how those fit into the world created by a God of love is not always, from the human perspective, very easy. But we are as children to parents. Things parents need do often appear unreasonable from a child's time, space, and personal perspective, but they are done for the good of the child and are usually not nearly as sacrificial or painful for the child as the kid might perceive it in the moment.

Fear is both of the mind and of the heart. In the mind, it is a perspective, paradigm, and point of view. In the heart, fear is an experience and is meant to be a protective, cautioning emotion. The heart ought to only follow the mind. But if allowed to, the mind will follow the heart. And the heart is deceitful indeed (Jer. 17:9). If our logical, mental perspective of God is wrong, our heart's response will naturally be wrong. If we allow our mind to merely follow our deceitful, often illogical, heart, our mind will begin to believe terrible lies about God.

To relate to God effectively, the mind must see God aright for the heart to respond to him appropriately.

Perfect love, that is, a right perspective of and relationship with God, drives away the bad kind of fear—"There is no fear in love. But perfect love drives out fear, because fear has to do with punishment. The one who fears is not made perfect in love" (1 John 4:18). Perfect love however instills the reverent, respectful, and worshipful fear of the beloved child—"Therefore, since we are receiving a kingdom that cannot be shaken, let us be thankful, and so worship God acceptably with reverence and awe" (Heb. 12:28), and "Follow God's example, therefore, as dearly loved children and walk in the way of love, just as Christ loved us and gave himself up for us as a fragrant offering and sacrifice to God" (Eph. 5:1–2).

If we have the right kind of fear, it will drive away the wrong kind of fear. If we succumb to the wrong kind of fear, our hearts condemn us as not knowing God at all! We fear and worship someone who actually does not exist. This kind of fear will, rather than supporting a godly life, in actuality overwhelm healthy reverence for God and deter our right relationship to him. Those who do not know God should indeed fear him for they are opposing him—"Why do you insist on going against the grain?" (Acts 26:14). Those who do not develop a healthy respect from God must fear God, as they live in grave danger living in conflict with the God of heaven and earth.

A Prayer:

> Cast the evils of fear from me, God, and defeat within me
> their effects and scars.
> Make my only fear be that of reverence and awe of you.
> Help me not to fear him that does only evil, but only to
> revere you who does good and can give life!

36
Fear and Anger

Fear and anger are emotional control mechanisms of our fleshly nature. Neither is helpful for long and often not helpful at all.

In your anger do not sin (Eph. 4:26).

FEAR AND ANGER are deep-seated emotions of the human animal. They are chemically, psychologically, and physiologically induced. Our bodies may induce them from within, but we must not be seduced by them from without! Rather if we live by the Spirit, he will bring them under his control—"So I say, walk by the Spirit, and you will not gratify the desires of the flesh" (Gal. 5:16). Either we will allow the Spirit within us to control fear and anger or they will control us. Sadly, these two emotions ultimately control countless people, even among Christians.

Many have wrongly assumed that giving vent to anger relieves it. This is a very wrong assumption—"Fools give full vent to their rage, but the wise bring calm in the end" (Prov. 29:11). Venting anger only stokes the fires of it. Maintaining anger causes us to be foolish and irrational—"Do not be quickly provoked in your spirit, for anger resides in the lap of fools" (Eccles. 7:9). The most heinous deeds are done in anger. The annals of history bear witness to the insanity of unabated anger.

There are two kinds of anger—first, the emotion that is chemically triggered in our brain and second, the long-term anger that festers in our hearts and minds and infects our whole being. Jesus warns of the deadly peril of this latter—"You have heard that it was said to the people long ago, 'You shall not murder, and anyone who murders will be subject to judgment.' But I tell you that anyone who is angry with a brother or sister will be subject to judgment" (Matt. 5:21–22). Jesus speaks of the second kind of anger—the persisting, seething anger of one possessed by it. It is most dangerous, injurious, and even murderous. It brings on us the judgment of God, because it is deadly and not of him.

The emotion of anger is a thought from the heart. It is designed to provoke us to action. It is a good thing if it is rightly held captive—"We take captive every thought to make it obedient to Christ" (2 Cor. 10:5). It can help us focus and address sinful and unhelpful situations. Thus, we must "refrain from anger and turn from wrath; do not fret—it leads only to evil" (Ps. 37:8).

Fear too is an emotion generated by the human biological self. It is a protective response to a perceived danger. Within itself it is good, as it too helps us respond to threats and dangers. But it must not be allowed to rule; only Jesus must rule. There is no more frequently echoed command in scripture than the one to not be afraid or fearful—"Peace I leave with you; my peace I give you. I do not give to you as the world gives. Do not let your hearts be troubled and do not be afraid" (John 14:27).

Unmitigated fear is antithetical to faith in God. God is near, and he wants our hearts and actions to reflect that reality—"Have I not commanded you? Be strong and courageous. Do not be afraid; do not be discouraged, for the LORD your God will be with you wherever you go" (Josh. 1:9). Jesus is in complete control of heaven and earth, and he has promised us as Christians that he will be with us in our mission—"And surely I am with you always, to the very end of the age" (Matt. 28:18–20).

No matter where we may be forced to walk, our fearlessness must be a witness to our faith in him—"Even though I walk through the darkest valley, I will fear no evil, for you are with me; your rod and your staff, they comfort me" (Ps. 23:4). God feels very strongly about the cowardly, as cowardice thwarts faith, and the fate of the fearful is not favorable—"But the cowardly, the unbelieving, the vile, the murderers, the sexually immoral, those who practice magic arts, the idolaters and all liars—they will be consigned to the fiery lake of burning sulfur. This is the second death" (Rev. 21:8).

The emotions of fear and anger generated from within must be taken captive and made obedient to Christ. But doing so can only be accomplished through the Spirit of God—"If by the Spirit you put to death the misdeeds of the body, you will live" (Rom. 8:13). Rather than listening to the momentary reactions that are generated biologically and psychologically from within us, we must listen to the spiritual ones that stand against them and are also generated within us, but by the Holy Spirit himself—"So I say, walk by the Spirit, and you will not gratify the desires of the flesh. For the flesh desires what is contrary to the Spirit, and the Spirit what is contrary to the flesh. They are in conflict with each other, so that you are not to do whatever you want" (Gal. 5:16–17).

When fear or anger are felt or perceived, we must stop and refuse to react to their mere fleshly instincts. Rather we must consider carefully God's will and the inner urging of the Holy Spirit and react only to God. Of paramount importance, we must not allow a momentary anger reaction to turn into a root of bitterness and hate. Neither must we allow a momentary fear reaction to turn into pervasive cowardice or foolishness.

The only fear we must succumb to is that of reverence and respect of God—"Fear God and keep his commandments, for this is the duty of all mankind" (Eccles. 12:13).

A Prayer:

Help me not, O Lord, to be controlled by another's or my own fear or anger.

And help me never to seek to control others with these emotions.

Help me to see their potential destructiveness, when given reign in our lives, and to cast them away through the power of your word and Spirit.

37
Fear and Negativity

Fear and negativity are first cousins and are enemies of the faith and the believer's heart.

Whatever is true, whatever is noble, whatever is right, whatever is pure, whatever is lovely, whatever is admirable—if anything is excellent or praiseworthy—think about such things (Phil. 4:8).

FAITH IN GOD produces hope, and hope dispels fear and negativity. Negative, fearful Christians are weak Christians who stymie the Holy Spirit's fire—"Do not quench the Spirit" (1 Thess. 5:19). Both fear and negativity can be tricky things for the Christian to understand and deal with.

Fear can be a momentary thing that startles us, either justifiably or unjustifiably. Fear can also grow within us into a veritable emotional monster that bullies and controls us. Anxiety itself is a form of possessing, progressive, and protracted fear. Some have an inclination toward fear and anxiety while others do not. Yet for those who do, these emotions can control them and thwart the will of God in their lives.

Negativity may also be a momentary realization or thought that too may be justified or unjustified by circumstances. But it can also morph into a monster that clouds one's spiritual reality and spoils our every thought and feeling.

As it is with every sort of sin, certain people have a greater propensity to sinful fear and negativity, while others may struggle little with them. Each of us has our own natural proclivities. But we must never use our natural inclinations as an excuse to sin! Not for one single minute!

The apostle Paul gives the progression away from fear and negativity, and it begins with the simple command to "Rejoice in the Lord always. I will say it again: Rejoice!" (Phil. 4:4). To rejoice in a thing is to tap into your hope concerning it. Hope, as used biblically, is generally about expectations, not mere wishes. To hope for a thing is to expect it to come to pass or into being. Rejoicing in the Lord is to celebrate the unmatched hopefulness that comes into reality when we enter into him!

Such rejoicing ignites our hopefulness and reminds us of the existential reality of Christ. It calms our troubled spirits and reminds us who is in control. It brings a gentleness, which in this context means an unhurried, un-fearful calmness and confidence—"Let your gentleness be evident to all. The Lord is near" (Phil. 4:5). Such calmness and confidence are produced by the constant reality of our faith that the Lord is always near—"He is not far from any one of us" (Acts 17:27).

The spiritual antidote to fearfulness, anxiety, and negativity is submitting our concerns to God—"Do not be anxious about anything, but in every situation, by prayer and petition, with thanksgiving, present your requests to God" (Phil. 4:6). And our prayers for those things that bother us must be awash with thankfulness, as does our whole life—"Rejoice always, pray continually, give thanks in all circumstances; for this is God's will for you in Christ Jesus" (1 Thess. 5:16–18). Such a prayer is not seeking to control God by giving him instructions on how to fix my life, rather is seeking to surrender to God and therefore be prepared to handle whatever he may come.

The result is glorious—"And the peace of God, which transcends all understanding, will guard your hearts and your minds in Christ Jesus" (Phil. 4:7). There is a peace that comes from our faith and hope that transcends what mere humans are capable of fostering or understanding. It is a part of the fruit of the glorious Holy Spirit within us—"But the fruit of the Spirit is love, joy, *peace*, forbearance, kindness, goodness, faithfulness, gentleness and self-control" (Gal. 5:22–23, italics added).

Our further participation in sustaining such peace from the Spirit is in taking captive evil thoughts that flow from fear and negativity—"We take captive every thought to make it obedient to Christ" (2 Cor. 10:5). Making our thought life obedient to Christ requires a most intentional, hopeful, and positive focus—"Finally, brothers and sisters, whatever is true, whatever is noble, whatever is right, whatever is pure, whatever is lovely, whatever is admirable—if anything is excellent or praiseworthy—think about such things" (Phil. 4:8).

And it also requires a constant commitment to putting into practice, as best we can, all the things we learn from scripture, the insights and prompts we get from the Holy Spirit, and the examples of other faithful Christian leaders and friends—"Whatever you have learned or received or heard from me, or seen in me—put it into practice. And the God of peace will be with you" (Phil. 4:9).

With the God of peace at the helm, we find the ability to be content, free from fear and negativity, in all situations—"I have learned to be content whatever the circumstances" (Phil. 4:11). We get the best outcome our physical and spiritual self is capable of. And we find the ability to endure, face, and handle everything the world may throw at us—"I can do all this through him who gives me strength" (Phil. 4:13).

Stop making excuses for your fear and negativity, and commit to following the way of the Spirit in their regard. You will be very thankful for the outcome.

A Prayer:

> Father, help me to focus on things that are excellent and praiseworthy rather than to allow my face to be rubbed in the world's rubbish.
> Give me a heart to see beauty and a mind to find the good in situations.
> Help me to be a spark of positive energy rather than to drain those around me with my fear and negativity.
> Help me to stop doubting your ability to turn even the bad into good in my life and to truly believe.

38
Forgiveness

If we haven't forgiven others, we haven't yet accepted forgiveness from God. If we have accepted his forgiveness, we will become more and more forgiving.

For if you forgive other people when they sin against you, your heavenly Father will also forgive you. But if you do not forgive others their sins, your Father will not forgive your sins (Matt. 6:14–15).

AS FAR AS humanity is concerned, God's ability and desire to forgive is arguably his greatest, most-loving attribute—"Who is a God like you? You forgive sin and overlook the rebellion of your faithful people. You will not be angry forever, because you would rather show mercy. You will again have compassion on us. You will overcome our wrongdoing. You will throw all our sins into the deep sea" (Mic. 7:18–19). And because we are created in his image, we too have this marvelous capacity!

Both forgiveness and the lack thereof, which ever we generally mete out, have ricochet effects of sorts—we get back whatever we give out. This is notably true in our relationship with God—"For if you forgive other people when they sin against you, your heavenly Father will also forgive you. But if you do not forgive others their sins, your Father will not forgive your sins" (Matt. 6:14–15). And it tends to be true in all our other relationships as well—"Do not judge, or you too will be judged. For in the same way you judge others, you will be judged, and with the measure you use, it will be measured to you" (Matt. 7:1–2).

All sins create debt, whether toward God or others. If there is a debtor, there is a creditor. Unabated debt accrues and becomes burdensome for those who owe—"The borrower is slave to the lender" (Prov. 22:7). Just as debt of capital has to be paid back, sin, as spiritual debt, requires recompensing, as well. Our sin must be repaid in kind—"Life for life, eye for eye, tooth for tooth, hand for hand, foot for foot, burn for burn, wound for wound, bruise for bruise" (Exod. 24:23–25). Unless, of course, it is simply forgiven by the one owed, whether it be God or perhaps another.

The word generally used for "sin" literally means to "miss the mark" or "to fail" (*hamartia*, Greek). In the case of humanity, we miss the mark by falling short of God's glory and goodness, as we were originally designed to be—"All have sinned and fall short of the glory of God" (Rom. 3:23). Sin is to be thought of both in general, as in our overall problem, for example, "The wages of sin…" (Rom. 6:23), or specifically as particular kinds of sins, for example, the sin of adultery.

In the Bible, sin is also sometimes called iniquity (*anomia*, Greek), meaning lawlessness or disobedience. Sins are also sometimes called transgressions (*parabasis*, Greek), meaning overstepping, deviating, or going aside. Just different words for basically the same thing.

Sin can be a transgression of not doing something we are commanded to do, sometimes called a sin of omission. Sin can also be something we do that we are commanded not to do, sometimes called a sin of commission. Sin can involve our hearts, our minds, and our bodies, individually or in combinations.

Since the first sin of Adam and Eve, all humanity has fallen into sin—"I was guilty of sin from birth, a sinner the moment my mother conceived me" (Ps. 51:5, New English Translation). Therefore all of us suffer sin's consequences—"Sin came into the world because of what one man did. And with sin came death. So this is why all people must die—because all people have sinned" (Rom. 5:12, Easy-to-Read Version).

The inevitability of sin is the bad news. Bad news gives opportunity for good news—gospel. In our case, "the" gospel or the good news of Christ. The good news, given our pervasive sin problem, is that God is a forgiving God—"Praise the Lord, my soul; all my inmost being, praise his holy name. Praise the Lord, my soul, and forget not all his benefits—who *forgives all your sins* and heals all your diseases, who redeems your life from the pit and crowns you with love and compassion, who satisfies your desires with good things so that your youth is renewed like the eagle's. The Lord works righteousness and justice for all the oppressed" (Ps. 103:1–6, italics added).

The gospel is not first about what God *does for* us; it is first about who God *is* and its implications to us! Christ did what he did in dying on the cross for us because he manifests in human form who God has always been and always will be—"In your relationships with one another, have the same mindset as Christ Jesus: Who, being in very nature God, did not consider equality with God something to be used to his own advantage; rather, he made himself nothing by taking the very nature of a servant, being made in human likeness. And being found in appearance as a man, he humbled himself by becoming obedient to death—even death on a cross!" (Phil. 2:5–8).

God did not change his basic nature when he died on the cross in order to forgive us; he *revealed* his nature to us so that we would trust him and not try to trust in our own "knowledge of good and evil" and ability to live it all out. Whatever he accomplished within himself in order to atone for our sins, the cross for us is God showing his merciful compassionate nature to us and inviting us back to him, the Tree of Life!

God *does* for us all he *is* to us—"Because of his great love for us, God, who is rich in mercy, made us alive with Christ even when we were dead in transgressions—it is by grace you have been saved" (Eph. 2:4–5). And our connection to that forgiveness is our trust and faith in him—"For it is by grace you have been saved, through faith—and this is not from yourselves, it is the gift of God—not by works, so that no one can boast" (Eph. 2:8–9).

Before we come to Christ, we are said to be *lost*, that is separated from the life and direction of God, because we have sin that has not yet been forgiven, or in other words, we have debt to God that has not been repaid. We are *saved* when that sin is forgiven, or the debt has been paid back. At the cross, Christ put the "payback" for our sin debt into an escrow account of sorts, and we access the payback that is in the escrow when we come to faith in Christ. Thus, God considers our debt paid—"I will forgive their wickedness and will remember their sins no more" (Heb. 8:12, Jer. 31:34).

Surely, it is not that God literally forgets that we ever sinned, for that would negate his omniscience. Actually, his forgiveness is an even greater thing. The debt owed for every sin is death itself—"The wages of sin is death" (Rom. 6:23). Oh, he indeed remembers we once owed it, but he has cancelled that debt by repaying it himself—"Christ's love compels us, since we have reached this conclusion: If One died for all, then all died" (2 Cor. 5:14, Holman's Christian Standard Bible). The sacrifice on the cross is apparently an existential reality of our Loving God!

Christ died for us, so that we wouldn't have to die eternally and so that we could live with him forever, as we were originally designed to do—"He died for all so that those who live should no longer live for themselves, but for the One who died for them and was raised"

(2 Cor. 5:15, Holman's Christian Standard Bible), and "The *gift of God is eternal life in Christ Jesus our Lord*" (Rom. 6:23, italics added).

God will forgive us if we will but trust him, because he is and has always been a forgiving God. We connect to his grace by trusting him (coming to faith). And our willingness to freely forgive others is a mere manifestation of the reality of our having been forgiven ourselves—"Freely you have received; freely give" (Matt. 10:8).

As the first verse of a song says:

He paid a debt He did not owe
I owed a debt I could not pay
I needed someone to wash my sins away
And now I sing a brand new song
Amazing Grace
Christ Jesus paid a debt that I could never pay
(1977 Ellis J. Crum, Publisher, Admin. by Sacred Selections R.E. Winsett LLC, 1977.)

Another verse could be added:

He paid a debt He did not owe
I owed a debt I could not pay
Should I then expect others to me repay
For the little sins they do to me
For shame, for shame
When Christ paid the awful debt that I could never pay

A Prayer:

> Lord, as I behold your glory and goodness seen in Christ, may your Spirit transform me to be more and more like him.

Help me not for a moment to choose my own comfort and rights over showing mercy to others.
Make the cross an ever-present reality in my heart and mind so that I always remember that your forgiveness was offered to me before I ever sinned, and that I will therefore do the same with others' sins against me.
May I be slow to see others' sins, slow to make judgments toward them, and quick to forgive.
Help me to forgive in imitation of Christ's mercy to me.
May I never regard another differently than the way that you regard me in Christ Jesus.
Amen.

39
Freedom in Christ

Until we are unobligated to the world, we will not finally be liberated from it.

Owe no one anything, except to love each other (Rom. 13:8, English Standard Version).

THE ONLY REAL freedom that humanity can know is through Christ—"If you hold to my teaching, you are really my disciples. Then you will know the truth, and *the truth will set you free*" (John 8:31–32, italics added). All other alleged forms of freedom are short-term or are merely shams.

Because we are finite and limited, we will be subject to either God or to the evil spiritual powers of the universe—"Don't you know that when you offer yourselves to someone as obedient slaves, you are slaves of the one you obey—whether you are slaves to sin, which leads to death, or to obedience, which leads to righteousness?" (Rom. 6:16). We have no choice beyond these two. If we do not choose Christ, we choose evil by default.

One choice however brings oppression and slavery, while the other brings freedom. We have an obligation—a debt of sin—that must be paid off, and one choice brings forgiveness and freedom from the debt, while the other piles it on and oppresses us through it. The former forgives debt; the latter accuses us constantly. This battle for freedom we fight is not against anything of this world—"For our struggle is not against flesh and blood, but against the rulers, against the authorities, against the powers of this dark world and against the spiritual forces of evil in the heavenly realms" (Eph. 6:12).

Our real battle is against Satan—the Evil One—the instigator of humanity's fall. He wants to own us in order to oppress us, to press us into his mold, and to use us in his hateful rebellion against God and all that is good! Although he is defeated and his final fate determined, he is an angry beaten enemy living out his last days seeking to do as much damage to God's beloved humanity as he possibly can before his final, eternal fate is sealed—"Your enemy the devil prowls around like a roaring lion looking for someone to devour" (1 Pet. 5:8). Only slavery and death is found in him. And all apart from God are in subjection to him.

Until we turn to Christ with it, Satan holds our debt of sin in his own charge. And he extracts payment from us day-by-day, moment by moment, by his oppression and all that he selfishly imposes on us. On the other hand, when we turn to God, Christ takes our sin burden as his own. He paid our debt off through his death on the cross. At the cross, the best of God squared off with the worst of man, and God won! God's presence in our lives brings freedom from evil's bondage and oppression—"Now the Lord is the Spirit, and where the Spirit of the Lord is, there is freedom" (2 Cor. 3:17).

However, Satan lures us in and holds us into subjection to him by falsely promising us God-like powers, independence, and self-determination—"'You will not certainly die,' the serpent said to the woman. 'For God knows that when you eat from it your eyes will be opened, and you will be like God, knowing good and evil'" (Gen. 3:4–5). But Christ calls us into subjection to him in order to liberate us from slavery—"It is for freedom that Christ has set us free" (Gal. 5:1), and "So if the Son sets you free, you will be free indeed" (John 8:36).

When we obligate ourselves to anyone other than the debt to love one another, we return again to slavery—"The borrower is slave to the lender" (Prov. 22:7). God calls us to owe one another only love, just as Christ did—"Follow God's example, therefore, as dearly loved children and walk in the way of love, just as Christ loved us and gave himself up for us as a fragrant offering and sacrifice to God" (Eph. 5:1–2).

Because of Christ we are no longer slaves, but we are God's children—"For those who are led by the Spirit of God are the children of God. The Spirit you received does not make you slaves, so that you live in fear again; rather, the Spirit you received brought about your adoption to sonship. And by him we cry, '*Abba,* Father.' The Spirit himself testifies with our spirit that we are God's children" (Rom. 8:14–16). This changes everything, as through Christ we move from slavery to sin to being a child of God and from being owned to being heirs to the ownership of everything.

Freedom is our calling from God—"You, my brothers and sisters, were called to be free" (Gal. 5:13). Christ turns our relationships to God from ones of shameful guilt and hiding to that of unashamed, unabashed children, from slaves to free, from debtors to debt free, and from pitiful to powerful—"In him and through faith in him we may approach God with freedom and confidence" (Eph. 3:12).

There is, however, responsibility that comes with freedom—"Live as free people, but do not use your freedom as a cover-up for evil; live as God's slaves" (1 Pet. 2:16). We must not abuse our freedom to the point of our losing it if and when the Spirit withdraws from us—"Do not cast me from your presence or take your Holy Spirit from me" (Ps. 51:11). For our freedom comes from the Spirit's presence in our lives—"Where the Spirit of the Lord is, there is freedom" (2 Cor. 3:17).

We must protect ourselves against whatever would adhere us to this present world and whatever might try to bring an obligation or expectation beyond that of expressing the love of God to any and all. We must hold dear and protect the freedom we have in

Christ by refusing all the other bogus offers Satan floods the market with—"It is for freedom that Christ has set us free. Stand firm, then, and do not let yourselves be burdened again by a yoke of slavery" (Gal. 5:1).

A Prayer:

> Daily breathe your Spirit on us, dear Lord, that we may feel your glorious freedom.
> Make repugnant to us any sense of returning to that which enslaves us.
> Draw us to you and into you that we no longer live in fear and shame.
> May our freedom bring a deep sense of our responsibility to love one another.
> May our freedom also make us live as debtors to those who are not yet free.
> And may our freedom make us overflow with thankfulness and praise to you, our deliverer and liberator!

40
Friendship

It is not very hard to be many people's best friend, because most people don't have a best friend.

One who has unreliable friends soon comes to ruin, but there is a friend who sticks closer than a brother (Prov. 18:24).

FRIENDSHIP IS OF God, but if not given over to God, just as other forms of love, it will be to varying degrees selfish, worldly, abusive, and evil. Friendship grows out of God's nature and goodness. And godly friendship is a priceless thing.

Friendship may begin with philia (*philía or phileo*, friendship or brotherly love, Greek), but godly friendship, although driven by philia is ultimately governed by agape (*agápē*, the love of God, Greek). Of the three "natural" loves, including sexual love (*erōs*, Greek) and family love (*storgē*, Greek), philia is the highest order of the three. But God's love is heavenly and spiritual and therefore even higher. It is the essence and nature of God—"Whoever does not love does not know God, because God is love" (1 John 4:8). Agape takes philia out of a mere earthly experience and into the godly.

It is the love of God that rules the friendships of the sincere believer. Those without the Spirit of God can rarely, if ever, exhibit such love—"The person without the Spirit does not accept the things that come from the Spirit of God but considers them foolishness, and cannot understand them because they are discerned only through the Spirit" (1 Cor. 2:14). Godly friendship is from God and thus is spiritually discerned and spiritually operated. Those without the Spirit can little love like God. However, those with the Spirit are fully capable of loving with the love of God.

It is an amazing thing—a wonder of God—that Jesus considers us, as his followers, his friends—"I no longer call you servants, because a servant does not know his master's business. Instead, I have called you friends, for everything that I learned from my Father I have made known to you" (John 15:15). Jesus is a best friend to all of us, but a lot of people just don't get that. The kind of friendship Christ shows us is born out of the nature of God, and when we are like God, we can freely offer up such friendship.

Unbelievers and detractors called Jesus a friend of sinners—"The Son of Man came eating and drinking, and you say, 'Here is a glutton and a drunkard, a friend of tax collectors and sinners'" (Luke 7:34). His godly friendship to even the worst of sinners was obviously quite evident. However, contrary to the false accusations of the self-righteous, Jesus did not stoop to the level of those he befriended; rather, he raised them to his.

The best at any endeavor is the one who elevates the life and efforts of those around them, and Jesus did just that with those who would believe. Godly friends do not participate in the destruction of the other; rather they deliver them from it.

Because few really discover the life of Jesus (Matt. 7:13–14), few ever experience the level and quality of friendships inspired by Jesus. And that is where the child of God enters the picture. As the present incarnation of Christ, we as the body of Christ, or the church, are also to be the friend of sinners, starting with ourselves.

And it is only through a Spirit-filled believer that any of us can experience the friendship, affection, and unselfish, unconditional loyalty that come only from the ultimate friend of sinners, Jesus Christ. Many, if not most, rarely, if at all, experience such love. And that is the great opportunity and open door found in the world by the child of God.

Jesus came and became our friend, so we would go and become the friend of others, believer and unbeliever alike—"Greater love has no one than this: to lay down one's life for one's friends. You are my friends if you do what I command" (John 15:13).

Jesus has sent us to love the world, as he loved the world—"For God so loved the world that he gave his one and only Son, that whoever believes in him shall not perish but have eternal life" (John 3:16). We too are to give ourselves for the sake of the world. We are to be in the world as its friend, not its foe.

We have a source of life that is not of this world, and thus we are enabled not to have to draw further from the meager resources of the spiritually arid human landscape. We can bring something to the world that's not of the world, and without Christians faithfully giving it, it will not be in the world—that is the love of God, imbued by the Spirit of God.

Thus the reality truly is that it is not hard for the believer in Christ to be another's best friend, because many, if not most, never experience such friendship—"A [godly] friend loves at all times, and a brother is born for a time of adversity" (Prov. 17:17).

"A friend in need is a friend indeed."

A Prayer:

> Father, help me to be a true friend, one that sticks closer than a brother.
> Teach me to be a friend and brother in adversity and not one who flees trouble.

Help me to be a friend of others the way that Jesus is a friend to me.
And through my friendships may the love of Christ be shown.

41
Generosity Toward God

Our genuine generosities reveal whom we acknowledge as our "god(s)."

"This is how it will be with whoever stores up things for themselves but is not rich toward God" (Luke 12:21).

GOD WANTS US all, and especially the more blessed among us, to be generous and rich in good deeds—"Command them to do good, to be rich in good deeds, and to be generous and willing to share" (1 Tim. 6:18). Ultimately, our generosity—the depth of it and the recipients of it—is most telling of our faith itself.

Our words—our claims and such—can be shallow and deceptive, both to ourselves and to others. Less deceptive however are our actions—"Show me your faith without deeds, and I will show you my faith by my deeds" (James 2:18). Utter sincerity will be found in the depth and nature of our material investments, however.

God wants us to have the trust of the animals—"Look at the birds of the air; they do not sow or reap or store away in barns, and yet your heavenly Father feeds them. Are you not much more valuable than they?" (Matt. 6:26). He desires that we display the unworried splendor of the wild flowers—"And why do you worry about clothes? See how the flowers of the field grow. They do not labor or spin" (Matt. 6:28).

Yet we are often malcontented and fritter away our existence allowing the trivialities to dominate us while the most important things languish in neglect. And we invest our resources and wealth in the inconsequential and momentary matters, while depriving those areas that involve the greatest consequence and eternal significance.

We can easily spend hours pleasuring ourselves and enjoying luxuries and privilege, in fact, so much that we lose track of time. We demonstrate ourselves most ungenerous toward God when in matters of serving God, we prioritize them last, spend on them the least, and count the minutes until we can stop and get back to serving ourselves and those things that matter most to us.

Ultimately, if God is not first in our lives, he will refuse to be in our lives at all—"But seek first his kingdom and his righteousness..." (Matt. 6:33). If God is not preeminent in our hearts, he will reject our lesser affections—"Anyone who loves their father or mother more than me is not worthy of me; anyone who loves their son or daughter more than me is not worthy of me" (Matt. 10:37).

Our treasures will indeed be where our hearts are, but too, our hearts will follow our treasures wherever we place them—"Do not store up for yourselves treasures on earth, where moths and vermin destroy, and where thieves break in and steal. But store up for yourselves treasures in heaven, where moths and vermin do not destroy, and where thieves do not break in and steal. For where your treasure is, there your heart will be also" (Matt. 6:19–21). We develop our affections toward the things we spend our time, money, and resources on.

The wise person of God learns quickly to eschew the selfish natural heart, prone to self-centeredness and self-interest, in favor of the generous, others-centered inclination of our spirit made in God's image. We learn that the great blessing is not in selfishness and accumulation but in giving generously and unselfishly, as the apostle explained, "In everything I did, I showed you that by this kind of hard work we must help the weak, remembering the words the Lord Jesus himself said: 'It is more blessed to give than to receive'" (Acts 20:35).

It is amazing what we will do for our "god," whether that god is self, others, another "god," or Yahweh, as revealed to us in the Lord Jesus Christ. Our true generosities will be telling of the actualities and realities of whom we choose as our God in this life. Whom we acknowledge as our God in this life is who will decide our fate in the next one.

A Prayer:

Dear Father, I pray that you will give me a generous heart toward you.
May there be nothing of me or in me that I fail to surrender up to you.
Give me the same spirit of generosity toward all others that you have toward me.

42
Giving and Receiving

It is impossible to out-give God.

No one who has left home or brothers or sisters or mother or father or children or fields for me and the gospel will fail to receive a hundred times as much in this present age (Mark 10:30).

THE KINGDOM OF God is about receiving and giving, giving and receiving.

God is a God of grace. He always has been, and he always will be. It's who he is. Our relationship with him is founded squarely upon his grace for us—"For it is by grace you have been saved, through faith—and this is not from yourselves, it is the gift of God" (Eph. 2:8). He offers this grace to each of us—"The grace of God has appeared that offers salvation to all people" (Titus 2:11).

God's grace flows from his very essence—his love—"God is love. Whoever lives in love lives in God, and God in them" (1 John 4:16). He loves us, and he has extended his grace to us in Christ Jesus—"For God so loved the world that he gave his one and only

Son, that whoever believes in him shall not perish but have eternal life" (John 3:16). Jesus is the human revelation of Yahweh, and in revealing God, Jesus shows him to be full of grace and truth—"The Word became flesh and made his dwelling among us. We have seen his glory, the glory of the one and only Son, who came from the Father, full of grace and truth" (John 1:14).

The word "grace" is used in a number of ways in scripture, but in all of them, its use conveys the various aspects of the generous, giving nature of God. Grace means a free gift, an unmerited favor, and an unearned blessing. That God is graceful means that he is a generous, giving God. He is so unlike the pagan conceptions of self-indulgent, impetuous, self-willed gods who are made in the image of fallen humanity and propagated by and made in the image of the Prince of Darkness himself. They are false gods. Unreal, untrue, and thankfully not in control.

Yahweh is the all-powerful Creator God of the world. He is preeminent in all things. And thankfully, all that he is and does is about giving, a virtue of God that is at the very foundation of the creation itself. He has given humankind the creation in all its abundance and splendor. He gave it to us, and he gave us to it as its caretakers—to use it but not to abuse it and to bless it as he has blessed it.

He will give us every physical blessing we need if we but acknowledge him as Lord in our heart and life—"But seek first his kingdom and his righteousness, and all these things will be given to you…" (Matt. 6:33). And he has, as well, given us, as his children, every spiritual blessing in Christ—"Praise be to the God and Father of our Lord Jesus Christ, who has blessed us in the heavenly realms with every spiritual blessing in Christ" (Eph. 1:3).

In fact he has saved us and set us up before the world as an ongoing and living example of the extent of his grace to us—"And God raised us up with Christ and seated us with him in the heavenly realms in Christ Jesus, in order that in the coming ages *he might show the incomparable riches of his grace, expressed in his kindness to us in Christ Jesus*" (Eph. 2:6–7, italics added).

God's grace emanates from his love, and only his Spirit can strengthen us and help us fully grasp the magnitude of God's grace—"I pray that out of his glorious riches he may strengthen you with power through his Spirit in your inner being, so that Christ may dwell in your hearts through faith. And I pray that you, being rooted and established in love, may have power, together with all the Lord's holy people, to grasp how wide and long and high and deep is the love of Christ, and to know this love that surpasses knowledge—that you may be filled to the measure of all the fullness of God" (Eph. 2:16–19). We need him to help us to fully see him!

God freely gives because he is full of grace. God is generous because he is rich in grace. And he wants us to be full of grace too—"Be strong in the grace that is in Christ Jesus" (2 Tim. 2:1). He wants us to be strengthened by his grace—"It is good for our hearts to be strengthened by grace" (Heb. 13:9). He wants us as his regents and ambassadors in the world to give freely from his overflowing fountain of graciousness—"Freely you have received; freely give" (Matt. 10:8).

And, for the child of God, receiving the grace of others is just as much an act of grace as giving—"Not that I desire your gifts; what I desire is that more be credited to your account" (Phil. 4:17). We must receive so that others may give. We must graciously both give and receive. It is at the root of our obligation to God. He teaches us to give to and serve him by giving to others—"Whatever you did for one of the least of these brothers and sisters of mine, you did for me" (Matt. 25:40).

And we should be constantly reminded of the admonition of the apostle—"Remember this: Whoever sows sparingly will also reap sparingly, and whoever sows generously will also reap generously. Each of you should give what you have decided in your heart to give, not reluctantly or under compulsion, for God loves a cheerful giver. And God is able to bless you abundantly, so that in all things at all times, having all that you need, you will abound in every good work" (2 Cor. 9:6–8).

A Prayer:

> Give me a generous heart, Lord,
> Help me to give as you give,
> Make me a statement of your grace, God,
> In the ways that I speak and I live.
>
> Keep me from yielding to self-interest,
> Rather let me be all-in for you.
> Help me to get only by giving,
> And selfishness fully eschew.
>
> You are the giver of life, God,
> You are the teacher of grace,
> May your goodness be seen in me daily,
> Your generosity fully embraced.

43
Giving What Has Been Given

We can only give to another what has first been given to us.

You will be enriched in every way so that you can be generous on every occasion, and through us your generosity will result in thanksgiving to God (2 Cor. 9:11).

THE DISCERNING CHILDREN will eventually learn that the gifts they give to others, even to their parents, derive only from what has already been given to them. Because giving is God's nature and humankind's original essence. We are to give because it is who we are and how we are wired. It is in our DNA. To not give is to deny and defy who we really are.

The greater blessing is not in receiving but in giving—"It is more blessed to give than to receive" (Acts 20:35). In fact, for the Christian receiving from another is but an act of giving to another. We receive so that another can give. We allow ourselves to be served so that others can serve. We allow ourselves to be loved so that others can love. It is a testimony to the reality of our following Christ—"By this everyone will know that you are my disciples, if you love one another" (John 13:35).

We however need not trust in humankind for our needs, because God, in his own wisdom and design, gives us everything we need in order to live a godly life, and we trust him for it—"His divine power has given us everything we need for a godly life through our knowledge of him who called us by his own glory and goodness" (2 Pet. 1:3). The reality is that every good gift that any of us receives, even from others, comes from him, no matter the channel of its delivery—"Every good and perfect gift is from above, coming down from the Father of the heavenly lights, who does not change like shifting shadows" (James 1:17).

The wise servant takes no credit for their gifts and service—"So you also, when you have done everything you were told to do, should say, 'We are unworthy servants; we have only done our duty'" (Luke 17:10). When all has been stripped away from us, we will all see as the ancient Job saw when all he loved, possessed, and enjoyed were gone—"Naked I came from my mother's womb, and naked I will depart. The Lord gave and the Lord has taken away; may the name of the Lord be praised" (Job. 1:21).

The Lord said in his Second Coming that he would separate humanity into two groups—sheep and goats. The sheep are depicted as those who were givers in life—"For I was hungry and you gave me something to eat, I was thirsty and you gave me something to drink, I was a stranger and you invited me in, I needed clothes and you clothed me, I was sick and you looked after me, I was in prison and you came to visit me" (Matt. 25:35–36). The goats are conversely depicted as those who were not—"For I was hungry and you gave me nothing to eat, I was thirsty and you gave me nothing to drink, I was a stranger and you did not invite me in, I needed clothes and you did not clothe me, I was sick and in prison and you did not look after me" (Matt. 25:42–43). A simple illustration about a simple truth.

Children of God are givers because they live by trust in and in imitation of the ultimate giver—God. Those who are not children of God ultimately scrounge for themselves, because they have no sense of trusting another to provide for them. Children of God are as energy giving stars that shine brightly and are an energy source for those near and far. Those who are not children of God are as black holes that have so imploded in on themselves that nothing escapes them, including light and energy. It has nothing to give, but it only receives.

Children of God carry a positive energy charge because they bask in the abundant life-giving light of God. They exude the life-giving energy of the Holy Spirit—"Whoever believes in me, as Scripture has said, rivers of living water will flow from within them" (John 7:38). They exhibit real joy flowing from genuine thankfulness. Those who are not children of God carry a negative life charge. They have no energy to give but only some to barter for equal exchange. They have little to nothing to actually give because they exist only from a spiritually meager subsistence.

The one following Christ will be a true and free giver. The one who does not follow Christ cannot be.

A Prayer:

> Lord, help me to have a generous heart and an open hand.
> Clear from my heart the greed and selfishness that robs me of this precious gift.
> Help me to trust that you will give me all I need if I give in your name all I have.
> Transform me to be a person of grace—a free giver of all good things!

44
God's Work in Us

God works through us is often in spite of us, and he is in no way limited by us.

Therefore, my dear friends, as you have always obeyed—not only in my presence, but now much more in my absence—continue to work out your salvation with fear and trembling, for it is God who works in you to will and to act in order to fulfill his good purpose (Phil. 2:12–13).

COMING TO FAITH is a freeing of us from mere mortal thinking. It is the most foolish assumption ever to assume that the world is centered on any one of us! Such is the original sin—"...you will be like God..." Atheism is the greatest immorality of all, because God existence is the greatest moral truth of all—"The fool says in his heart, 'There is no God'" (Ps. 14:1).

That one cannot believe in a thing does not preclude that thing's existence, and therefore, that one refuses to believe in God does not preclude his existence. Neither is God's truth and goodness open to human scrutiny—"Oh, the depth of the riches of the wisdom and knowledge of God! How unsearchable his judgments, and his paths beyond tracing out!" (Rom. 11:33). That we often do not understand his purposes and actions is a statement not about God whatsoever but it is a demonstration of our own human limitations and inadequacies.

God predetermined to work in and through humanity. As caretakers of creation, he breathed into humankind his own spirit of life—"The Lord God formed a man from the dust of the ground and breathed into his nostrils the breath of life, and the man became a living being" (Gen. 2:7). Humanity's original mold is God himself—"So God created mankind in his own image, in the image of God he created them; male and female he created them" (Gen. 1:27). Jesus is the mold for the new humanity that God is at present recreating in the church—"For those God foreknew he also predestined to be conformed to the image of his Son, that he might be the firstborn among many brothers and sisters" (Rom. 8:29), and "His purpose was to create in himself one new humanity out of the two, thus making peace" (Eph. 2:15).

Although fallen humans maintain the mortal breath of life for their lifetimes in the here and now, God's breath of life is taken from us early on by sin. But God regenerates believers through our faith Christ Jesus—"We were therefore buried with him through baptism into death in order that, just as Christ was raised from the dead through the glory of the Father, we too may live a new life" (Rom. 6:4). He promises to everyone he calls the blessing of his Spirit to live within us—"Repent and be baptized, every one of you, in the name of Jesus Christ for the forgiveness of your sins. And you will receive the gift of the Holy Spirit. The promise is for you and your children and for all who are far off—for all whom the Lord our God will call" (Acts 2:38–39).

It is through the redemptive work of Christ's life, death, and resurrection that God affects his final regenerative work in each believer—"While we were God's enemies, we were reconciled to him through the death of his Son, how much more, having been reconciled, shall we be saved through his life!" (Rom. 5:10). And it is because of his eternal plan that no force outside of him and ourselves can separate us from him—"Who shall separate us from the love of Christ?" (Rom. 8:35). The evidence of our new humanness in Christ Jesus is found in the reality of our singular belief in him—"The Spirit himself testifies with our spirit that we are God's children" (Rom. 8:16).

God thus sent Christ so that we would be collectively recreated in him as his own bride. And it is through his new creation that he has chosen to work—"All this is from God, who reconciled us to himself through Christ and gave us the ministry of reconciliation: that God was reconciling the world to himself in Christ, not counting people's sins against them. And he has committed to us the message of reconciliation" (2 Cor. 5:18–19). He does this not because of our goodness but because of his.

And it is not because of what we are capable of, but because of what he is capable of working within us—"Now to him who is able to do immeasurably more than all we ask or imagine, according to his power that is at work within us, to him be glory in the church and in Christ Jesus throughout all generations, for ever and ever!" (Eph. 3:20–21).

Our ultimate conquest in him is not of our own doing and can never be; it is of his doing. Our victory is not the result of our own conquest, rather it is the result our yielding to the loving and gracious God who is building his kingdom within us.

A Prayer:

> Father, help mine be a faith that works—serving you in all I do.
> Let my faith be one that extends from beginning to end; that I live my whole life by faith.

As I believe in your work to redeem and justify me, help me believe in your work to sanctify me and work through me.

Help me to "work out my salvation" with full assurance that you are working in me.

Help me to see that you prepared in advance the good works you give me to do.

45
Good Deeds

The smallest act of good exceeds the greatest intention of good.

For we are God's handiwork, created in Christ Jesus to do good works, which God prepared in advance for us to do (Eph. 2:10).

GOD RECREATES US in Christ in order for us to do his good work. Certainly our good works in no way merit salvation—"It is by grace you have been saved" (Eph. 2:5). Good works do not save us, but we are certainly saved by God in order for us to do the good work he has foreordained for us. Our salvation, in fact, is a good work of God himself! Our own good works are a testimony of his goodness and not of our own.

Jesus himself is the example of God's appointment of us and his leadership for us in going about doing good—"God anointed Jesus of Nazareth with the Holy Spirit and power, and how *he went around doing good* and healing all that were under the power of the devil, because God was with him" (Acts 10:38, italics added).

It is all too easy for us to not do the small good deed in front of us when we allow ourselves to be overwhelmed by all the profound needs around us. What most defines us is found in the daily and the menial, not in the intermittent and mighty. Indeed we should not walk away from significant opportunities to undertake great projects that may help the masses and gain the even gain the possible unwanted attention of well-wishers. However, many, if not most, of our opportunities are simple, spontaneous, and often will go unappreciated or even unnoticed by others and even the ones we serve.

But the good we do will never go unnoticed by God, that is, if it is truly done for God—"Truly I tell you, whatever you did for one of the least of these brothers and sisters of mine, you did for me" (Matt. 25:40). That is why the works we do must truly be done for his purposes and his glory—"And whatever you do, whether in word or deed, do it all in the name of the Lord Jesus, giving thanks to God the Father through him" (Col. 3:17).

Everything that the Christian is and does is for God, even that which might otherwise seem secular and nonreligious. Thus, we are to work at everything we do as if for God—"Whatever you do, work at it with all your heart, as working for the Lord, not for human masters" (Col. 3:23). And at judgment God will not forget the works we have done for him—"Blessed are the dead who die in the Lord from now on…they will rest from their labor, for their deeds will follow them" (Rev. 14:13).

The scripture itself was handed down to us in order to fully equip us for good work—"All Scripture is God-breathed and is useful for teaching, rebuking, correcting and training in righteousness, so that the servant of God may be thoroughly equipped for every good work" (2 Tim. 3:16–17). And to fail in our obedience to that which we have been equipped for is itself sinful—"If anyone, then, knows the good they ought to do and doesn't do it, it is sin for them" (James 4:17).

It was not the religious priest and Levite, who were rushing to perform their religious duties, that were commended by Jesus. Rather Jesus commended the busy Samaritan, one of those resented and rejected by the Jews, who took of his own time and resources to care for one fallen (Luke 10:25–37). It was by the example of the Good Samaritan that Jesus concluded that we should "go and do likewise" (Luke 10:37).

God does not want us to be sparing in our good deeds, rather he instructs us to "do good, to be rich in good deeds, and to be generous and willing to share" (1 Tim. 6:18).

And, "As we have opportunity, let us do good to all people, especially to those who belong to the family of believers" (Gal. 6:10).

To the outsider to the faith, the testimony of the good we do generally far outshines the good we speak—"Live such good lives among the pagans that, though they accuse you of doing wrong, they may see your good deeds and glorify God on the day he visits us" (1 Pet. 2:12). We should, in fact, be thoughtful to encourage others to do good as well—"And let us consider how we may spur one another on toward love and good deeds" (Heb. 10:24).

In serving our Lord, we must remember that Jesus takes very personally our actions toward others—"For I was hungry and you gave me something to eat, I was thirsty and you gave me something to drink, I was a stranger and you invited me in, I needed clothes and you clothed me, I was sick and you looked after me, I was in prison and you came to visit me." (Matt. 25:35–36).

And, in order to please God, we must do the good we are called to do most discreetly—"Be careful not to practice your righteousness in front of others to be seen by them. If you do, you will have no reward from your Father in heaven" (Matt. 6:1). Also, lest we grow tired and give up, we should remember that the fruit of our good actions may come much later, and oftentimes even after we have gone to be with the Lord, but good will come of it—"Let us not become weary in doing good, for at the proper time we will reap a harvest if we do not give up" (Gal. 6:9).

To all then, even to one's enemies, we must remember the simple admonition of the Lord: "On the contrary: 'If your enemy is hungry, feed him; if he is thirsty, give him something to drink. In doing this, you will heap burning coals on his head.'" (Rom. 12:20).

Carefully, considerately, purposefully, and lovingly, just do it. Perhaps our greatest regrets in the end might not be the evil things we might have done, but the good things we neglected to do.

A Prayer:

> Help me, O Lord, to respond to your work for me by hard work for you.
> Let me not merely say "I will"; help me, Father, to actually do!
> Break down my stubborn will, God, that thinks first of me,
> And to be diligent always and in your mission and service.
>
> Prune my branch so that I can bear abundant fruit for you,
> Clean my heart and clear my schedule of the chaff that I accrue,
> Help me make my ultimate priority serving you daily, Lord,
> And be always obedient to the things you teach in your word.

46
Graceful Living

Some wonder about the Sermon the Mount and its seeming lack of grace. However, the Sermon on the Mount is not about receiving grace but about giving it; it is about graceful living.

Blessed are the merciful, for they will be shown mercy (Matt. 5:7).

IN OUR FLIGHT from the sinful life, we find ourselves desperate for the grace of God. We witness, sometimes as mere observers, the battle between our sinful and spiritual natures, and we feel the pain of our all-too-frequent failures—"I do not understand what I do. For what I want to do I do not do, but what I hate I do" (Rom. 7:15). Our faithful reception of his grace thus is God's most important work in us—"The work of God is this: to believe in the one he has sent" (John 6:29).

We can, however, become so obsessed with the receiving of grace that we forget that we are to be conduits of it and not simply receptacles of this glorious gift! Indeed we must faithfully receive it, but in our eager reception, we must as well generously extend it to others—"Freely you have received; freely give" (Matt. 5:8).

Grace is not merely mercy. Mercy is certainly an expression of it. "Grace" means "gift." To be graceful is to be giving of all good things. To be graceful is to be generous in all aspects of life. A great witness of genuine conversion is the transforming of a person from being a *taker* to being a *giver*. God is a giver, and to be like God is for us to be a giver.

The gospel is not just about the honest, graceful essence of God as exuded and extended to us by Jesus—"We have seen his glory, the glory of the one and only Son, who came from the Father, full of grace and truth" (John 1:14). The gospel is a freeing of us to again be like God and to, as well, exude this same grace to the world around us—"For we are God's handiwork, created in Christ Jesus to do good works, which God prepared in advance for us to do" (Eph. 2:10). In his love, God is reaching out to the lost world through us as his people—"We are therefore Christ's ambassadors, as though God were making his appeal through us" (2 Cor. 5:20).

It is in the essence of the Spirit of God on display through us that our status as his children is finally revealed—"And God raised us up with Christ and seated us with him in the heavenly realms in Christ Jesus, in order that in the coming ages he might show the incomparable riches of his grace, expressed in his kindness to us in Christ Jesus" (Eph. 2:6–7). And this fallen creation anxiously, but often unknowingly, waits the revealing of God's graceful people—"For the creation waits in eager expectation for the children of God to be revealed" (Rom. 8:19).

Jesus's Sermon on the Mount, appearing at the very beginning of the New Testament scriptures, appears to many to lack the expression of the grace of God. However, God's grace is expressed through the life of Jesus himself. Jesus is the gospel. Jesus is the extending of God's grace to us through the redemptive work performed in Christ, namely his miraculous life, death, burial, resurrection, and ascension to heaven so that we could be forgiven and receive God's Holy Spirit. The good news of Christ is that God offers us reconciliation to himself in accordance with his grace and our faith in him.

The Sermon on the Mount, then, is Jesus's telling us how, after receiving grace, to extend it to the world and not just receive it. He begins it as if to say, "To be of God's kingdom and extend his grace to the awaiting world, you must be poor toward yourself while rich toward others"—"Blessed are the poor in spirit, for theirs is the kingdom of heaven" (Matt. 5:3). And also, you must genuinely care for the desperate pain of the lost world—"Blessed are those who mourn" (Matt. 5:4). You must, as well, be humble and not proud—"Blessed are the meek" (Matt. 5:5).

Continuing, you must be dying of a thirst and hunger for God—"Blessed are those who hunger and thirst for righteousness" (Matt. 5:6). You must, too, be one who freely extends the mercy generously extended to you—"Blessed are the merciful" (Matt. 5:7). Too, your heart must be solely about God, not about you—"Blessed are the pure in heart" (Matt. 5:8). And you must extend to others the same peace-loving grace and invitation of God that has been extended to you—"Blessed are the peacemakers" (Matt. 5:9). Finally, you must prepare for and rejoice in the same treatment doled out on Jesus by evil—"Blessed are those who are persecuted because of righteousness" (Matt. 5:10).

It is in this imitation of Christ that we become the ongoing embodiment of him in the world today—"You are the salt of the earth…You are the light of the world" (Matt. 5:13–14). We become his expression and extension: giving to those in need, loving the unloving, and meting out grace instead of judgment. We reject hating, hurting, and hitting in favor of loving, helping, and consoling. Indeed, as kingdom people and ambassadors of God, we fulfill the prophet's prediction—"They will beat their swords into plowshares and their spears into pruning hooks. Nation will not take up sword against nation, nor will they train for war anymore" (Isa. 2:4). In following, imitating, and obeying the Prince of Peace, we become his emissaries of peace.

We must be the people who extend generously the grace and mercy of God that has been freely extended to us—"Forgive as the Lord forgave you" (Col. 3:13). Thus, we must live lovingly and gracefully as did our Lord—"Follow God's example, therefore, as dearly loved children and walk in the way of love, just as Christ loved us and gave himself up for us as a fragrant offering and sacrifice to God" (Eph. 5:1–2).

A Prayer:

It is by your grace, Lord, that I am called and by your grace that I am chosen.
It is in your grace that I live daily and that I find refuge from sinful desires.
Even the good works that I do have been pre-prepared and given to me by your grace.
Help me then to feel a debt of gratitude to you that I repay in the grace I extend to others,
To forgive as you have forgiven me,
To love others has you have loved me,
To esteem others as you have esteemed me,
To serve others as you have serve me, and
To freely give as I have been freely given to.
Help me to be poor in spirit that the kingdom might be mine.
Help me to mourn for the sin and pain of the world so that I can be comforted by you.
Make me meek that I can receive your world as my inheritance.

Famish me, Lord, that I might hunger and thirst deeply for you.
Make me merciful that I might receive mercy.
Purify my heart by your word and Spirit so that I can see you.
Make me a peacemaker like Jesus that I might be called your child.
And fill up your suffering in me through persecution and sacrifice that I might possess the kingdom.
Shine on me, Lord, that I might shine on others for you by extending grace all around.

47
Growing Up and Maturing

It takes a little effort to grow old; however, it takes great effort to grow up.

For this very reason, make every effort to add to your faith goodness; and to goodness, knowledge; and to knowledge, self-control; and to self-control, perseverance; and to perseverance, godliness; and to godliness, mutual affection; and to mutual affection, love. For if you possess these qualities in increasing measure, they will keep you from being ineffective and unproductive in your knowledge of our Lord Jesus Christ (2 Pet. 1:5–8).

THE ASSUMPTION THAT age equates to wisdom is but a myth—"Getting old doesn't guarantee good sense" (Job 32:9, The Message). The worst fool is the oldest fool.

Growing in wisdom and stature is to be like the Lord and is of the Lord—"And Jesus grew in wisdom and stature, and in favor with God and man" (Luke 2:52). Growth is not just an outcome to be awaited, but it is an attitude and action of life to be sought and enacted—"Grow in the grace and knowledge of our Lord and Savior Jesus Christ" (2 Pet. 3:18).

The conception and growth of spiritual life in us begins and ends with God—"Then the Lord God formed a man from the dust of the ground and breathed into his nostrils the breath of life, and the man became a living being" (Gen. 2:7). From the inception of creation, life was his plan for humanity. Because of sin's curse, the outward life, as we experience presently, wastes away and diminishes around us. However, just as creation grew out of the eternal, the eternal grows out of creation, and thus we grow stronger in our pursuit of the eternity lies ahead—"Therefore we do not lose heart. Though outwardly we are wasting away, yet inwardly we are being renewed day by day. For our light and momentary troubles are achieving for us an eternal glory that far outweighs them all. So we fix our eyes not on what is seen, but on what is unseen, since what is seen is temporary, but what is unseen is eternal" (2 Cor. 4:16–18).

Our faith is first a work of God in us and then a work of us in God—"The work of God is this: to believe in the one he has sent" (John 6:29). The mystery of faith's conception within the few is ultimately a divine mystery—"For he chose us in him before the creation of the world to be holy and blameless in his sight" (Eph. 1:4). Thus, we, as the people of faith, must not divide over its understanding; rather we must unite around its reality.

The conception of salvation is an expression and outgrowth of the rich grace of the eternal God. The extension and invitation of grace to each one of us is by the express purpose of the God of grace himself—"In him we have redemption through his blood, the forgiveness of sins, in accordance with the riches of God's grace that he lavished on us" (Eph. 1:7–8). It is by his own will and purpose that he revealed this divine plan to us—"With all wisdom and understanding, he made known to us the mystery of his will according to his good pleasure, which he purposed in Christ" (Eph. 1:8–9).

His grace offered to us through Christ and by his divine election allows us to approach God without fear—"In him and through faith in him we may approach God with freedom and confidence" (Eph. 3:12). But his grace also teaches and challenges us, in our own present existence and state, to pursue the being and nature of God—"For the grace of God has appeared that offers salvation to all people. It teaches us to say 'No' to ungodliness and worldly passions, and to live self-controlled, upright and godly lives in this present age, while we wait for the blessed hope—the appearing of the glory of our great God and Savior, Jesus Christ, who gave himself for us to redeem us from all wickedness and to purify for himself a people that are his very own, eager to do what is good" (Titus 2:10–14).

Thus, it is our stated obligation to act on our faith in doing good—"[Be] eager to do what is good." We must "make every effort" to do so. And we must add knowledge to goodness and self-control to knowledge. Perseverance must be added to keep us from falling into ineffectiveness and mediocrity—"For if you possess these qualities in increasing measure, they will keep you from being ineffective and unproductive in your knowledge of our Lord Jesus Christ" (2 Pet. 1:8). This all must be blended not to produce a self-righteousness of our own, but rather godliness that begins and ends with faith in him and that is from God himself.

Godliness is ultimately expressed through us in the very essence of God—love. We must love one another as Jesus commanded—"A new command I give you: Love one another. As I have loved you, so you must love one another" (John 13:34).

It is not in knowledge and agedness that growth and wisdom from God are expressed; it is through godliness and love produced by the Spirit—"Apart from me [Jesus] you can do nothing" (John 15:5). Our wisdom and stature in the Lord is not conjured in us by our own human knowledge, work, and expertise but is built within us by the love of God—"We know that 'We all possess knowledge.' But knowledge puffs up while love builds up. Those who think they know something do not yet know as they ought to know. But whoever loves God is known by God" (1 Cor. 8:1–3).

Our efforts to pursue wisdom and growth are summed up by and found in our pursuit of Jesus himself. It is that end that we must forcefully pursue—"And we all, who with unveiled faces contemplate the Lord's glory, are being transformed into his image with ever-increasing glory, which comes from the Lord, who is the Spirit" (2 Cor. 3:18).

And thus, we must never equate our spiritual maturity with our longevity in Christ or our age.

A Prayer:

> Finish your work in me, Lord, and mature me fully.
> Help my efforts to grow be aligned to your efforts to mature me.
> Give me spiritual teeth to eat meat that I may grow beyond spiritual infancy.
> Help me to not just grow old in you, but to grow up in you!

48
The Heart, Part 1

The human heart is deceitful, not first because it tells lies, but because it believes them. Thus, it must be carefully watched over and also watched out for.

Above all else, guard your heart, for everything you do flows from it (Prov. 4:23).

TO LIVE THE full life, we must know ourselves better. We are intricately and marvelously designed and created—"I am fearfully and wonderfully made" (Ps. 139:14). We exist in a *body* that is a master-machine run by an incomparable supercomputer! We have been given a *mind* to think. We have had created within us a *heart* to perceive, feel, and experience. We have been given a *soul* as the personality and expression of our being and existence. And, we have been given a *spirit* that breathes into us the full breath of God's life and being and connects us to him.

These are all intricately bound up together and somehow humanly inseparable. But they are not inseparable by God; all that comprises us is fully visible and accessible to him—"For the word of God is alive and active. Sharper than any double-edged sword, *it penetrates even to dividing soul and spirit, joints and marrow*; it judges the thoughts and attitudes of the heart. Nothing in all creation is hidden from God's sight. Everything is uncovered and laid bare before the eyes of him to whom we must give account" (Heb. 4:12–13).

Our facades do not deceive God, but he recognizes us for who we are in our inner being—"The Lord does not look at the things people look at. People look at the outward appearance, but the Lord looks at the heart" (1 Sam. 16:7). We can fool ourselves as to who we really are inside. We may also fairly easily fool others in that regard. But we cannot fool God. With God, the one who seeks to fool only plays the fool! God knows us fully and completely as we presently are. In our eternal, post redemption state, so will we—"Now I know in part; then I shall know fully, even as I am fully known" (1 Cor. 13:12).

Left to itself the human heart can be foolish and deceiving—"The heart is deceitful above all things and beyond cure. Who can understand it?" (Jer. 17:9). However, sometimes alarmingly, our life ultimately betrays to those around us our deception as to what is actually in our hearts—"As water reflects the face, so one's life reflects the heart" (Prov. 27:19).

The heart is not so much first deceiving as it is deceived. The heart does indeed have its own filtration. For the unbeliever, the conscience, to whatever degree it is effectively functional, guards the heart. Although apart from Christ, it will indeed be seared by sin and can be overcome by fleshly desires. For the Christian, the word and Spirit of God are its protectors, although the Spirit can be quenched and the word quieted within. And as the heart can be deceived, it can indeed prove most deceiving concerning its inner realities—"These people honor me with their lips, but their hearts are far from me. They worship me in vain; their teachings are merely human rules" (Matt. 15:8–9).

But it is not what goes into it that most defiles us; it is what emerges from it that is most defiling and dangerous to us—"Don't you see that whatever enters the mouth goes into the stomach and then out of the body? But the things that come out of a person's mouth come from the heart, and these defile them. For out of the heart come evil thoughts—murder, adultery, sexual immorality, theft, false testimony, slander. These are what defile a person; but eating with unwashed hands does not defile them" (Matt. 15:17–20).

Our minds can easily and quickly believe the lies our hearts tell us. Our "feelings" are real, experiential, and compelling. But to feel something internally does not make it real externally. Our idealism, romanticism, desires, and infatuations can easily dash reality against the concrete wall of what we *want* to believe to be true about ourselves and others, as well as the world around us. We must not however stand for it. We must take these "thoughts of the heart" captive by the word and the Spirit and align them with the truth and reality of Christ—"We demolish arguments and every pretension that sets itself up against the knowledge of God, and we take captive every thought to make it obedient to Christ" (2 Cor. 10:5).

We must fix our minds and our hearts on the eternal, objective realities of God—"Since, then, you have been raised with Christ, set your *hearts* on things above, where Christ is, seated at the right hand of God. Set your *minds* on things above, not on earthly things" (Col. 3:1–2). We must defer to God's sentries of our inner being, the Spirit and the word, walking by his Spirit and engraving his word on our hearts—"Walk by the Spirit, and you will not gratify the desires of the flesh" (Gal. 5:16), and "I have hidden your word in my heart that I might not sin against you" (Ps. 119:11).

Indeed, by these two gifts from God, the Spirit and the word, we must, as the first priority, reserve our hearts—our "Most Holy Places"—for God's presence and work alone—"Above all else, guard your heart, for everything you do flows from it" (Prov. 4:23).

A Prayer:

> You, God, are the owner and master of my heart.
> Rule in me that I might live in you.
> Judge and purify my heart by your Spirit and word and keep me from being fooled by its deceitfulness.

49
The Heart, Part 2

Our hearts "glow in the dark" to God.

I the Lord search the heart and examine the mind, to reward each person according to their conduct, according to what their deeds deserve (Jer. 17:10).

GOD SEES AND knows us as we really are, not merely by how we may appear outwardly. As he observes our outward actions and behaviors, he as well regards how we think and feel as behavior too. Thus, he commands us to love him with our hearts and minds (Matt. 22:37). And this complete love he commands of us (*agape*, Greek) is an active love that wills and does what is right regardless of our heart's desires.

God looks at who we are in our hearts to assess our inner and ultimate reality. The heart may be deceived, and it as well may seek to deceive, but God can indeed know what will be our outward conduct by what he sees inwardly within us—"The Lord does not look at the things people look at. People look at the outward appearance, but the Lord looks at the heart" (1 Sam. 16:7), and "For the mouth speaks what the heart is full of" (Luke 6:45).

Who we are, what we are, and what we think and feel are fully splayed before God—"Nothing in all creation is hidden from God's sight. Everything is uncovered and laid bare before the eyes of him to whom we must give account" (Heb. 4:13). It is he, and he alone, through the all-surpassing power of his Spirit and word within us who can purify our hearts. We must look to him for such renewal—"Create in me a pure heart, O God, and renew a steadfast spirit within me" (Ps. 51:10).

The heart may control behavior, but it is the mind that controls the heart. Thus, we find transformation of the heart through the renewal of our mind and manner of thinking—"Do not conform to the pattern of this world, but be transformed by the renewing of your mind. Then you will be able to test and approve what God's will is—his good, pleasing and perfect will" (Rom. 12:2).

Our heart will gravitate toward what we choose to invest ourselves in—"Where your treasure is, there your heart will be also" (Matt. 6:21). And we can only present to God and others what it is that we have shelved, intentionally or unintentionally, in our heart's storehouse—"A good man brings good things out of the good stored up in his heart, and an evil man brings evil things out of the evil stored up in his heart. For the mouth speaks what the heart is full of" (Luke 6:45).

Whatever is stored in the heart will inevitably come out of the heart. Thus, God purifies his people—"I will put the third part [those I choose to be mine] into the fire; I will refine [purify] them like silver and test them like gold. They will call on my name and I will answer them; I will say, 'They are my people,' and they will say, 'The Lord is our God'" (Zech. 13:9, Common English Bible, bracket comments added).

And it is those he has chosen to purify and make singly his who will be blessed—"Blessed are the pure in heart, for they will see God" (Matt. 5:8). That which is pure consists of but one thing. The pure heart is then wholly and solely of God. Pure hearts are the ones that are receptive to God's healing of our fallen, sinful, duplicitous selves—"Teach me your way, Lord, that I may rely on your faithfulness; give me an undivided heart, that I may fear your name. I will praise you, Lord my God, with all my heart; I will glorify your name forever" (Ps. 86:11–12).

It is those with pure hearts who will see God (Matt. 5:8). In fact, it is only those with pure hearts who may come into God's holy presence—"Who may ascend the mountain of the Lord? Who may stand in his holy place? The one who has clean hands and a pure heart, who does not trust in an idol or swear by a false god" (Ps. 24:3–4).

We must surrender to the word and the Spirit to become strong inwardly. Our inner hope and rejoicing must be only about the reality of God and never about any trust in ourselves or what is human—"Be strong and take heart, all you who hope in the Lord" (Ps. 31:24). In such submission to him, we will find our hearts guarded by the protector of our souls, Jesus Christ, our Lord. His peace will then guard our hearts from this present world's tumult—"The peace of God, which transcends all understanding, will guard your hearts and your minds in Christ Jesus" (Phil. 4:7). Amen.

A Prayer:

Purify my heart, God,
Conform it completely to you,
Refine from it all impurity,
Sanctify it through and through.

50
The Holy Spirit and God

The Holy Spirit is most real. He is God. He is a person, not an "it" or a thing. His presence is more assured than the ground beneath and the air around us. He underlies everything and hovers over all that is. And he lives inside believers in Christ.

The Spirit of God was hovering over the waters (Gen. 1:2).

GOD IS THE "God Almighty" (*El Shaddai*, Hebrew). He is the "Great I AM" (*Yahweh*, Hebrew). He is the Majestic Glory that the apostles heard on the Mount of Transfiguration (Matt. 17:5, 2 Pet. 1:17). He is the God of Gods and of all heavenly hosts—the "Elohim" (plural of "El," or "God"), as opposed to the multiplicity of false gods contrived by Satan and those of false religion—"God said, 'Let *us* make mankind in *our* image, in *our* likeness'" (Gen. 1:26, italics added).

As the universe is vast beyond human imagination, so it is that God, his divinity and power, is infinitely vast beyond our imagination—"Now to him who *is able to do immeasurably more than all we ask or imagine*" (Eph. 3:20, italics added). His infinite power and goodness are ultimately incomprehensible to finite humanity—"Oh, the depth of the riches of the wisdom and knowledge of God! How unsearchable his judgments, and his paths beyond tracing out!" (Rom. 11:33).

God reveals himself in scripture as what has come to be known as the "Trinity," the Father, the Son, and the Holy Spirit—"May the grace of the *Lord Jesus Christ*, and the love of *God*, and the fellowship of the *Holy Spirit* be with you all" (2 Cor. 13:14). Three "persons" in one? It seems an impossibility in this present earthly realm; however, it is shown to be a reality in the heavenly one.

All three were active in creation—"In the beginning *God created* the heavens and the earth. Now the earth was formless and empty, darkness was over the surface of the deep, and *the Spirit of God was hovering* over the waters" (Gen. 1:1–2, italics added). Of Jesus's role in creation, the Bible says, "In the beginning was the Word [the Son of God, Jesus Christ, see John 1:14], and the Word was with God, and the Word was God. He was with God in the beginning. *Through him all things were made; without him nothing was made that has been made*" (John 1:1–3, italics added).

Jesus was the bodily personification of all three persons of the Trinity—"For in Christ all the fullness of the Deity lives in bodily form" (Col. 2:9). His birth was a miracle performed by God through the Holy Spirit—"The angel answered [to Jesus's mother-to-be, the virgin, Mary], 'The Holy Spirit will come on you, and the power of the Most High will overshadow you. So the holy one to be born will be called the Son of God'" (Luke 1:35). Jesus was God come to the earth—"'The virgin will conceive and give birth to a son, and they will call him Immanuel' (which means 'God with us')" (Matt. 1:23).

While on earth, Jesus promised that after he returned to heaven, he would send the Holy Spirit to be with and in his believers, the church—"I will ask the Father, and he will give you another advocate to help you and be with you forever—the Spirit of truth. The world cannot accept him, because it neither sees him nor knows him. But you know him, for he lives with you and will be in you" (John 14:16–17), and "Unless I go away, the Advocate will not come to you; but if I go, *I will send him to you*" (John 16:7, italics added). In fact, Jesus promised the Holy Spirit would literally flow out of believers—"Whoever believes in me, as Scripture has said, rivers of living water will flow from within them" (John 7:38).

Jesus "anoints" believers with the Holy Spirit, and the Spirit then gives us the ability to recognize of the voice of Christ—"My sheep listen to my voice; I know them, and they follow me" (John 10:27). He also gives us the ability to avoid the voices of spirits other than Jesus—"But they will never follow a stranger; in fact, they will run away from him because they do not recognize a stranger's voice" (John 10:5).

It is this anointing of the Spirit that gives believers a sense of "knowing," both how to follow Jesus and how stay "in" him—"Remain in me, and I will remain in you" (John 15:4, Common English Bible), and "*You have an anointing from the Holy One*, and all of you know the truth…As for you, the anointing you received from him remains in you, and you do not need anyone to teach you. But as his anointing teaches you about all things and as that anointing is real, not counterfeit—*just as it has taught you, remain in him*" (1 John 2:20, 27, italics added).

Therefore, the work of Jesus was and is the work of the fullness of the "Trinity," as God has come to be seen and described in orthodox Christianity. And when Jesus gave the Great Commission to the apostles, handed down to the church of each generation, he commissioned that believers be baptized by the authority of all three—"Therefore go and make disciples of all nations, baptizing them in the name of *the Father* and of *the Son* and of *the Holy Spirit*" (Matt. 28:19). Thus, to be baptized in the name of Jesus is to be baptized in the name of the Father, the Son, and the Holy Spirit—"Repent and be baptized, every one of you, in the name of Jesus Christ for the forgiveness of your sins" (Acts 2:38). When it comes to the Trinity, then, the authority of the one is the authority of all and the authority of all is the authority of the one—"I and the Father are one" (John 10:30).

The Holy Spirit is to this present age what Jesus was to the time in which he lived—the representation, agent, and emissary of God on earth. The Holy Spirit is given to those who through faith obey God, seeking his presence—"How much more will your Father in heaven *give the Holy Spirit to those who ask him*!" (Luke 11:13), and "We are witnesses of these things, and so is the Holy Spirit, whom *God has given to those who obey him*" (Acts 5:32).

The Spirit is God's seal of ownership on us, in the spiritual realms—"Now it is God who makes both us and you stand firm in Christ. He anointed us, set his seal of ownership on us, and put his Spirit in our hearts as a deposit, guaranteeing what is to come" (2 Cor. 1:21–22). And, void of the Spirit, one simply does not belong to God—"You, however, are not in the realm of the flesh but are in the realm of the Spirit, if indeed the Spirit of God lives in you. And *if anyone does not have the Spirit of Christ, they do not belong to Christ*" (Rom. 8:9, italics added).

It is through the Spirit's work in ministering Christ to us that God saves us—"But when the kindness and love of God our Savior appeared, he saved us, not because of righteous things we had done, but because of his mercy. *He saved us through the washing of rebirth and renewal by the Holy Spirit*, whom he poured out on us generously through Jesus Christ our Savior, so that, having been justified by his grace, we might become heirs having the hope of eternal life" (Titus 3:4–7). And it is by the Spirit's working that we, as Christ's followers, are transformed to look more and more like Jesus—"And we all, who with unveiled faces contemplate the Lord's glory, are being transformed into his image with ever-increasing glory, *which comes from the Lord, who is the Spirit*" (2 Cor. 3:18, italics added).

Thus the apostle Peter makes clear at the outset of his address to Christians that it is through the Holy Spirit that the fullness of the deity of God continues to work in the elect, those called by God—"To God's elect…who have been chosen according to the foreknowledge of *God the Father*, through the sanctifying work of *the Spirit*, to be obedient to *Jesus Christ* and sprinkled with his blood" (1 Pet. 1:1–2, italics added).

Christians, individually as well as collectively as the church, are the temple of the Holy Spirit of God on earth—"Do you not know that your bodies are *temples of the Holy Spirit*, who is in you, whom you have received from God?" (1 Cor. 6:19, italics added), and, "Consequently, you are no longer foreigners and strangers, but fellow citizens with God's people and also members of his household, built on the foundation of the apostles and prophets, with Christ Jesus himself as the chief cornerstone. In him the whole building is joined together and rises to become a holy temple in the Lord. And in him you too *are being built together to become a dwelling in which God lives by his Spirit*" (Eph. 2:19–22, italics added).

As we live for and walk with God, the Holy Spirit intercedes for and helps us—"The Spirit helps us in our weakness. We do not know what we ought to pray for, but the Spirit himself intercedes for us through wordless groans. And he who searches our hearts knows the mind of the Spirit, because the Spirit intercedes for God's people in accordance with the will of God" (Rom. 8:26–27). Through him flows to us and through us the love of God—"God's love has been poured out into our hearts through the Holy Spirit, who has been given to us" (Rom. 5:5).

The Spirit gives us various gifts and in many ways, and he places us in the body according to God's own will. And it is his greatest and enduring gifts that we should thus desire—"Now eagerly desire the greater gifts" (1 Cor. 12:31), and "And now these three remain: faith, hope and love. But the greatest of these is love" (1 Cor. 13:13).

A Prayer:

> Holy Spirit of God, through Jesus I ask that you fill me, consume me, and flow from me.
> Grow me to be more and more like the Son, Jesus Christ.
> Transform my heart of flesh into a heart for God.
> Manifest yourself through me and bring glory to God in my mortal life here.
> Amen.

51
Hope and Strength

It is in our hope in God that we find the strength of God.

We have this hope as an anchor for the soul, firm and secure (Heb. 6:19).

IN THE MODERN sense, to hope means to wish. On the contrary, in scripture, to hope (*elpis*, Greek) means to expect. Our hope is what we expect because it derives from what we believe. For instance, we believe Jesus will return for the final redemption because of the eyewitness accounts of his resurrection from a brutal death and his release from a sealed, guarded tomb. An angel told them that Jesus had ascended into heaven and that he would return similarly—"This same Jesus, who has been taken from you into heaven, will come back in the same way you have seen him go into heaven" (Acts 1:11).

It is through our faith in Christ that we have salvation and hope of life eternal—"He [Jesus] saved us through the washing of rebirth and renewal by the Holy Spirit, whom he poured out on us generously through Jesus Christ our Savior, so that, having been justified by his grace, we might become heirs having the hope of eternal life" (Titus 3:5–7). Because of what Jesus did and demonstrated, we possess a hope that is real, living, and substantive—"Praise be to the God and Father of our Lord Jesus Christ! In his great mercy he has given us new birth into a living hope through the resurrection of Jesus Christ from the dead" (1 Pet. 1:3).

What we hope for, or expect, is what we are, in our lives, drawn to and by. When our hope is based on what is false and thus fails us, we can certainly become disenchanted and generalize it to other or all areas of our lives. We become hopeless. Hopelessness leads to despair. Despair leads us to bad places.

But our hope is anchored in history and in real events witnessed by those, such as the apostle Peter, who ultimately died defending what they had seen and heard—"For we did not follow cleverly devised stories when we told you about the coming of our Lord Jesus Christ in power, but we were eyewitnesses of his majesty" (2 Pet. 1:16). Thus in the end we will not be disappointed—"Hope does not put us to shame, because God's love has been poured out into our hearts through the Holy Spirit, who has been given to us" (Rom. 5:5).

God created the world in the hope (expectation) of the salvation of many—"He predestined us for adoption to sonship through Jesus Christ, in accordance with his pleasure and will" (Eph. 1:5). It is through his plan affected in Christ that God is "bringing many sons and daughters to glory" (Heb. 2:10).

And our firm conviction brings tremendous confidence that God will deliver on all his promises—"I know whom I have believed, and am convinced that he is able to guard what I have entrusted to him until that day" (2 Tim. 1:12). Such hope brings steadiness to our lives lived in this already unsteady world—"Let us hold unswervingly to the hope we profess, for he who promised is faithful" (Heb. 10:23).

Our hope in the promises of God anchors us in the eternal and divine realities. And though the storms of life will indeed surely beat down upon us, our foundation in Christ will hold us firm till the end—"The rain came down, the streams rose, and the winds blew and beat against that house; yet it did not fall, because it had its foundation on the rock" (Matt. 7:25).

Thus the admonition of the apostle Paul should be heeded by all of us who would seek the godly, meaningful life—"Be joyful in hope, patient in affliction, faithful in prayer" (Rom. 12:12). Thus, the beautiful prayer of hopeful blessing for us: "May the God of hope fill you with all joy and peace as you trust in him, so that you may overflow with hope by the power of the Holy Spirit" (Rom. 15:13).

A Prayer:

> Help me to seek and find pure truth wherever it is to be found.
> I firmly believe that Jesus is the truth and therefore the giver of truth.
> Purify and sanctify my heart and mind so that I can see you, believe in you, trust you, and live in you.
> Help my conviction to be strong that my hope may be sure.
> I believe, Father, help my unbelief; defeat my doubt with the pure water of truth.
> Lord, come quickly!

52
Human Value

Our problem is often not that we believe God is not powerful enough to take care of our problems and concerns or to meet our needs. The real problem is often that we do not believe we are valued enough by him for him to help us.

For God so loved the world (John 3:16).

WE LIVE IN a blessed paradise—a marvelous mansion with a beautiful garden. God's creation. We have been given countless abilities to delight in its bounties and enjoy its opportunities and pleasures—"We may eat fruit from the trees in the garden…" (Gen. 3:2). Yet we continue to ogle the forbidden fruit in the middle of our paradise; the tree whose fruit God told us would prove deadly to us—"You must not eat fruit from the tree that is in the middle of the garden, and you must not touch it, or you will die" (Gen. 3:2). Its fruit is toxic and its effects are deadly.

This deadly fruit is from the Tree of the Knowledge of Good and Evil. Yet, in spite of the warning and the compelling evidence not to, we continue to dine on it almost daily. The world apart from God has its own grafted versions and even the world religions outside of Christ are variations of it as well. All these variations are philosophies, traditions, and belief systems devoid of Yahweh, as shown to us through Jesus Christ. Still, sadly, this forbidden tree is often planted squarely in our Christian sanctuaries and hearts. Because of it, we can come to believe we will ultimately be saved because, or if, we are "right" about the right things. In such a way, Christianity can become to us another philosophical world religion that tries to define a bit differently the "knowledge of good and evil." But there is no life in that. Outside of the church, in the secular world and in the religions apart from Christ, any concept of salvation whatsoever likely doesn't, or rarely, exists. Although many do idealize some sort of nirvana, religiously or generally, in the present or in the future, it must ultimately be attained through somehow being right about things.

But within Christendom, salvation, although somewhat disputed in meaning and form, is the ideal. And salvation to most, in some way, means a right relationship with God resulting in regeneration from our dead spiritual states. It offers life. But sadly, the way of Christ is also often fashioned by humanity into that fruit of human self-rightness that seems so inviting to us in our prideful conditions. Yet, it is so deadly—"When the woman saw that the fruit of the tree was good for food and pleasing to the eye, and also desirable for gaining wisdom, she took some and ate it. She also gave some to her husband, who was with her, and he ate it" (Gen. 3:6). Because of the original lie—"you will be like God," that led to the original sin—"she took some and ate and gave some to her husband and he ate," they were banished from the garden and their experiential relationship to God, and their fate has been handed down to all the generations to this very day that are without Christ—"Therefore, just as sin entered the world through one man, and death through sin, and in this way death came to all people, because all sinned" (Rom. 5:12).

Often our statements of faith and creeds seem to be more assertions of *rightness* than they are humble statements of understanding, discussion, clarity, and orthodoxy. Yet, we continue to find our value by our *membership* in this church or that church, or this denomination or that denomination, or no denomination at all. We feel righteousness comes from our own rightness about things. And we find security in this assumed rightness by belonging to a reassuring tribe of some sort that agrees with us.

But inside we feel this roiling of the truth about our actual "unrightness" deep in the fiber of our flesh and bones—"Surely I was sinful at birth, sinful from the time my mother conceived me" (Ps. 51:5). We just know that, although in our spirits we desire what is higher, in our flesh still dwells all that is base and carnal—"For I know that nothing good dwells in me, that is, in my flesh. For I have the desire to do what is right, but not the ability to carry it out" (Rom. 7:18, English Standard Version).

And the sad admission and the subsequent question it begs naturally follow: "What a wretched man I am! Who will rescue me from this body that is subject to death?" (Rom. 7:24). The correct answer is: not me or my accomplishments, and especially not my own "goodness" or "rightness." Nor can any other human being or institution, including the church, rescue us. There is only one right answer, not many—"I am the way and the truth and the life. No one comes to the Father except through me" (John 14:6).

Only Christ can deliver us from this inner sinfulness—"Thanks be to God, who delivers me through Jesus Christ our Lord!" (Rom. 7:25). Our job in the relationship is to trust him and not ourselves or our right religiosity—"Therefore, since we have been justified through faith, we have peace with God through our Lord Jesus Christ, through whom we have gained access by faith into this grace in which we now stand" (Rom. 5:1–2). He is the truth; we are not—"Let God be true, and every human being a liar" (Rom. 3:4).

Because of what Christ has done for us and can do through us, we are not judged on the basis of our goodness, or lack thereof, but on the basis of his rock-solid goodness. Subsequently, our firm trust in this eternal reality—"Therefore, there is now no condemnation for those who are in Christ Jesus, because through Christ Jesus the law of the Spirit who gives life has set you free from the law of sin and death" (Rom. 8:1–2).

What we simply cannot do—be completely good—Christ has done for us—"For what the law was powerless to do because it was weakened by the flesh, God did by sending his own Son in the likeness of sinful flesh to be a sin offering. And so he condemned sin in the flesh, in order that the righteous requirement of the law might be fully met in us, who do not live according to the flesh but according to the Spirit" (Rom. 8:3–4). In our trust in him, he can put his trust back in us—"He has trusted us with this message of reconciliation" (2 Cor. 5:19, Common English Bible).

Hallelujah! Our attainment of goodness is simply no longer the basis of our rightness with God! His goodness is. And it is his goodness that deems us priceless, not worthless, for in God's way of thinking, we are worth more than the whole world—"What good is it for someone to gain the whole world, and yet lose or forfeit their very self?" (Luke 9:25).

We are, then, most certainly valuable enough to him for him to help us with our present needs and concerns. He proved it by dying for us in regard to all our concerns both temporal and eternal!

A Prayer:

> Help me see myself, Lord, through your sweet eyes,
> Help me find my worth in what *you* say,
> Instill within my heart the gospel message,
> Show me my soul's worth in the life that you paid.

May I never, God, go by the world's price tags and valuations—
Their high costs of the worthless, and the cheap tags on the priceless.
May I never venture again to find my value through what is earthly,
Or trust the world's philosophies that are clearly Christ-less.

Thank you, Lord, for living out in Jesus the message of my value,
Thank you, for paying for us all the highest price,
Show me in my mind's eye and heart the truth revealed in your Son,
Help me measure my worth only through Jesus Christ!

53
Humanism

Humanism itself is the greatest demonstration not of humanity's independence *from* God but it is ultimately the greatest testimony of humanity's desperate need *for* God.

They did not think it worthwhile to retain the knowledge of God (Rom. 1:28).

MODERN HUMANISM IS in actuality as old as the Garden of Eden. Humanism is a belief that humans can serve as their own god—"When you eat from it your eyes will be opened, and you will be like God, knowing good and evil" (Gen. 3:5). It is no more or no less just one more expression of the fruit of the Tree of the Knowledge of Good and Evil.

Relying on the ingenuity and reason of humanity alone, as expressed in religion in general, Christianity in particular, or in the completely secular, has shown itself over and over again to be futile—"So I tell you this, and insist on it in the Lord, that you must no longer live as the Gentiles [those apart from God] do, in the futility of their thinking. They are darkened in their understanding and separated from the life of God because of the ignorance that is in them due to the hardening of their hearts. Having lost all sensitivity, they have given themselves over to sensuality so as to indulge in every kind of impurity, and they are full of greed" (Eph. 4:17–19).

Many cite examples of misguided religion, and even Christianity in particular, as their reason for spurning the pursuit of divine guidance in favor of pursuing mere human reasoning. The abuse of a thing should in no way limit the use of it; rather the abuse of it only admits that it actually exists. The mere illogic and lunacy of such an idea should startle us. Yet that is exactly what many choose—the human over the divine, the mortal over the immortal, the temporal over the eternal, and the pitiful over the powerful.

Human solutions and approaches, be they secular or religious, always fail—"Cursed is the one who trusts in man, who draws strength from mere flesh and whose heart turns away from the Lord" (Jer. 17:5). Certainly, human-centered approaches pervade among humanity, but sadder still is how pervasive it can be even within the heart the most solid believer.

The sincere king Asa, after mostly relying on God, suddenly turned to man in his own military leadership and was rebuked by the prophet Hanani. He thus suffered a great failure—"Because you relied on the king of Aram and not on the Lord your God, the army of the king of Aram has escaped from your hand" (2 Chron. 16:7). The lesson delivered to King Asa is completely lost on those who would insist on trusting in humanity—"For the eyes of the Lord range throughout the earth to strengthen those whose hearts are fully committed to him. You have done a foolish thing, and from now on you will be at war" (2 Chron. 16:9).

Even though science is presently the religion of humanism—reason over revelation, it is claimed—and thus scientists and philosophers are humanism's priests, the reality is that what science studies is but that which was designed and created by the divine—"For since the creation of the world God's invisible qualities—his eternal power and divine nature—have been clearly seen, being understood from what has been made, so that people are without excuse" (Rom. 1:20). The true end of science and reason is not that which is unreasonable—unbelief and trust in what is human. The true end of science and reason is faith itself. True science and philosophy honors the faith that exists within it, just as true faith honors the science and reason from which it derives.

There is a divine wisdom, as experienced through the ages, that defies all that is human and proves incomparably superior—"Those who trust in themselves are fools, but those who walk in wisdom are kept safe" (Prov. 28:26). Humanism at its core denies the existence of God, and that is the least wise thing of all—"The fear of the LORD is the beginning of knowledge, but fools despise wisdom and instruction" (Prov. 1:7).

Indeed there is a pseudo wisdom that flows from pseudo knowledge and pseudo faith. However, that in no way discounts or discredits the genuine wisdom that flows from the genuine faith—"Out in the open wisdom calls aloud, she raises her voice in the public square; on top of the wall she cries out, at the city gate she makes her speech. 'How long will you who are simple love your simple ways? How long will mockers delight in mockery and fools hate knowledge?'" (Prov. 1:20–22).

Jesus did not trust in humanity—"But Jesus would not entrust himself to them, for he knew all people. He did not need any testimony about mankind, for he knew what was in each person" (John 2:24–25). And neither should we trust in humanity—its motives, its purposes, its reasoning, and its selfish ends.

The fruit of the forbidden tree is so very tempting, and it grows near each one of us. It grows inside of us. It is especially tempting now, when the misguidance of humanity is so well documented for us. But for very human reasons, it still appears good for food.

It still can appear so pleasing to the eye, with its false promises and the self-aggrandizement it offers. And it is ever so tempting to think that it can make us like God, or rather make us a god. It will not, however, gratify our spiritual hunger, but it will most definitely gratify our human ego.

Rather let it be that, "He put a new song in my mouth, a hymn of praise to our God. Many will see and fear the Lord and put their trust in him" (Ps. 40:3). The promise of faith is reasoned and sound—"Blessed is the one who trusts in the Lord, who does not look to the proud, to those who turn aside to false gods" (Ps. 40:4).

We must never allow humanity's distortions of the divine to cause us to turn to humanity as the divine.

A Prayer:

> Help me never, Lord, trust in what is merely human,
> Let me not be swayed by what mere humankind might say,
> Keep me from the fruit that makes me trust in human rightness,
> Show me clearly the Christ who is the truth, the life, the Way!

54
Humbling Oneself Before God

Humble pie is often not so sweet and tasty, but it is very nourishing.

Humble yourselves before the Lord, and he will lift you up (James 4:10).

WHAT *TASTES* GOOD to us is often not that which *is* good for us. What may seem to us good and right might prove to be completely bad and wrong—"There is a way that appears to be right, but in the end it leads to death" (Prov. 14:12).

The ways of God are mostly paradoxical to the ways of humanity apart from God—"'For my thoughts are not your thoughts, neither are your ways my ways,' declares the Lord" (Isa. 55:8). In God's way of thinking, it is the poor who are rich. It is the mourner who is comforted. It is the meek who win out. It is those who are starving who are satisfied. It is the merciful who find mercy. It is the oppressed and persecuted who can rejoice and win in the end. It is in complete surrender and death that real victory and life are found.

There is great woe in the failure to accept reality in favor of believing the lies—"Woe to those who call evil good and good evil, who put darkness for light and light for darkness, who put bitter for sweet and sweet for bitter" (Isa. 5:20). Appearances can be most deceiving, especially when we are looking through the lens of mortal humanity—"Stop judging by mere appearances, but instead judge correctly" (John 7:24).

Humility is a decision that is a direct outcome of the deeper and more foundational decision of faith itself. Humility is a decision of true faith. The truth of who God is makes apparent who we as mere mortals are and who we are not—"Can a mortal be more righteous than God? Can even a strong man be more pure than his Maker?" (Job 4:17). Humility is a command to be obeyed out of trust in God—"Humble yourselves, therefore, under God's mighty hand, that he may lift you up in due time" (1 Pet. 5:6). God is in fact the template of what humanity-done-right-should-look-like, and God is humble—"I am gentle and humble in heart" (Matt. 11:29).

Those who come closest to seeing God are those who are most humble. Unless we get this fact, we will never *get* him. A close relationship with God is not found in those who may know the most about God but it will be found in those who know God the most. And those who know God the most will not be puffed up by mere knowledge but will be filled up with the love that flows from the knowing of—the experiencing of—our incomparably beautiful Maker—"Knowledge puffs up while love builds up" (1 Cor. 8:1).

The great prophet, rather than expressing delight and distinction at seeing God in a vision, expressed great distress and felt nothing but utter humility—"'Woe to me!' I cried. 'I am ruined! For I am a man of unclean lips, and I live among a people of unclean lips, and my eyes have seen the King, the Lord Almighty'" (Isa. 6:5).

Humility is the result of a realization of who God is and who I am not. Humility brings the only real freedom that exists for anyone. Humility is the key antidote of stress, fear, anxiety, and all the troubling emotions we experience. As opposed to the destructiveness of pride, humility opens the door to real wisdom—"When pride comes, then comes disgrace, but with humility comes wisdom" (Prov. 11:2).

Jesus says it is the meek (humble) who will, "Inherit the earth" (Matt. 5:5). Humility begins with the recognition of who God is, and it ends in the true riches of that which is immortal—"Humility is the fear of the Lord; its wages are riches and honor and life" (Prov. 22:4).

A humble stature before God is among humanity's weightiest concerns, because it is an essential element to any relationship with him. Humility is something God requires—"He has shown you, O mortal, what is good. And what does the Lord require of you? To act justly and to love mercy and to walk humbly with your God" (Mic. 6:8). And although it is an expressed requirement of those who would serve God, it is an oft-neglected virtue even among believers, who are sadly and ironically prone to feed their egos on the altar of God's humility.

Thus, we must boldly choose humility and spurn pride—"'Let not the wise boast of their wisdom or the strong boast of their strength or the rich boast of their riches, but let the one who boasts boast about this: that they have the understanding to know me, that I am the Lord, who exercises kindness, justice and righteousness on earth, for in these I delight,' declares the Lord" (Jer. 9:23–24).

The reality and the subsequent admonition is that, "'God opposes the proud but shows favor to the humble.' Submit yourselves, then, to God. Resist the devil, and he will flee from you. Come near to God and he will come near to you. Wash your hands, you sinners, and purify your hearts, you double-minded. Grieve, mourn and wail. Change your laughter to mourning and your joy to gloom. Humble yourselves before the Lord, and he will lift you up" (James 4:6–10).

A Prayer:

Let the mirror through which I see myself be the one hanging from the Cross, Lord.
Let the standard by which I measure be the benchmark, not be the dross, but your word,
Show me the greatness of my last-ness and the pricelessness of the least,
Not settle for the world's meager, when I'm invited to your feast!

55
Humility

Humility comes from the recognition of reality. To be humble is to be in touch with reality.

God opposes the proud but shows favor to the humble (James 4:6).

HUMILITY IS VERY important to God. And it should be very important to us in regard to our relationship with God. Its presence can bring God's grace to us—"God…shows favor to the humble" (James. 4:6). Its absence can bring God in opposition to us—"God opposes the proud" (James. 4:6). In this current fallen world, humility is not natural to any of us and is seemingly quite foreign to many.

The word "humble" (*tapeinóō*, Greek) means to make low, to humble, or to humiliate (taken from http://biblehub.com/greek/5013.htm on Sept. 19, 2017, Strong's Exhaustive Concordance, 5013). Humble is used both as an adjective and a verb, something we are and something we do. As a trait, it is often referred to as "humility," which literally means "lowliness of mind."

Humility is a synonymous noun to humble, sharing with it the same root. Being humble (or possessing humility) is a result of reason and sensibility, not from poor self-esteem. In Christ we are to be covered with humility—"Therefore, as God's chosen people, holy and dearly loved, clothe yourselves with compassion, kindness, humility, gentleness and patience" (Col. 3:12).

A trait related to humility is "meekness" (*praus*, Greek). To be meek means to be gentle. However, in the original language, meekness implies much more—"This difficult-to-translate root (*pra-*) means *more than* 'meek.' *Biblical* meekness is *not weakness* but rather refers to exercising *God's strength* under *His control*—i.e. demonstrating power without undue harshness" (taken from http://biblehub.com/greek/4239.htm on Sept. 19, 2017, Strong's Exhaustive Concordance, 4239). In fact, Jesus says that it is the meek who will in the end prevail—"Blessed are the meek, for they will inherit the earth" (Matt. 5:5).

Humans are not gods. Our influence and control is quite limited, individually and collectively. Pride however puffs us up and makes us want to behave as if we are gods and in control. Pride is the opposite of humility. And our pride can even fool us into thinking we are actually humble!

The New Testament word for pride (*huperéphania*, Greek) derives from a Greek word that means to overestimate one's own power or merit, and thus, look down on and treat others with contempt and disdain. Rather than accept the reality of God and therefore the subsequent reality of ourselves, in our foolishness, we get it backward and try to impose our own delusional "reality" on God. Thus, we trade the truth for a lie, logic for illogic, and reality for fantasy—"They exchanged the truth about God for a lie, and worshiped and served created things rather than the Creator—who is forever praised" (Rom. 1:25).

By default we attempt to play "God" of our own world! The effort always ends up badly.

Pride is the precursor of all kinds of problems, and even ruin—"Pride goes before destruction, a haughty spirit before a fall" (Prov.

16:18). When one becomes haughty and proud, the connection with reality is lost. Losing touch with reality is by definition insanity. Unbelief then is insanity. Thus, to be prideful is to be insane—out of touch with reality. Crazy is; crazy does.

To be humble is to be in touch with reality. Humility allows us to think rationally about ourselves—"Do not think of yourself more highly than you ought, but rather think of yourself with sober judgment" (Rom. 12:3). We must be humble to get God right in our thinking, revering and respecting him and his infinite goodness and wisdom—"Wisdom begins with the fear of the LORD, but fools despise wisdom and instruction" (Prov. 1:7, Common English Bible). Humility allows us to grow in wisdom—"When pride comes, then comes disgrace, but with humility comes wisdom" (Prov. 11:2). On the other hand, humility flows from wisdom—"Who is wise and understanding among you? Let them show it by their good life, by deeds done in *the humility that comes from wisdom*" (James 3:13, italics added).

Humbling ourselves before God is a command given to us by God. It is something we must do before him, and only in doing so will we receive the esteem of God—"Humble yourselves, therefore, under God's mighty hand, that he may lift you up in due time" (1 Pet. 5:6). We must also humble ourselves in regard to others—"Honor one another above yourselves" (Rom. 12:10), and "Do nothing out of selfish ambition or vain conceit. Rather, in humility value others above yourselves" (Phil. 2:3). Humility prevents us from developing the kind of pride that causes us to look down on and exclude others from the graciousness of God's fellowship—"Live in harmony with one another. Do not be proud, but be willing to associate with people of low position. Do not be conceited" (Rom. 12:16).

God wants us to be humble, because he is humble, and we are made in his image—"I am gentle and humble in heart" (Matt. 11:29–30), and "Be completely humble and gentle; be patient, bearing with one another in love" (Eph. 4:2). We were made to be humble. When we are otherwise, we go against our created nature.

Jesus said our humility should be as that of a child—"Truly I tell you, unless you change and become like little children, you will never enter the kingdom of heaven. Therefore, whoever takes the lowly position of this child is the greatest in the kingdom of heaven" (Matt. 18:3–4). In reality, children can be rowdy, selfish, prideful, and so forth. However, their lack of humility is due to human instinct rather than human intention. They are helpless to varying degrees and know it. Thus, they generally willingly rely on an adult. This is how God wants us to rely on him. Before God we are all his children, and when we walk with him, we will walk in humility.

A Prayer:

> Lord, I come to you in humility seeking greater humility.
> In my reverence before you, please give me wisdom from which flows true humility.
> Give my mind and my heart spiritual sanity that I see myself rightly, in view of you and in regard to others.
> I bow before you now as a servant, as the least and as the worst, seeking your mercy and favor.
> Exalt yourself in my lowliness.
> Amen.

56
Hypocrisy, Part 1

Our hypocrisy is often best seen in our indignations.

Be on your guard against the yeast of the Pharisees, which is hypocrisy. There is nothing concealed that will not be disclosed, or hidden that will not be made known. What you have said in the dark will be heard in the daylight, and what you have whispered in the ear in the inner rooms will be proclaimed from the roofs (Luke 12:1–3).

HYPOCRISY CAN BE a difficult thing to wrap our minds around. It is a thing—a whole-being malady—that creeps upon us and wraps itself around us. Hypocrisy invades our soul. It blinds us to the truth and corrupts us to believe anything that exalts us over all others, including God, really.

Hypocrisy is more than a mere pretense of superiority; it is a claiming of it. Thus, we begin to think ourselves more knowledgeable, spiritual, accomplished, and worthy. And the subtle, deceptive esteeming of our own self eats away at our sensibility and humility;

it does so through the fuel obtained from our inner devaluing of all others.

Some would argue that our greatest need is to be loved, and one could hardly argue against that. Yet, it begs the question: "What is it within us that causes us to need to feel loved so?" The answer is that at the core of our being we need to fully grasp our real identity and worth. We need to know who we are in the larger perspective of the universe. Are we but a breathing speck that accidentally evolved on a relatively small rock hurtling through a seemingly endless and purposeless universe? Or are we a special and unique part of a carefully and divinely designed creation?

Are we relatively worthless or are we relatively priceless? Perhaps, our greatest need then is not love but to feel our real worth by recognizing our real identity—"So God created man in his own image" (Gen. 1:27). And the unconditional love emanating into the creation from its Creator is the substance of our knowing it—"For this reason I bow my knees before the Father, from whom every family in heaven and on earth is named, that according to the riches of his glory he may grant you to be strengthened with power through his Spirit in your inner being, so that Christ may dwell in your hearts through faith—that you, being rooted and grounded in love, may have strength to comprehend with all the saints what is the breadth and length and height and depth, and *to know the love of Christ that surpasses knowledge, that you may be filled with all the fullness of God*" (Eph. 3:14–19, italics added).

God wants to grant us the ability, by the power of his Holy Spirit, to fully grasp and experience the love he has for us. He wants us to know our worth to him, and thus what others' worth ought to be to us. He is the divine appraiser of value, and he has deemed us all priceless. He expressed his assessment by giving his best for us at our worst—"For God so loved the world, that he gave his only Son, that whoever believes in him should not perish but have eternal life" (John 3:16). He did not pay the ultimate price of his own life here in the supreme expression of love because we are worthless. He did it because to him we are priceless—"For while we were still weak, at the right time Christ died for the ungodly. For one will scarcely die for a righteous person—though perhaps for a good person one would dare even to die—but God shows his love for us in that while we were still sinners, Christ died for us" (Rom. 5:6–8).

The essence of the gospel is the answer to this gnawing inner need all humans have. We are divinely priceless when we seem humanly worthless. Through the cross the best of God conquered the worst of humanity. And the cross answers the questions of who we are, whose we are, what is our purpose, and what is each of our own value in the creation equation.

God affirms our pricelessness through the ultimate sacrifice that he made on the cross. It is in our faithful recognition of the reality of who God really is that we find salvation—"Come to me, all who labor and are heavy laden, and I will give you rest. Take my yoke upon you, and learn from me, for I am gentle and lowly in heart, and you will find rest for your souls" (Matt. 11:28–29). It is finally in *getting* God that we finally get the valuation we are so desperately looking for. His statement of our pricelessness to him is punctuated with an exclamation mark written in his own blood.

Yet, when we fail to grasp this reality and continue to trust in our own interpretations and accomplishments, hypocrisy finds its entrée into us. And it will not stop until it possesses us. There has always only been two macro-choices for us and nothing in between—accept Yahweh as God, as revealed in Jesus Christ, or attempt to play God ourselves through some alleged knowledge of and performance concerning good and evil, discovered and possessed within our own selves independently of God and all others.

Thus, we take on the pretentious and utterly false identity of self-worthiness and goodness—hypocrisy. And in our judgments we are indignant and offended when others act otherwise, even when their actions are those of God himself.

A Prayer:

> Help me see myself, Lord, in the face of the Pharisee,
> Not in the broken tax collector I might merely appear to be,
> Help me not think I'm the person whom everyone seems to see,
> Help me see who I really am through what's seen by you in secrecy.

57
Hypocrisy, Part 2

Hypocrisy is a silent killer of the human soul. When its deception is complete, it will have obliterated any right perception of the reality of who God is and thus who we are to him.

Many will say to me on that day, "Lord, Lord, did we not prophesy in your name and in your name drive out demons and in your name perform many miracles?" "Then I will tell them plainly, 'I never knew you. Away from me, you evildoers!'" (Matt. 7:22-23).

TRAGICALLY, THE ULTIMATE revelation of hypocrisy, even among those of us who call ourselves Christians, might come in the final judgment and revelation of the identity we assumed in our lives here. However the identities we assume may prove counter to the identity God gave to us. Will my assumed identity prove rooted in the truth of God, or in the end will it prove to have been rooted in my own assumed rightness and good works?

But the revelation of such foolishness and senselessness need not wait until it is too late for us. The immediate revelation can be seen well in what offends us—what causes us to be "indignant." The hyper religious Pharisees were quickly outed by Jesus as being hypocrites—"Woe to you, teachers of the law and Pharisees, you hypocrites!" (Matt. 23:13). Thus we read of their indignation at Jesus's association with known sinners—"The Pharisees were indignant. 'Why does your teacher associate with men ["many tax collectors and sinners"] like that?'" (Matt. 9:11, The Living Bible).

The history of the Christian church is wrought with the stories of the contentiousness and indignation of Christians, one against another and each claiming to be eating from the "correct" Tree of the Knowledge of Good and Evil. Often each subsequently violating the very essence of the nature of God and humanity as his image-bearers in defense of their own presumed rightness about this or that! Arrogance, hatred, and insolence sadly seem bred into the DNA of many of the Christian church.

The all-surpassing "new command" of Jesus is thus obliterated on the rocks of human self-rightness among these—"A new command I give you: Love one another. As I have loved you, so you must love one another. By this everyone will know that you are my disciples, if you love one another" (John 13:34–35). The belief then must be that some Christians suppose that true discipleship is seen not in sacrificial, humble, unconditional love but rather in the stubborn defense of one's own rightness about some self-decided, supposed fundamental truths of the knowledge of good and evil—"Isaiah was right when he prophesied about you hypocrites; as it is written: 'These people honor me with their lips, but their hearts are far from me'" (Mark 7:6).

But human appearances and the judgments of mere mortals are useless in the eternal reality of things—"Woe to you, teachers of the law and Pharisees, you hypocrites! You are like whitewashed tombs, which look beautiful on the outside but on the inside are full of the bones of the dead and everything unclean. In the same way, on the outside you appear to people as righteous but on the inside you are full of hypocrisy and wickedness" (Matt. 23:27–28). For God's judgments are right, good, and without guile—"Nothing in all creation is hidden from God's sight. Everything is uncovered and laid bare before the eyes of him to whom we must give account" (Heb. 4:13). So then, "Be careful not to practice your righteousness in front of others to be seen by them. If you do, you will have no reward from your Father in heaven" (Matt. 6:1).

So, when our indignation is ignited over the supposed "wrongs" of others rather than our experiencing godly sadness (mourning) over their possible failings and yes, even in what may otherwise appear incorrect, we must grapple with the reality of perhaps the most egregious sin of all within us—hypocrisy. Else, why would the emotion of indignation spawned from the sin of unrighteous judgment be there in the first place—"If anyone thinks they are something when they are not, they deceive themselves" (Gal. 6:3)?

There is first the judgment of discernment within the church and the family of humanity, to which the children of God are gifted and called—"What business is it of mine to judge those outside the church? Are you not to judge those inside?" (1 Cor. 5:12). And further, "Do you not know that the Lord's people will judge the world?" (1 Cor. 6:2).

Then there is the judgment of condemnation to which no one is called—"Do not judge, or you too will be judged. For in the same way you judge others, you will be judged, and with the measure you use, it will be measured to you" (Matt. 7:1–2). The final judgment is reserved only for the just and righteous God who alone is worthy—"My conscience is clear, but that does not make me innocent. It is the Lord who judges me. Therefore judge nothing before the appointed time; wait until the Lord comes. He will bring to light what is hidden in darkness and will expose the motives of the heart. At that time each will receive their praise from God" (1 Cor. 4:4–5).

Jesus's commands emanate from God's very essence, that of love—"Everyone who believes that Jesus is the Christ is born of

God, and everyone who loves the father loves his child as well. This is how we know that we love the children of God: by loving God and carrying out his commands" (1 John 5:1–2). Jesus's commands are not the burdensome ones of human rightness, works, and attainment—"In fact, this is love for God: to keep his commands. And his commands are not burdensome" (1 John 5:3).

We are, in fact, without defense or excuse when we feel offended and indignant concerning the conditions of others against the backdrop of our own supposed rightness—"You, therefore, have no excuse, you who pass judgment on someone else, for at whatever point you judge another, you are condemning yourself, because you who pass judgment do the same things" (Rom. 2:1).

Thus, the admonition, "Do not merely listen to the word, and so deceive yourselves. Do what it says" (James 1:22).

A Prayer:

> Help my self-perception not be based on human pretense but of godly substance.
> Help my presentation of myself be modest and humble not showy and ostentatious.
> Search me out God and reveal to me what in me is insincere, untrue, and disingenuous.
> Transform me to be a person of godly reality, sincerity, and truth.
> Utterly defeat in me all hints of evil hypocrisy that I might stand before others as I stand before you!
> Amen.

58
Identity

Our identity is not to be found merely by the flesh and its desires but rather through the word and the Spirit of God.

Or do you not know that wrongdoers will not inherit the kingdom of God?...And that is what some of you were. But you were washed, you were sanctified, you were justified in the name of the Lord Jesus Christ and by the Spirit of our God (1 Cor. 6:9–11).

THE MODERN POPULAR notion is understandable that what must define us is to be determined by what we might desire or feel, but it is horribly misguided. The idea that we must be defined by and identify with our natural inclinations is not only socially dangerous, it is morally absurd.

By God's plan and design, we are rather to be defined by the template of his own nature, because we are like him—"So God created mankind in his own image, in the image of God he created them; male and female he created them" (Gen. 1:27). In that Jesus shows us the image of God, he shows us what our own image is to be—"The Son is the radiance of God's glory and the exact representation of his being" (Heb. 1:3). It is he who renews within our minds and hearts the correct template of who we were made to be and what, in Christ, we are being remade to look like.

Sin has corrupted the world and in each of us it disrupts, distorts, and subverts God's plan. Sin has a damning progression, both in the specific and in general, taking us away from our God image—"When tempted, no one should say, 'God is tempting me.' For God cannot be tempted by evil, nor does he tempt anyone; but each person is tempted when they are dragged away by their own evil desire and enticed. Then, after desire has conceived, it gives birth to sin; and sin, when it is full-grown, gives birth to death" (James 1:13–15).

On the other hand, transformation back into the original image of God also has a progression. First, we are called to God by the gospel through an act of his own grace—"No one can come to me unless the Father who sent me draws them" (John 6:44). Second, we are chosen by God, divinely elected, according to his own plan, based on the faithful heart we offer to him—"Many are invited, but few are chosen" (Matt. 22:14), and "People look at the outward appearance, but the Lord looks at the heart" (1 Sam. 16:7).

God justifies each of us on the basis of Christ's sacrifice—"Therefore, since we have been justified through faith, we have peace with God through our Lord Jesus Christ" (Rom. 5:1). He justifies us, declaring us as just and right, holy and blameless, when, in fact, we are not within ourselves that at all—"God…gives life to the dead and calls those things which do not exist as though they did" (Rom. 4:17, New King James Version).

Justification is what God does to bring us into a right relationship with him. Our salvation is an act of God; it is his bidding and his doing—"We were therefore buried with him through baptism into death in order that, just as Christ was raised from the dead through the glory of the Father, we too may live a new life" (Rom. 6:4). And our role is to trust him in what he wills to do within us—"Your whole self ruled by the flesh was put off when you were circumcised by Christ, having been buried with him in baptism, in which you were also raised with him through your faith in the working of God, who raised him from the dead" (Col. 2:11–12). Everything is then based on our faith in his working, not our own—"Everything that does not come from faith is sin" (Rom. 14:23).

Our salvation is not, therefore, at all about trust in ourselves—in our own goodness, our good deeds, or certain performance standards, rather it is about trusting in the goodness and "working of God." He comes into us by the Holy Spirit he gives us upon our faithful repentance and acceptance of him—"Repent and be baptized, every one of you, in the name of Jesus Christ for the forgiveness of your sins. And you will receive the gift of the Holy Spirit" (Acts 2:38).

Then as we focus on and follow Christ, the Holy Spirit within us transforms us back into the original template stamped on us, that of God himself—"And we all, who with unveiled faces contemplate the Lord's glory, are being transformed into his image with ever-increasing glory, which comes from the Lord, who is the Spirit" (2 Cor. 3:18). The Spirit himself works within us to sanctify us. Thus we become saints. To be sanctified is to be made holy or set apart for God's use—"He gave me the priestly duty of proclaiming the gospel of God, so that the Gentiles might become an offering acceptable to God, sanctified by the Holy Spirit" (Rom. 15:16).

In the flesh, our feelings and inclinations are carnal and bear little resemblance to what we are made to be. It is Christ and Christ alone who shows us the truth of where we came from, where we are going, who we are to be, and what we are to be doing—"I am the way and the truth and the life. No one comes to the Father except through me" (John 14:6).

When we choose Christ and his way, we have already chosen our identity based on him. Our work is then to seek him and find out what we are to be—"The work God wants you to do is this: to believe in the one he sent" (John 6:29, Easy-to-Read Version).

A Prayer:

> Lord, I find my identity in you, thus I identify with you.
> It is you that I seek and it is you I seek to imitate.
> Let me never be numbered with those who choose only to live for this present age.
> I choose you, O Lord; I choose your eternal kingdom over this present darkness.
> Help me to be a living testimony to your glory and goodness, both through your mercy you show me in my weaknesses and through your Spirit's transformation of me to look more like you.

59

In the Trenches

Following Christ means serving in the trenches—in gutters and alleyways and other hard-to-reach places.

Go out quickly into the streets and alleys of the town and bring in the poor, the crippled, the blind and the lame (Luke 14:21).

AS CHRISTIANS, WE can easily begin to take the attitude of some of the leaders identified by Jesus who considered themselves exempt from menial kingdom tasks and lowly associations. And thus, we end up looking just like the world outside of Christ—"Not so with you. Instead, whoever wants to become great among you must be your servant, and whoever wants to be first must be your slave—just as the Son of Man did not come to be served, but to serve, and to give his life as a ransom for many" (Matt. 20:26–28).

We can learn to love the bests seats, positions, parking spots, offices, and titles—"They love the place of honor at banquets and the most important seats in the synagogues" (Matt. 23:6). Thus, we look no different than the world. Because we are, in fact, worldly.

We can come to savor our titles and our esteem among those not so esteemed or privileged, for whatever reason we might foolishly justify it—"They love to be greeted with respect in the marketplaces and to be called 'Rabbi' by others" (Matt. 23:7). But such is not the path of the one following closely behind Christ. Jesus intentionally and consistently went to the outcasts of society. And he was hated by those who would have the kingdom of God be otherwise.

Jesus led in the fashion of King David, whose throne he was assuming—"He will be great and will be called the Son of the Most High. The Lord God will give him the throne of his father David" (Luke 1:32). And David began his kingship campaign leading the lowliest of armies—"All those who were in distress or in debt or discontented gathered around him, and he became their commander" (2 Sam. 22:2).

Jesus too chose to do his extraordinary work through ordinary people—"When they saw the courage of Peter and John and realized that they were unschooled, ordinary men, they were astonished and they took note that these men had been with Jesus" (Acts 4:13). Often still, the most ardent and devoted followers of Jesus are not those from among the elite but those from among the lowly—"Brothers and sisters, think of what you were when you were called. Not many of you were wise by human standards; not many were influential; not many were of noble birth" (1 Cor. 1:26).

Those of us who might otherwise consider ourselves above the more common among us, because of our lifelong Christian involvement, education, standard of living, or community or church status, can easily forget the mountain of sins that we too have been forgiven of and are still being forgiven of daily. We can also forget the responsibility that has been laid upon those who are most blessed—"From everyone who has been given much, much will be demanded; and from the one who has been entrusted with much, much more will be asked" (Luke 12:48).

Jesus used a story to make the point that those who feel forgiven of the most will love and serve the most (Luke 7:36–50). It was to the apparently prosperous Pharisee, Simon, in whose home Jesus had gone for dinner and with whom he was eating, that he told the story. The prompt was that a "sinful" woman from that town had burst into the dinner and begun to wipe Jesus's feet with her tears and to anoint them with expensive perfume.

Seeing the obvious offense taken by the hypocritical Pharisee, Jesus told of two who owed debts, one a great amount and the other a small amount. Neither debtor, however, could pay back their debt, and both debts were subsequently forgiven. Jesus asked Simon the question, "Now which of them will love him more?" (Luke 7:42). Simon answered correctly, saying it would be the one forgiven the most. Jesus then noted that Simon had done nothing to serve him, while the poor woman had not stopped washing and anointing his feet. He summarized Simon's situation, and sadly too many of ours, saying, "Whoever has been forgiven little loves little" (Luke 7:47).

It is God's own choosing to use the common and the ordinary, even the base, to shame the allegedly blessed, prosperous, and strong—"But God chose the foolish things of the world to shame the wise; God chose the weak things of the world to shame the strong" (1 Cor. 1:27). In fact, it was through and to the lowly that he did most of his work. And it has never changed. The kingdom of God has been built on the backs of and is carried mostly by commoners. And those who realize that we are all, in fact, "commoners" before God.

Jesus was born in a glorified barn (Luke 2:4–7). He was raised by common people in a despised city (Matt. 2:19–22, John 1:46). He was said not to be particularly handsome (Isa. 53:2). And he began his kingdom among the lowly, common people of Galilee through twelve ordinary men and others similar to them.

As had John the Baptist, his forerunner, Jesus grew up, lived, and ministered in the trenches of Israel. He made his home and his ministry among the lowly. In his story of the great banquet, he told of those blessed ones who refused to come because of their blessings (Luke 14:15–24). The host, who obviously mirrors God, was most frustrated with those self-absorbed ones who refused his invitation in favor of enjoying their own good fortunes. Hence, he sent his servants to invite the lowly of all the surrounding area—"Go out to the roads and country lanes and compel them to come in, so that my house will be full. I tell you, not one of those who were invited will get a taste of my banquet" (Luke 14:23–24).

And it is to the commoners, those in the trenches and those who recognize that we are all commoners and equals in God's sight, that he has sent us as his ambassadors and emissaries.

A Prayer:

Help me to find honor in the lowly, God.
Help me never to glory in anything human, but only in you.
Show me the trail Jesus left to those who are marginalized and rejected.
Help me to see myself as one of them, not as one who is privileged.
Help me see my pathways as alleys and byways, not the boulevards and freeways.

60
Indebtedness and Entitlement, Part 1

A truly converted heart feels not a sense of entitlement but a deep abiding sense of indebtedness.

This is love: not that we loved God, but that he loved us and sent his Son as an atoning sacrifice for our sins (1 John 4:10).

CONVERTED BELIEVERS CAN scarcely, from the day faith takes over within us, feel any sense of entitlement but only indebtedness. When a Christian feels entitlement, pride has taken over again.

Before one comes to real faith, one can only feel some sense of earthly entitlement to "life, liberty, and the pursuit of happiness." They believe the humanist position of certain "inalienable rights." This is because they have not yet come to understand their own personal part of the insurmountable debt that was paid for by Christ in his sacrifice on the cross. Thus in unbelief they go about to collect the debts owed to them and to assert the rights that are inherently theirs.

On the contrary, one who sees and believes the message of God's gospel will come to lay no claim to any "rights" to anything. We owe God everything; he owes us nothing—"'Who has ever given to God, that God should repay them?' For from him and through him and for him are all things" (Rom. 11:35–36).

At the recognition of Christ's sacrifice on the cross, God's core nature as a humble giver and lover rather than as a prideful taker is clearly demonstrated—"But God demonstrates his own love for us in this: While we were still sinners, Christ died for us" (Rom. 5:8). God is a God of grace. "Grace" means "gift." Thus a graceful person—a person full of grace—is a giving person. We are converted from our worldly status as a taker, a *net-negative person*—one who always takes more than he or she gives. A taker gives only in order to get. Apart from Christ, one can, in reality, only be a barterer, giving in order to get. There will always be a trade-off and an expectation.

On the other hand, one converted to Christ becomes a giver, a *net-positive person*—one who gives more than he or she takes. A true disciple expects nothing and barters for nothing. God provides all his or her needs, and disciples give God the credit—"Every good gift, every perfect gift, comes from above. These gifts come down from the Father, the Creator of the heavenly lights, in whose character there is no change at all" (James 1:17). Because of what has been given by God, a giver gives thanks to him by giving to others, even those who despise them—"And if you lend to those from whom you expect repayment, what credit is that to you? Even sinners lend to sinners, expecting to be repaid in full. But love your enemies, *do good to them, and lend to them without expecting to get anything back*. Then your reward will be great, and you will be children of the Most High, because he is kind to the ungrateful and wicked" (Luke 6:34–35, italics added).

The presumption of entitlement can show up in us in several key ways. The first is the belief that we are somehow owed earthly things, such as a certain measure of material wealth, a measure of physical health, certain kinds of relationships, and things that others have. The second is that for some reason, we feel we should be treated differently or special. The third is that we believe we have inherent "rights" owed to us by either God or society. The fourth is that we think that we are somehow exempt from responsibilities and obligations. These expressions of the sense of entitlement may present themselves variously and to different degrees through such things as arrogance, presumptuousness, greed, selfishness, elitism, discontent, hedonism, disobedience, divisiveness, and so forth.

Entitlement is an ugly thing. It leans away from the unselfish, graceful nature of God and leans toward the ugly nature of evil. It engenders strife, racism, nationalism, sectarianism, mistreatment of others, and all sorts of other evils.

God has promised us much. However many, if not most, of his promises are conditional, because, while God's love is unconditional toward us, his grace and blessings are not—"I am the Lord your God, who teaches you what is best for you, who directs you in the way you should go. If only you had paid attention to my commands, your peace would have been like a river, your well-being like the waves of the sea" (Isa. 48:17–18). *If only you had listened*—conditional.

Entitlement always expresses itself in presumptuousness. To presume is to assume or take for granted. But, since we have not even a promise of tomorrow, to presume anything beyond what God has promised is unmitigated pride—"Now listen, you who say, 'Today or tomorrow we will go to this or that city, spend a year there, carry on business and make money.' Why, you do not even know what will happen tomorrow. What is your life? You are a mist that appears for a little while and then vanishes. Instead, you ought to say, 'If it is the Lord's will, we will live and do this or that.' As it is, you boast in your arrogant schemes. All such boasting is evil" (James 4:13–16).

Jesus spoke of a rich fool who, in his greed and self-centeredness, presumed a long, merry life of enjoying his wealth. However, his presumption and sense of entitlement was most ill-advised—"But God said to him, 'You fool! This very night your life will be demanded from you. Then who will get what you have prepared for yourself?'" (Luke 12:20).

Most assuredly, King David, in perhaps his most dastardly sin, presumed that he was entitled to the lovely Bathsheba, who was not his wife but another's (2 Sam 12). This belief in his entitlement brought God's hand down harshly upon him—"But because by doing this you have shown utter contempt for the Lord, the son born to you will die" (2 Sam. 12:14).

Jesus, in a rebuke of the chief priests and Pharisees, told a parable of a landowner who planted a vineyard, rented the vineyard to some sharecroppers, and went away (Matt. 21:33–46). After the harvest he sent his servants to collect his share of the harvest as rent, but one servant the tenants beat, another they stoned, and a third they killed. He then sent his son to collect, thinking surely they would respect the landowner's own son and give to the son and heir the landowner's share of the harvest. Instead, the tenants presumed that by killing the heir, they could simply take the son's land inheritance from him. So they killed him. They obviously felt entitled to the land they had worked. But with God things don't work that way.

Jesus expressed God's wrath at such presumptuousness and sense of entitlement through his conclusion of the story. He asks a question and then answers it—"Therefore, when the owner of the vineyard comes, what will he do to those tenants? He will bring those wretches to a wretched end" (Matt. 21:40–41).

Don't presume things upon God. We are not entitled to anything.

A Prayer:

Lord, may I expect nothing of you beyond the greatest gift already given—Jesus Christ!
May I never presume to be owed anything, but may I trust that you will provide what I need.
Convert my ungrateful heart, still my quivering want, loose me from the grip of greed, and defeat my lust for more.
Forgive me, my Lord, for my disappointment when I do not receive those things that I expect from you, and defeat within my constant lusts.
Help my heart to focus rather on those things I have received, and on the ultimate outcome of my hope—that which I fully expect—the eternal life of final bliss with you!
Amen.

61
Indebtedness and Entitlement, Part 2

The gratitude we feel and express toward God is but an expression of the measure of our realization of the debt we, as believers, had previously accrued, but that he completely paid off for us in his sacrifice on the cross.

For it is by grace you have been saved, through faith—and this is not from yourselves, it is the gift of God—not by works, so that no one can boast (Eph. 2:8–9).

"**HE PAID A** debt he did not owe; I owed I debt I could not pay; I needed someone to wash my sins away. And now I sing a brand new song—'amazing grace'—Christ Jesus paid a debt that I could never pay" (Ellis J. Crum, Publisher, Sacred Selections, R. E. Winsett, LLC, 1977). Such simple lyrics about the profoundest truth of God!

And, the debt we owe the Lord for the favor he has given us can in no way involve a repayment in kind, for that is an impossibility.

The debt we owe him is simply the debt of love, living our lives as an extension of him in our own world—"For Christ's love compels us, because we are convinced that one died for all, and therefore all died. And he died for all, that those who live should no longer live for themselves but for him who died for them and was raised again" (2 Cor. 5:14–15).

The one grasping the essence of the gospel will find any sense of entitlement obliterated by the resounding force of deep inner gratitude. The believer will find by spiritual serendipity those deepest, inner blessings that can only be given by God to the one who simply and trustingly does his bidding. For it is only through the power of the Holy Spirit of God working in us that we can even begin to grasp the magnitude of the love of God, the greatest blessing of all and the one so few ever experience existentially—"And I pray that you, being rooted and established in love, may have power, together with all the Lord's holy people, *to grasp how wide and long and high and deep is the love of Christ, and to know this love that surpasses knowledge*—that you may be filled to the measure of all the fullness of God" (Eph. 3:17–19, italics added).

It is also only through our rejoicing and trusting in Christ that we can experience the kind of peace and contentment that come only as a direct work of God in our lives—"Rejoice in the Lord always. I will say it again: Rejoice! Let your gentleness be evident to all. The Lord is near. Do not be anxious about anything, but in every situation, by prayer and petition, with thanksgiving, present your requests to God. And the *peace of God, which transcends all understanding, will guard your hearts and your minds in Christ Jesus*…I have learned to be content whatever the circumstances…I can do [endure, weather, or handle] all this through him who gives me strength." (Phil. 4:4–7, 11, 13, italics added).

God wills that we not just hear or know about his love but also experience his love. Peace and contentment, those all-surpassing experiential elements that the world so slavishly seeks through artificial means but that are ultimately gained only through God, are simply given to us through our actual experience of God's incomparable love. It is this unselfish, universal expression of this essence of God, as demonstrated in the gospel message, that ultimately takes control of believers and causes us to live life on a different plane, in a different realm, and for a different reason—"Christ's love has moved me to such extremes. His love has the first and last word in everything we do" (2 Cor. 5:14, The Message). And "Because of his great love for us, God, who is rich in mercy, made us alive with Christ even when we were dead in transgressions—it is by grace you have been saved. And God raised us up with Christ and *seated us with him in the heavenly realms in Christ Jesus*, in order that in the coming ages he might show the incomparable riches of his grace, expressed in his kindness to us in Christ Jesus" (Eph. 2:4–7, italics added).

The reality is that any sense of human entitlement leads to anger, despair, resentment, and all sorts of other spiritual, mental, and emotional maladies. On the other hand, a sense of indebtedness, as elicited by God's love for and gift to us, brings thankfulness, peace, contentment, love, joy, goodness, and so forth. Such peace as seen in the sentiments of the ancient Job, who experienced both the worst of human suffering and the greatest of human blessings—"Naked I came from my mother's womb, and naked I will depart. The Lord gave and the Lord has taken away; may the name of the Lord be praised" (Job. 1:21).

Indebtedness trumps entitlement just as the beatitudes trump the Bill of Rights.

A Prayer:

> You are good, Lord, and all good things come from you.
> You turn even the bad in our lives into good.
> I trust you and submit myself to you.

I commit to be satisfied with the things I have and to not desire to be rich.
You satisfy me with the finest things and I dine on the richest fare.
To you be glory and honor.
I thank you, my Father, for your goodness and grace extended to me in Christ, my Lord!
Amen!

62
Jesus is Lord

The whole of scripture is by its very design written to bring us to the conclusion that "Jesus is Lord." Thus, the New Testament speaks throughout the language of total surrender.

For what we preach is not ourselves, but Jesus Christ as Lord, and ourselves as your servants for Jesus' sake (2 Cor. 4:5).

THERE IS NO grander or more profound statement or confession than "Jesus is Lord"—"If you declare with your mouth, 'Jesus is Lord,' and believe in your heart that God raised him from the dead, you will be saved. For it is with your heart that you believe and are justified, and it is with your mouth that you profess your faith and are saved" (Rom. 10:9–10). It is the summation of all that really matters in this age. And the confession of his Lordship can only be of the Holy Spirit—"No one can say, 'Jesus is Lord,' except by the Holy Spirit" (1 Cor. 12:3).

There was never any other plan—"He [Christ] was chosen before the creation of the world, but was revealed in these last times for your sake. Through him you believe in God, who raised him from the dead and glorified him, and so your faith and hope are in God" (1 Pet. 1:20–21). God determined before the creation to carry out his work for and through Jesus Christ—"For in him all things were created: things in heaven and on earth, visible and invisible, whether thrones or powers or rulers or authorities; all things have been created through him and for him" (Col. 1:16).

Jesus's ministry here was a kingdom campaign. Except that it was not a campaign concerning who would be king, for that had already been predestined. Rather it was a campaign to determine who would be the subjects in his kingdom. Jesus would be king by God's design and appointment. No one else could stand against him and no one else got a vote. His kingdom would surely come, and it would reign as chief among and above all earthly kingdoms—"All authority in heaven and on earth has been given to me" (Matt. 28:18). Although his kingdom has already been established, it continues to be built and advanced by Christ among those who accept him as Lord and Savior—"And in him you too are being built together to become a dwelling in which God lives by his Spirit" (Eph. 2:22). We, as believers, become a part of the kingdom by his calling and election of us.

Jesus is part and parcel with God—"In the beginning was the Word, and the Word was with God, and the Word was God. He was with God in the beginning. Through him all things were made; without him nothing was made that has been made" (John 1:1–3). Explaining what has come to be known as the Holy Trinity—Father, Son, and Holy Spirit is simply impossible. It would require explaining the infinite to the finite.

His infinite nature is only for us to behold and trust, not to fully understand, at least in this present life—"Oh, the depth of the riches of the wisdom and knowledge of God! How unsearchable his judgments, and his paths beyond tracing out!" (Rom. 11:33). Unbelief, however, is not an acceptable human option—"For since the creation of the world God's invisible qualities—his eternal power and divine nature—have been clearly seen, being understood from what has been made, so that people are without excuse" (Rom. 1:20).

Jesus was with God in the beginning and his coming was first revealed to humanity through God's curse on Satan after the Fall—"I will put enmity between you and the woman, and between your offspring and hers; he will crush your head, and you will strike his heel." His coming was the universal blessing promised to Abraham, Isaac, and Jacob—"I will make you into a great nation, and I will bless you; I will make your name great, and you will be a blessing. I will bless those who bless you, and whoever curses you I will curse; and all peoples on earth will be blessed through you" (Gen. 12:2–3).

He was the fulfillment of the great prophet promise Moses gave—"The Lord your God will raise up for you a prophet like me from among you, from your fellow Israelites. You must listen to him" (Deut. 18:15). He was not just a prophet, as were Moses and Elijah; he was God's only Son, as was revealed to Peter, James, and John, on the Mount of Transfiguration—"This is my Son, whom I love; with him I am well pleased. Listen to him!" (Matt. 17:5). He was the one promised to and through the prophet Isaiah, who would bring ultimate relief to humanity—"But he was pierced for our transgressions, he was crushed for our iniquities; the punishment that brought us peace was on him, and by his wounds we are healed" (Isa. 53:5).

The Old Testament writings pointed confidently to him. The whole of the New Testament writings point confidently to him as the fulfillment and enactor of the plan of God for all humanity—"For we did not follow cleverly devised stories when we told you about the coming of our Lord Jesus Christ in power, but we were eyewitnesses of his majesty" (2 Pet. 1:16). In Christ, all the prophetic messages pointing to his impending Lordship are crystallized and come to fruition—"We also have the prophetic message as something completely reliable, and you will do well to pay attention to it, as to a light shining in a dark place, until the day dawns and the morning star rises in your hearts" (2 Pet. 1:19).

"Jesus is Lord" is the summary statement of faith because Jesus is the revelation and representation of God in human form—"The Son is the radiance of God's glory and the exact representation of his being, sustaining all things by his powerful word" (Heb. 1:3). Christ did not just bring the truth or show the way or give life; he is in human form the personification of all three of these—"I am the way and the truth and the life. No one comes to the Father except through me" (John 14:6). Only in and through him do we discover and experience all three.

If Jesus can be our Lord, then he can be our Savior. Ours is but to accept and surrender to it—"Now, brothers and sisters, I want to remind you of the gospel I preached to you, which you received and on which you have taken your stand. By this gospel you are saved, if you hold firmly to the word I preached to you. Otherwise, you have believed in vain" (1 Cor. 15:1–2). Receive it, take your stand on it, and hold firmly to it.

Believe it—Jesus is Lord!

A Prayer:

That "Jesus is Lord," God,
Is all I need to know,
He's fully in charge,
Above and below!

His will is final,
His authority is complete,
His protection is ironclad,
His love for me replete.

I confess it with my tongue,
I believe it in my heart,
"Jesus is Lord!"
He has no counterpart!

63
Joy of the Lord

God's purpose for sending his word is so that we can be filled with the joy of the Lord.

You will go out in joy and be led forth in peace; the mountains and hills will burst into song before you, and all the trees of the field will clap their hands (Isa. 55:12).

GOD'S THOUGHTS AND ways are supremely more sophisticated and complex than our own—"As the heavens are higher than the earth, so are my ways higher than your ways and my thoughts than your thoughts" (Isa. 55:9). The loftiness of his being and purposes are beyond our ability to comprehend—"Oh, the depth of the riches of the wisdom and knowledge of God! How unsearchable his judgments, and his paths beyond tracing out!" (Rom. 11:33).

And his joy in us is the intended end of all that God teaches us to believe, do, and become—"I have told you this so that my joy may be in you and that your joy may be complete" (John 15:11). The kingdom of god is paradoxical but nonetheless true. We are told to be mourners, but that through mourning we will find comfort instead of pain—"Blessed are those who mourn, for they will be comforted" (Matt. 5:4). We are told that while we live in this world, we will have trouble but that we will not be overcome by it, because Christ has overcome the world—"In this world you will have trouble. But take heart! I have overcome the world" (John 16:33). Further, wealth is found in poverty; filling is found in starvation; conquest is found in surrender; to be first we must be last; and exaltation is found in humiliating ourselves.

Evil seeks only to rob us of our joy. Satan champions our demise. And only Christ can trump him—"The thief comes only to steal and kill and destroy; I have come that they may have life, and have it to the full" (John 10:10). And trump him he will surely do for us—"The one who is in you is greater than the one who is in the world" (1 John 4:4). Christ brings the full life, the abundant life, the joyful life, and the eternal life! All otherworldly promises of joy are but mirages.

Joy is not equal to happiness. Happiness is an emotion. It is situational and experiential in the moment. And it can be oh so fleeting and elusive! However the joy of the Lord runs much deeper and is much more existential. Joy has permanency and is independent of life situations. God's joy is a gift and is always at our fingertips. It is in fact commanded of us—"Rejoice in the Lord always. I will say it again: Rejoice! (Phil. 4:4). To rejoice means to take joy in. Even in trial we are to *take joy* in the Lord—"Consider it pure joy, my brothers and sisters, whenever you face trials of many kinds" (James 1:2).

Biblical joy is derived from our hope in God. Biblical hope is not the modern notion of hope either, which is that of a wish. Rather biblical hope is a full expectation of the good that is to come that is based on reason. When we expect ultimate good to come even from our suffering, joy is the result. Thus to rejoice means to take joy in the hope (expectation) that we have for the good that is to come in this life and the glory to come in the next.

The ultimate experience of joy is that which can only be given to us by the Holy Spirit—"But the fruit of the Spirit is love, joy, peace, forbearance, kindness, goodness, faithfulness, gentleness and self-control" (Gal. 5:22–23). The Spirit, whom we receive in coming to Christ, bears his fruit of joy in us—"You became imitators of us and of the Lord, for you welcomed the message in the midst of severe suffering with the joy given by the Holy Spirit" (1 Thess. 1:6).

Much strength is found in our joy in the Lord. Nehemiah and the other leaders instructed the Jews who had returned to Jerusalem from the exile, saying, "'This day is holy to the LORD your God. Do not mourn or weep.' For all the people had been weeping as they listened to the words of the Law…'Go and enjoy choice food and sweet drinks, and send some to those who have nothing prepared. This day is holy to our Lord. Do not grieve, for *the joy of the LORD is your strength*'" (Neh. 8:9–10, italics added). Even under trials, threats, and burdens, God's joy can be our sustaining strength in forging on.

God gives us instructions into the designed-in universal truths so that we can experience the deep joy that is a part of him. It is something that we are to do, and it is something we are to receive and experience. And God wills this deep, abiding joy for each of us. Through such deep, inner, abiding joy from the Lord, the world opens up before us to sing to us, applaud us, and give us peace—"You will go out in joy and be led forth in peace; the mountains and hills will burst into song before you" (Isa. 55:12). And perhaps we become beautiful to it—"All the trees of the field will clap their hands" (Isa. 55:12).

Thus God's earnest question for us and invitation to us: "Come, all you who are thirsty, come to the waters; and you who have no money, come, buy and eat! Come, buy wine and milk without money and without cost. Why spend money on what is not bread, and your labor on what does not satisfy? Listen, listen to me, and eat what is good, and you will delight in the richest of fare" (Isa. 55:1-2).

A Prayer:

I want you, Lord,
I need no other friend,
I seek you, Lord,
To meet you in the end.

Your peace, Lord,
Sustains my inner need,
Your will, Lord,
Is my only creed.

Your joy, Lord,
Is enough for me,
Your face, Lord,
Is what I long to see!

64
Knowing God

Our goal should not be to simply know the most about God; it should be to know God the most.

Those who boast should boast in this: that they understand and know me. I am the L*ORD* *who acts with kindness, justice, and righteousness in the world, and I delight in these things, declares the* L*ORD* (Jer. 9:24, Common English Bible).

EPISTEMOLOGY (FROM *EPISTĒMĒ*, Greek, meaning "knowledge") is the branch of philosophy that is concerned with the nature of knowledge—what we know and how we know it. Ontology is the branch of philosophy that deals with existence and being—what exists and how we know it exists. Because we are made in God's image, humanity has from our beginning been concerned with both epistemology (knowledge) and ontology (being). Although the words are foreign to many, their implications concern us all.

The creation story itself lays the biblical foundation and assertion for the source and reality of our existence as well as for the source of all knowledge—"In the beginning God created the heavens and the earth" (Gen. 1:1, Gen. 2 & 3). The Bible tells us that God generated and arranged creation, and that humanity, as the crown of God's creation, was made expressly in the image of God—"So God created mankind in his own image, in the image of God he created them; male and female he created them" (Gen. 1:27).

The scripture asserts that the knowledge of God's power and divinity is apparent through the creation itself—"For since the creation of the world God's invisible qualities—his eternal power and divine nature—have been clearly seen, being understood from what has been made, so that people are without excuse" (Rom. 1:20). And therefore, the psalmist asserts that to deny God's existence is utterly ridiculous—"The fool says in his heart, 'There is no God'" (Ps. 14:1).

The creation story answers the most basic questions of ontology and the rest of the Bible explains the rest. The Bible also answers the most basic questions of epistemology. However, no matter how much we can know in this life, there is much more that we cannot know—"Surely I spoke of things I did not understand, things too wonderful for me to know" (Job 42:3). Knowledge has never itself equaled peace, joy, success, love, and so forth. If we do not take care, our knowledge of God and the things of God can be counterproductive to us—"We know that "We all possess knowledge." But knowledge puffs up while love builds up" (1 Cor. 8:1).

It is inherit in our existence to practice practical philosophy concerning our own existence and knowledge. Too, one surely must ponder, the nature of our existence and the knowledge of the cosmos we exist in—was it created by God or was it somehow self-generated, has it always existed or did it have a beginning? How we answer the questions "Where did we come from?" "What are we doing here?" "And where are we going?" will ultimately determine how we live our life here and what will be its outcome.

Our views about (1) God and the cosmos, (2) self and the world around me, and (3) others and their lives and purposes form the core of the human belief system. How we answer the most basic questions concerning God and the cosmos will determine how we answer the questions of our own existence. And how we view ourselves will determine the outcome of our lives here, and how we view others will most certainly affect theirs. The gospel is a complete belief system, giving us a right perspective of God and creation, a right perspective of ourselves as human, and a right perspective of others outside of ourselves.

The apostle John explains that Jesus himself is the "Word of God" (John 1:1, 14). He is full of truth because he is the truth (John 1:14, John 14:6). Word (*logos*, Greek) comes from a philosophical Greek word generally meaning "a word, speech, divine utterance, or an analogy." Thus, John places Jesus squarely in the middle of the ancient discussion about epistemology and ontology, where he still remains—"*In the beginning was the Word, and the Word was with God, and the Word was God.* He was with God in the beginning. Through him all things were made; without him nothing was made that has been made. In him was life, and that life was the light of all mankind" (John 1:1–4, italics added). He is to us the ultimate of God's "word, speech, divine utterance, and analogy." Knowledge of him is the root of all knowledge (epistemology). And too, he is the definition of existence (ontology)—"I am the way and the truth and *the life*" (John 14:6, italics added).

Jesus is the human revelation and expression of God to humanity. It is he who maintains and sustains the universe in its present form—"The Son is the radiance of God's glory and the exact representation of his being, sustaining all things by his powerful word" (Heb. 1:3). Jesus Christ is the emanation of God, the Father, in human form—"Anyone who has seen me has seen the Father" (John 14:9).

The gospel's case for Christ begins with the fact that he was divinely predicted through scripture over hundreds of years before he came—"We also have the prophetic message as something completely reliable, and you will do well to pay attention to it, as to a light shining in a dark place, until the day dawns and the morning star rises in your hearts" (2 Pet. 1:19). It ends with the eyewitness accounts of his miraculous birth, his power-filled life, his brutal and unjust death, his unparalleled resurrection, and his stunning ascension back into heaven—"For we did not follow cleverly devised stories when we told you about the coming of our Lord Jesus Christ in power, but we were eyewitnesses of his majesty" (2 Pet. 1:16).

As proof positive of their accounts, all these eyewitnesses suffered humiliation, persecution, and mostly excruciating deaths for their refusal to renounce what they had seen and heard. Their confidence and resoluteness were notably impressive to those who saw and heard them—"When they saw the courage of Peter and John and realized that they were unschooled, ordinary men, they were astonished and *they took note that these men had been with Jesus*" (Acts 4:13, italics added). The apostles' answer to the Jewish leaders' order for them to stop preaching Jesus echoed all the way from the foundations of creation and resound all the way to the final resolution on judgment day—"It's up to you to determine whether it's right before God to obey you rather than God. As for us, we can't stop speaking about what we have seen and heard" (Acts 4:19–20).

Knowing God, the source of all knowledge and existence, is the greatest prize and accomplishment of our human endeavor—"Those who boast should boast in this: that they understand and know me. I am the Lord who acts with kindness, justice, and righteousness in the world, and I delight in these things, declares the Lord" (Jer. 9:24, Common English Bible). Knowing *of* God's existence and *about* his nature are both paramount to our successful existence in this life and on into the next. It is promised that if we diligently look for God through creation and revelation that we will existentially find him—"Ask, and it will be given to you; seek, and you will find; knock, and it will be opened to you. For everyone who asks receives, and *the one who seeks finds*, and to the one who knocks it will be opened" (Matt. 7:7–8, italics added).

Knowing God is much more than simply knowing about God though; it is about experiencing him by basking in his immeasurable love and goodness—"And I pray that you, being rooted and established in love, may have power, together with all the Lord's holy people, to grasp how wide and long and high and deep is the love of Christ, and *to know this love that surpasses knowledge*—that you may be filled to the measure of all the fullness of God" (Eph. 3:17–19, italics added). God wants us to experientially "know" him in a way and at a level that defies the limitations of human here-and-now knowledge, reason, and logic.

Many, both in history and at present, are ready and willing to attest to the reality that we can have a full and real experience of God in this present life—"Therefore, since *we are surrounded by such a great cloud of witnesses*, let us throw off everything that hinders and the sin that so easily entangles. And let us run with perseverance the race marked out for us, fixing our eyes on Jesus, the pioneer and perfecter of faith. For the joy set before him he endured the cross, scorning its shame, and sat down at the right hand of the throne of God" (Heb. 12:1–2).

Knowing God in Christ is the ultimate of epistemology and ontology. It is the greatest quest of life. It is the answer to all questions that matter. It is the solution to all problems that plague us. It explains the source and the destiny of all that exists. Knowing God is the priceless thing—"What is more, I consider everything a loss because of *the surpassing worth of knowing Christ Jesus my Lord*, for whose sake I have lost all things. I consider them garbage, that I may gain Christ" (Phil. 3:8, italics added). It is what drives the believing follower of Christ—"I want to know Christ—yes, to know the power of his resurrection and participation in his sufferings, becoming like him in his death, and so, somehow, attaining to the resurrection from the dead" (Phil. 3:10–11).

It is more than mere human information; it is real knowledge, knowledge that leads us to life, and not just into an endless cycle of human data and information—"We know that 'all of us possess knowledge.' This *knowledge* puffs up, *but love builds up*. If anyone imagines that he knows something, he does not yet know as he ought to know. But *if anyone loves God, he is known by God*" (1 Cor. 8:1–3, italics added). And the goal is not just for us to know God, but even more importantly for him to know us—"Many will say to me on that day, 'Lord, Lord, did we not prophesy in your name and in your name drive out demons and in your name perform many miracles?' Then I will tell them plainly, '*I never knew you*. Away from me, you evildoers!'" (Matt. 7:22–23, italics added). In the end, our fate will be determined according to the vote of only one—God. No one else, including our own selves, will have a say—"My conscience is clear, but that does not make me innocent. It is the Lord who judges me" (1 Cor. 4:4).

Knowing God and being known by him are not about what we know only intellectually but about whom we know experientially! We do not find life in the wrong tree—the Tree of the Knowledge of Good and Evil. Only death is found there. We find life in the Tree of Life. It is a truth revealed in a simple fashion in our simple creation story (Gen. 2 & 3). Thus, it is not who knows the most about God that matters but who knows God the most!

A little bit of God is worth infinitely more than a lot of anything else. To know God we must certainly know about God, but it should not end there. We can know *all about* God and *not know him at all*—"You study the Scriptures diligently because you think that in them you have eternal life. These are the very Scriptures that testify about me, yet you refuse to come to me to have life" (John 5:39–40). He, in fact, created the world and us so that we would reach out and experientially find him—"From one forefather he has created every race of men to live over the face of the whole earth. He has determined the times of their existence and the limits of their habitation, *so that they might search for God, in the hope that they might feel for him and find him*—yes, even though he is not far from any one of us. Indeed, it is in him that we live and move and have our being" (Acts 17:26–28). God wants us to reach out to him and find him. He promised us success if we only will—"Ask and it will be given to you; seek and you will find; knock and the door will be opened to you" (Matt. 7:7).

Real life—eternal life—is all about knowing God and being known by him. Nothing else matters much, unless knowing God matters the most—"Now this is eternal life: that they know you, the only true God, and Jesus Christ, whom you have sent" (John 17:3).

A Prayer:

> I want to know you, O God.
> I want to know all about you, but more than that I want to know you experientially.
> I want to sense and feel your presence in my every moment.
> Your beauty exceeds all else.
> Your love is unconditional, your grace immeasurable, your glory incomparable.
> I come to you in Jesus with freedom and confidence because of his goodness and your calling of me through him.
> Inform me, conform me, and transform me, O Lord!
> Amen.

65
Latent Faith

Latent faith is no faith at all.

As the body without the spirit is dead, so faith without deeds is dead (James 2:26).

OBEDIENCE—NECESSARY ACTION—IS INEXTRICABLY bound up in faith—"What good is it, my brothers and sisters, if someone claims to have faith but has no deeds? Can such faith save them?" (James 2:14). Faith that is not clearly manifested is no faith at all—"Faith by itself, if it is not accompanied by action, is dead" (James 2:17).

Genuine, biblical faith is based on substance, reason, and evidence—"Now faith is the *substance* of things hoped for, the *evidence* of things not seen" (Heb. 11:1, New King James Version, italics added). Real faith is substantive and evidential. And it is essential for one who would know God—"Without faith it is impossible to please God, because anyone who comes to him must believe that he exists and that he rewards those who earnestly seek him" (Heb. 11:6). And as faith is based on evidence, so faith itself is always evident—"You foolish person, do you want evidence that faith without deeds is useless?" (James 2:20).

The notion of an inner *latent* faith that gives us a connection to God but that is devoid of clear outward manifestation is a fallacious one. It is biblically and rationally illogical—"What good is it, my brothers and sisters, if someone claims to have faith but has no deeds? Can such faith save them?" (James 2:14). Faith, or belief, and obedience are part and parcel together—"And to whom did God swear that they would never enter his rest if not to those who *disobeyed*? So we see that they were not able to enter, because of their *unbelief*" (Heb. 3:18–19). Disobedience is evidence of unbelief; obedience is evidence of belief.

Conflicting, overpowering motives can certainly keep faith latent rather than active—"Yet at the same time many even among the leaders believed in him. But because of the Pharisees they would not openly acknowledge their faith for fear they would be put out of the synagogue; for they loved human praise more than praise from God" (John 12:42–43). It is from others that we hide our faith, and for all sorts of undesirable, albeit understandable, reasons. Yet, Jesus wants us to be salt and light. He wants us to be visible and noticeable for what should be obvious reasons to the believer. He predetermined to manifest himself through his people after his resurrection and return to heaven but to send his Holy Spirit to empower us for the cause.

Thus, Christ has no use for those who would believe and not manifest it through confession of life and lips—"Whoever acknowledges me before others, I will also acknowledge before my Father in heaven. But whoever disowns me before others, I will disown before my Father in heaven" (Matt. 10:32–33). When we find our confession of Christ somehow muted in our lives, we must ask ourselves, "Why is that so?" Be assured, the motive will never prove valid under the light of Jesus's inspection.

Jesus brings salvations, not to those with latent, hidden faith but to those who act on their faith by obeying him—"Son though he was, he learned obedience from what he suffered and, once made perfect, he became the source of eternal salvation for all who *obey* him" (Heb. 5:8–9, italics added). And faith in Christ is not manifested simply by religiosity or Christian behaviors—"Many will say to me on that day, 'Lord, Lord, did we not prophesy in your name and in your name drive out demons and in your name perform many miracles?' Then I will tell them plainly, 'I never knew you. Away from me, you evildoers!'" (Matt. 7:22–23). Rather faith is manifested in obedience—"Not everyone who says to me, 'Lord, Lord,' will enter the kingdom of heaven, but only the one who does the will of my Father who is in heaven" (Matt. 7:21). Christ's commands are first about coming to and living by faith in him, then about through the Spirit developing his character within us, and lastly about living out his life of love, service, and salvation.

One can no more claim to believe in Jesus, and it not be evident in their life, than one could claim to believe that the building they were sitting in was about to burn down and yet not get up and get out. It is logically inconsistent unless of course one just had a death wish, and arguably many seem to live with an eternal death wish. It is most foolish to hear of Jesus, hear his living message, and not actively and consistently respond—"Do not merely listen to the word, and so deceive yourselves. Do what it says. Anyone who listens to the word but does not do what it says is like someone who looks at his face in a mirror and, after looking at himself, goes away and immediately forgets what he looks like. But whoever looks intently into the perfect law that gives freedom, and continues in it—not forgetting what they have heard, but doing it—they will be blessed in what they do" (James 1:22–25).

Latent faith is no faith at all. Faith is by definition obedient and active. Don't be fooled.

A Prayer:

> Ignite my faith, God, so that I can be about your business.
> Incite me in my belief that I will be active and zealous for you.
> Defeat doubt within me that discourages my obedience.
> Help me not to just believe, help me believe and do.
>
> May I never claim to believe and not obey what you say.
> Or my faith ever be latent; lying asleep within my heart,
> May my life be consumed by completed faith, dear God,
> In the end, in the middle, from its very start!

66
Leadership

False leaders lead you to them; godly leaders lead you to Him.

Remember your leaders, who spoke the word of God to you. Consider the outcome of their way of life and imitate their faith (Heb. 13:7).

LEADERS CAN ONLY *lead us to where they are actually going.* Character is much more *caught* than it is *taught*. If even an unwise association can be harmful to our character, then most certainly following a bad leader can prove devastating to our inner self—"Do not be misled: 'Bad company corrupts good character'" (1 Cor. 15:33). Too many are those who end up in horribly frightening places in life because they naïvely followed bad leaders.

To be led by others means to be directed down a path by another, either by their showing us the way or telling us where to go. Leadership can be exerted on us either directly from the leader to us or indirectly from the leader through others. The leadership exerted on us by others can range in scope from quite broad to very limited, spiritually, religiously, morally, socially, politically, philosophically, and so forth. Leadership's impact is ultimately determined by the willingness of others to follow it. Worldly leaders are by definition corrupted from leading us God's way even though certain of their principles may even, within themselves, be good. However, all leadership is packaged and the bad comes mixed in with the good.

God has given each one of us individually the right to come into a relationship with and follow him, without any necessary approval of others—"Yet to all who did receive him, to those who believed in his name, he gave the right to become children of God—children born not of natural descent, nor of human decision or a husband's will, but born of God" (John 1:12–13). Further, he has given us, as his children, the wherewithal to hear his voice over and above the din of all others, and he expects us to follow his voice rather than others—"They will never follow a stranger; in fact, they will run away from him because *they do not recognize a stranger's voice*" (John 10:5, italics added). Our following another must always be based on their following Christ—"Follow my example, just like I follow Christ's" (1 Cor. 11:1, Common English Bible).

Thus it is the responsibility of each of us to take care who we follow—"*Watch out for false prophets.* They come to you in sheep's clothing, but inwardly they are ferocious wolves" (Matt. 7:15, italics added). Carelessness and naiveté on the front end of our following another can lead to disaster on the backend!

The test of authentic, godly leadership is in the long-term outcome, not in any short-term appearances. The one who leads best for God is the one who lives best for God—"Remember your leaders, who spoke the word of God to you. *Consider the outcome of their way of life* and imitate their faith" (Heb. 13:7). And the fruit of one's life is not to be measured by short-term appearances but rather by the long-term effects of our life on others. Short-term impressions can be most deceiving—"They come to you in sheep's clothing..."

Looking like a harmless, domesticated sheep does not make one a harmless, domesticated sheep. Let the *follower* beware.

Satan is a liar and a deceiver. Thus, so are those leaders who are, wittingly or unwittingly, being influenced by him—"For such people are false apostles, deceitful workers, masquerading as apostles of Christ. And no wonder, for Satan himself masquerades as an angel of light" (2 Cor. 11:13–14). Looks and words can be most deceiving. The test of a leader must then be the "outcome of their way of life," the only "fruit" that cannot be faked.

Godly leadership is the exact opposite of worldly leadership in all the basic ways. Worldly leadership seeks control; godly leadership seeks surrender. Worldly leadership seeks attention for itself; godly leadership eschews attention, rather seeking to call attention to God. Worldly leadership seeks personal gain; godly leadership seeks, in this life, nothing for itself. Worldly leadership follows in order to lead; godly leadership leads in order to follow. Worldly leadership seeks to be served; godly leadership seeks to serve. Worldly leadership is prideful, even if it may at first seem humble; godly leadership is humble, even if it may at first seem prideful.

The one who leads best for Christ is the one who follows Christ the best. Christ is the one who calls and places leaders among his people—"So Christ himself gave the apostles, the prophets, the evangelists, the pastors and teachers, to equip his people for works of service, so that the body of Christ may be built up until we all reach unity in the faith and in the knowledge of the Son of God and become mature, attaining to the whole measure of the fullness of Christ" (Eph. 4:11–13). Before we follow another, we must ask *whom* such a one follows and *how* he or she follows.

Christ's authentic leaders understand that their calling and appointment is from him, that it is not earned, that it is not a *right*, and that Christ is the supreme Lord and leader. Therefore, they understand that their purpose is to go make disciples of Christ and to mature those disciples in their ability to follow him, not them—"Therefore go and make disciples of all nations, baptizing them in the name of the Father and of the Son and of the Holy Spirit, and teaching them to obey everything I have commanded you" (Matt. 28:19–20). Although there is always weakness and humanness in all leaders, there will ultimately be no equivocation in the direction and purpose of a genuine Christ-appointed leader.

Bad leaders always lead followers; godly leaders lead leaders. Bad leaders want no rivals; therefore they mature others primarily in the skill of following *them* rather than maturing them in personally following *him* (Christ). Bad leaders are at their core filled with pride and will always seek to be at the center, in control, and recognized. Godly leaders are humble and are always seeking to elevate others to the leader's own spiritual maturity level and beyond—"The things you have heard me say in the presence of many witnesses *entrust to reliable people who will also be qualified to teach others*" (2 Tim. 2:2, italics added). The perfection of Christ is the goal and simply being like some human leader—"He is the one we proclaim, admonishing and teaching everyone with all wisdom, so that we may present everyone fully mature in Christ" (Col. 1:28).

Bad leaders lead from the top down; godly leaders lead from the bottom up—"You know that the rulers of the non-Jewish people love to show their power over the people. And their important leaders love to use all their authority over the people. But it should not be that way with you. *Whoever wants to be your leader must be your servant. Whoever wants to be first must serve the rest of you like a slave.* Do as I did: The Son of Man did not come for people to serve him. He came to serve others and to give his life to save many people" (Matt. 20:25–28, Easy-to-Read Version, italics added). Godly leaders strive to look and lead like Christ and therefore serve others on behalf of Jesus.

The test of leadership is in the long-term outcome, not in the short-term appearance. Bad leaders may at first be willing and eager but in the end are actually fearful and insecure, as was King Saul (1 Sam.

15:24). Godly leaders may at first seem unwilling and unconfident but in the end will show themselves to be most surrendered and supremely bold, as was Moses (Exod. 3:11). Godly leaders will, in the end, see themselves as the *least*, the *last*, and the *worst* because they see Christ as the greatest, the first, and the best (1 Cor. 15:9, Matt. 20:16, 1 Tim. 1:15).

Godly leaders will also always be seeking God's approval by careful regard for scripture and the leading of the Holy Spirit—"Do your best to present yourself to God as one approved, a worker who does not need to be ashamed and who correctly handles the word of truth" (2 Tim. 2:15), and "For those who are led by the Spirit of God are the children of God" (Rom. 8:14).

Because of the seriousness of the responsibility, godly leaders will choose to lead out of humility before God and will do so only after carefully considering if such a role is God's will or not—"Not many of you should become teachers, my fellow believers, because you know that we who teach will be judged more strictly" (James 3:1).

And godly leadership will be most careful in the charge of leading others to and for God—"Watch your life and doctrine closely. Persevere in them, because if you do, you will save both yourself and your hearers" (1 Tim. 4:16). Because godly leaders are seeking to lead us to him and not just to them.

All in all, godly leaders not only look like Jesus, they are like Jesus, and the outcome of their ways will bring life to those who listen to and follow them—"The thief comes only to steal and kill and destroy; I have come that they may have life, and have it to the full" (John 10:10).

A Prayer:

> Lord, help me to follow only those who follow you.
> And help me to influence and lead others only to follow you.

Give me trusting eyes that are wary only in the right way.
Give me a careful heart that discerns rightly.
Be my only supreme leader, and lead me to life everlasting!
Amen.

67
Learning, Part 1

The mind that has never significantly changed is of a life that has never significantly grown.

Don't become like the people of this world. Instead, change the way you think. Then you will always be able to determine what God really wants—what is good, pleasing, and perfect (Rom. 12:2, GOD'S WORD Translation).

THE LIFE CHRIST calls us to is all about learning and growing. And when we only feel the need to shore up our inherited or often blindly accepted worldviews or opinions, we have by default chosen spiritual, social, and intellectual dwarfism. When we march to the masses' drumbeat of self-centeredness and closed-mindedness, we become numb and closed off to any reality outside of ourselves. Thus, we can only implode into subjective foolishness, and it is foolishness, no matter how profoundly wise it may seem when so many others seem to agree. For those on this path, only a kind of worldly growth is, at best, even possible—the spiritual and intellectual obesity of arrogant ignorance, pseudo intellectualism, and self-righteousness. We don't grow up; we only grow out. We don't get better; we merely get blinder.

Significant spiritual learning and growth has always caused individuals to appear freakish—too obtrusive—to the overpopulated spiritual munchkin societies that have dominated since the fall. Most humans are eventually, at least at times, lulled into living to the mind-numbing beat of a death march of ignorance and narrow-mindedness, whether religious or irreligious, rather than choosing the real life that is lived in the pursuit of authentic, unadulterated truth—"For wide is the gate and broad is the road that leads to destruction, and many enter through it" (Matt. 7:13). In choosing the way of the masses, we likely choose a Pied Piper doctrine of some well-worn, perhaps popular, but human-centered agenda rather than choosing to listen for the eternal, priceless, God-centered call of truth himself.

Sadly, most dare not look too far beyond our present self-interests lest it be admitted that none of us are—can ever be—the god of our own world, internally or externally. Churches, religions, families, societies, governments, and political blocs of all kinds are the fiercest defenders of the often-diminutive minds they seek to close, stunt, manipulate, and control. And simply reviewing what we read, watch, and give our time and money to, as well as, whom we listen to, and whom we spend our time with will clue us in to where we are in this regard.

We are too often fools before those who entertain us—athletes and actors alike; preachers and praise leaders as well. We are frequently suckers to those who flatter us and charmed by those who tell us what we want to hear—"For the time will come when people will not put up with sound doctrine. Instead, to suit their own desires, they will gather around them a great number of teachers to say what their itching ears want to hear" (2 Tim. 4:3).

The follower of Christ has, however, chosen the better way. As Jesus attested, Mary showed us that way, sitting at his feet when the opportunity arose, learning the most important life lessons rather than being bothered by the seemingly important things of this life—"Mary has chosen what is better, and it will not be taken away from her" (Luke 10:42).

Choosing Christ is in reality a call to freedom of thought—"a renewal of the mind." It is the freedom to seek and serve only the truth no matter how offensive it might be to the current tastes of the savoir-faire, and likely will be, to the ever-present, all-knowing power brokers of the shallow philosophical guilds of the day. Choosing Christ is choosing to be a lifelong learner. Christ delivers to us the foundational truths we need to know to live as God designed us to live—"His divine power has given us everything we need for a godly life through our knowledge of him who called us by his own glory and goodness" (2 Pet. 1:3).

As well as with our hearts, God wants us to love him with all of our minds—"Love the Lord your God with all your heart and with all your soul and with all your mind" (Matt. 22:37). How can we say we do this when our minds, in reality, belong to something other than to him? Rather than using our minds to seek him more fully and exactly, we busy ourselves in shoring up and supporting what we already believe, which may, in fact, be quite contrary to Christ's will and way!

Truth is found first in seeking truth, wherever it may be found and from whomever it may be acquired. And Jesus's contention is that whoever seeks truth ultimately finds him—"Everyone who is of the truth [who is a friend of the truth and belongs to the truth] hears *and* listens carefully to My voice" (John 18:37, Amplified Bible). Because his claim is that he *is* the truth—"I am the way and the truth and the life" (John 14:6). Jesus promised that those who seek truth will find it—"Ask and it will be given to you; seek and you will find; knock and the door will be opened to you" (Matt. 7:7). Every believer is a testimony to the reliability of his promise.

In finding Jesus, then, and learning and obeying his teaching, we are set free—"If you keep on obeying what I have said, you truly are my disciples. You will know the truth, and the truth will set you free" (John 8:31–32, Contemporary English Version). In finding the truth of God, we are liberated from the humanistic lie swallowed by most of humanity, because of our self-seeking, self-centered quests—"They gave up the truth about God for a lie, and they worshiped God's creation instead of God, who will be praised forever" (Rom. 1:25, Contemporary English Version).

Thus the kind of learning we must seek is not only *informational*, as information is just a tool. The kind of learning we must seek is more importantly *transformational*. It is ultimately that of knowing Christ, who is truth personified—"I want to know Christ—yes, to know the power of his resurrection and participation in his sufferings, becoming like him in his death, and so, somehow, attaining to the resurrection from the dead" (Phil. 3:10–11). The knowledge we must seek is the gateway to the experience for which we were designed—that of experiencing the life of God—"Now *choose life*, so that you and your children may live" (Deut. 30:19, italics added).

When we find Jesus, we find wisdom personified and knowledge energized—"The heart of the discerning acquires knowledge, for the ears of the wise seek it out" (Prov. 18:15). For it is the wisdom of God, which is revealed in Jesus, that calls out to all humanity, drawing us to God, through creation itself—"I cry out to you, people; my voice goes out to all of humanity. Understand skill, you who are naive. Take this to heart, you fools. Listen, for I speak things that are correct; from my lips comes what is right. My mouth utters the truth; my lips despise wickedness. All the words of my mouth are righteous; nothing in them is twisted or crooked. All of them are straightforward to those who understand, and upright for the knowledgeable. Take my instruction rather than silver, knowledge rather than choice gold. Wisdom is better than pearls; nothing is more delightful than she" (Prov. 8:4–11, Common English Bible).

However sadly, churches, which ought to be the leaders of open-minded, genuine learning and growth, have too often become as bad in closing and controlling minds as anything seen outside of Christianity. The very human conceptions of God himself are mostly the constrained or even misguided ideas of earlier generations of the various social and Christian clusters. These kinds of ideas about God have been repeatedly wrapped in scores, centuries, and even millennia of closed-minded mental plastic wrap originally designed to preserve and protect specific conceptions of God from decay but that now serve only to incubate, within its warm, closed confines, the festering, insufficient, and sometimes patently false, ideas of a previous day and time.

Simply put, diligent, open-minded, and truth-seeking learning is essential to the one who would know God and not be pulled away by false suitors.

A Prayer:

> Lord, help me to be resolute in seeking truth with all of my heart and mind, wherever it is to be found.
> Give me the strength of will to seek only you and let all my other loves and endeavors be guided by this.
> Quicken my heart to open my mind that I may give my life in this quest.
> Free me from all constraints that I may seek you with my all, freely and fully!
> Amen!

68
Learning, Part 2

Learning is a lifelong process. The more we know, the more we can know. The best of knowing and experiencing God is always yet to come, for he is limitless, and thus our relationships to him are limitless!

Let the wise listen and add to their learning, and let the discerning get guidance (Prov. 1:5).

BEING A LEARNER is in actuality an outgrowth of true humility. We never know what we do not already know, but should be ever aware that we know infinitely less than there is to know.

"Christian" is the word we use most to describe ourselves as believers, however, this word has become in modern times generic and fairly nondescript. Disciples (of Christ) were what the original followers of Jesus were known as. In fact, "Christian" is likely what outsiders called the early Christ followers—"The disciples were called Christians first at Antioch" (Acts 11:26).

To be a disciple is to be a follower or an adherent to a person or a view. It implies being an imitator and a conformer to the life and ways of a certain teacher or teaching, not just an information gatherer. To be a genuine follower of the literal manifestation of God, Jesus Christ our Lord, is to be a lifelong learner about him, for surely all must admit that God's knowledge is limitless—"Oh, the depth of the riches of the wisdom and knowledge of God! How unsearchable his judgments, and his paths beyond tracing out!" (Rom. 11:33)

Too many fall sway to the courting of denominations and movements of Christians bent on advancing what they are convinced is the right, and often believe to be the only *right*, way of following Christ, when in fact its outcomes may seem quite dissimilar to his. But we as believers must grow up in faith and knowledge so that we are not unstable in our faith and beliefs—"That we may no longer be children, tossed to and fro by the waves and carried about by every wind of doctrine, by human cunning, by craftiness in deceitful schemes" (Eph. 4:14). We must not confuse church marketers with genuine disciplers.

God sent his son to unite all heaven and earth under one Lord and Savior, Jesus Christ—"He [God] made known to us the mystery of his will according to his good pleasure, which he purposed in Christ, to be put into effect when the times reach their fulfillment—to bring unity to all things in heaven and on earth under Christ" (Eph. 1:9–10). Yet, in the name of Christ, denominated Christians have too often exploited those who might want to follow only Christ and dragged them into following them, playing unwittingly into the hands of the Evil One.

However still, Christ gives each who comes to him the knowledge of his voice. As sheep in his flock we can, if we are determined to, actually listen with a spiritual ear and ferret out that which is not of him from that which is—"The sheep listen to his voice. He calls his own sheep by name and leads them out. When he has brought out all his own, he goes on ahead of them, and his sheep follow him because they know his voice" (John 10:3–4).

There is a spiritual "knowing" given to each believer by the anointing of the Holy Spirit. This knowing is not of all the information there is to know about God, but it is a knowing of Christ's voice. It is a knowing of Christ himself—"But you have an anointing from the Holy One, and all of you know the truth…the anointing you received from him remains in you, and you do not need anyone to teach you. But as his anointing teaches you about all things and as that anointing is real, not counterfeit—just as it has taught you, remain in him" (1 John 2:20, 27). The Spirit gives us the ability to be unobstructed from the voice of the shepherd and undeterred in following him!

And as we may know him by this precious gift given personally to us by him, we can also grow by the power of his Spirit to know him better and better—"I keep asking that the God of our Lord Jesus Christ, the glorious Father, may give you the Spirit of wisdom and revelation, so that you may know him better" (Eph. 1:17). He can open the eyes of our minds and hearts wider and wider as we grow in him—"I pray that the eyes of your heart may be enlightened in order that you may know the hope to which he has called you, the riches of his glorious inheritance in his holy people, and his incomparably great power for us who believe" (Eph. 1:18–19). If we follow the Spirit, we will increase our learning capacity as we increase in our learning.

In knowing rightly about Christ, we can be thrust into God's spiritual space, so that we can know Christ in an experiential way that far surpasses knowing him only intellectually and academically—"I pray that out of his glorious riches he may strengthen you with power through his Spirit in your inner being, so that Christ may dwell in your hearts through faith. And I pray that you, being rooted and established in love, may have power, together with all the Lord's holy people, to grasp how wide and long and high and deep is the love of Christ, and *to know this love that surpasses knowledge*—that you may be filled to the measure of all the fullness of God" (Eph. 3:16–19, italics added).

We thus dedicate not just our hearts but also our minds to Christ Jesus—"We demolish arguments and every pretension that sets itself up against the knowledge of God, and we take captive every thought to make it obedient to Christ" (2 Cor. 10:5). *We choose* what we think rather letting the cursed, negative world around us choose for us—"Finally, brothers and sisters, whatever is true, whatever is noble, whatever is right, whatever is pure, whatever is lovely, whatever is admirable—if anything is excellent or praiseworthy—think about such things" (Phil. 4:8). When our minds are changed and set only on the goodness and grace of Christ, our hearts follow in succession to thus crave his pure truth—"Like newborn babies, crave pure spiritual milk, so that by it you may grow up in your salvation, now that you have tasted that the Lord is good" (1 Pet. 2:2–3).

A Prayer:

> Father, help me, as a newborn baby, to crave your pure spiritual truth.
> Help me to grow as a learner, able to learn more and more rather than being sated by mere human information about you.
> May my antenna be turned toward you and may you be the channel I am attuned to.
> Fill my mind with your knowledge and guide my heart to follow.
> Transform me by the renewal of my mind.
> Amen!

69
Learning, Part 3

To truly know Christ is to genuinely want to know more and more about him. Christ promises power and strength to those who hear his message and put it to practice.

Let the word of Christ dwell in you richly (Col. 3:16).

KING DAVID WAS said to be "a man after God's own heart" (1 Sam. 13:14). He didn't do a lot of things right, but he seemed to have done the right things right. God wants us all to have hearts like his. After coming to faith itself, no component of spiritual growth is more important than learning more about God and his word. We must have our hearts engraved with his truth—"I have stored up your word in my heart, that I might not sin against you" (Ps. 119:11, English Standard Version).

Although God gives believers the ability to recognize the Good Shepherd's voice and to know what we need to know to remain in Christ, our experience of Christ can grow in proportion to our increasing knowledge about him—"For this very reason, make every effort to add to your faith…knowledge" (2 Pet. 1:5). Knowledge doesn't equate to spiritually, but at least some knowledge is required for it. Following Christ requires us to hear and obey his teaching—"If you hold to my teaching, you are really my disciples. Then you will know the truth, and the truth will set you free" (John 8:31–32).

The one who presumes to know everything knows nothing. The one who presumes to be right about everything is wrong about the most important thing.

Believers must seek to be constant, lifelong learners, learning as much about God as humanly possible. But we must, of course, never take pride in or boast about our knowledge. The ultimate goal of all knowledge about God is to learn it in order to know God better and better—"This is what the LORD says: 'Let not the wise boast of their wisdom or the strong boast of their strength or the rich boast of their riches, but *let the one who boasts boast about this: that they have the understanding to know me*, that I am the LORD, who exercises kindness, justice and righteousness on earth, for in these I delight,' declares the LORD" (Jer. 9:23–24, italics added).

We can indeed know scripture and not know God at all—"You study the Scriptures diligently because you think that in them you have eternal life. These are the very Scriptures that testify about me, yet you refuse to come to me to have life" (John 5:39–40). Indeed, we can know a lot about scripture and still not know God at all. However, we cannot know God well and not know the truths revealed in scripture about him and his will for us!

When it comes to learning and inculcating truth into our lives, *repetition is the friend of the adult learner.* We must consider the word of God our daily bread, always remembering that our learning about God enables us to know him better, for Christ is that bread—"I am the living bread that came down from heaven. Whoever eats this bread will live forever. This bread is my flesh, which I will give for the life of the world" (John 6:51). We must first take in the words *from* God that we may through them find the word *of* God, and then we must ruminate on it (him), digesting it as we do the food that we eat—"You thrill to God's Word, you chew on Scripture day and night" (Ps. 1:2, The Message).

To be a good servant of Christ, we must make the careful effort to know and understand his will and ways—"Do your best to present yourself to God as one approved, a worker who does not need to be ashamed and who correctly handles the word of truth" (2 Tim. 2:15). The scriptures were revealed to thoroughly provide us as disciples with all that we need to live for God—"All Scripture is God-breathed and is useful for teaching, rebuking, correcting and training in righteousness, so that the servant of God may be thoroughly equipped for every good work" (2 Tim. 3:16–17). But as we do with other necessary provisions for life, we must stock up on the words of God in order to utilize them in our daily lives.

Reading, understanding, and remembering God's word must become our daily need and practice. The unlearned Christian is a stunted, vulnerable Christian. And truly knowing and understanding what God's will is requires giving our whole selves to him—"Therefore, I urge you, brothers and sisters, in view of God's mercy, to *offer your bodies as a living sacrifice*, holy and pleasing to God—this is your true and proper worship. Do not conform to the pattern of this world, but be transformed by the renewing of your mind. *Then you will be able to test and approve what God's will is*—his good, pleasing and perfect will" (Rom. 12:1–2).

Growing disciples are not those who learn most of what they know early on and then coast along, assuming they know enough. They are those who truly "get it" and grow as learners. True disciples are eager learners because they know that equipping themselves with greater knowledge enables them to have a deeper and richer relationship with the Father in Heaven! Growing disciples grow not less hungry as they eat the bread of life, but they grow even hungrier, and they are blessed for their constant need of him—"Blessed are those who hunger and thirst for righteousness, for they will be filled" (Matt. 5:6).

Many are the Christians who were most eager in their learning in the beginning but most complacent in the end. This should not be the case. We should grow hotter in our learning about Christ, not colder. The fire should burn brighter, not grow dimmer as we age.

And we must put his word into action, not merely store it up as information, or worse yet hear it and let it slip away from us—"Do not merely listen to the word, and so deceive yourselves. Do what it says" (James 1:22). We deceive ourselves or rather allow ourselves to be deceived by the Evil One, when we say we know Christ but fail to obey him—"We know that we have come to know him if we keep his commands. Whoever says, 'I know him,' but does not do what he commands is a liar, and the truth is not in that person. But if anyone obeys his word, love for God is truly made complete in them. This is how we know we are in him: Whoever claims to live in him must live as Jesus did" (1 John 2:3–6).

Or, as Jesus said, "Now that you know these things, you will be blessed if you do them" (John 13:17).

For the disciple learning is doing and doing is learning.

A Prayer:

> Father, let me know more about you, that I may know you
> more,
> Let me see your glorious virtues, all you have in store,
> Grow my mind daily that it be only yours,
> That I may eat forever, the bread that e'er endures.

70
Life Done Right

Jesus is "what-humanity-done-right-looks-like."

But so the world might know how thoroughly I love the Father, I am carrying out my Father's instructions right down to the last detail (John 14:31, The Message).

THERE IS AN old expression in process management that says we must show those we teach "what-done-right-looks-like." In sending Jesus to live among us, God did this very thing for us, showing us what humanity-done-right-looks-like—"I am the way and the truth and the life" (John 14:6). Jesus not only brought true teachings to us but also *the* truth was personified in himself! He showed us what the life of God looks like in the life of humanity.

In Christ, we behold the wonders of God in human form—"We have seen his glory, the glory of the one and only Son, who came from the Father, full of grace and truth" (John 1:14). Jesus shows us what God looks like and thus what being and doing right looks like—"The Son is the radiance of God's glory and the exact representation of his being" (Heb. 1:3).

We are made in God's image, but the curse of sin deeply mars and scars us from within, rendering our resemblance to God as fairly unrecognizable. Jesus came to show us what God looks like in human form and thus what we are to look like as our sin is removed and we are healed of its damage and ongoing malignancy.

Through the power and work of the Holy Spirit that Christ gives to believers, we are then transformed gradually and deliberately back to what and who we are to be when we are finally and completely "done right" again—"And we all, with unveiled face, *continually* seeing as in a mirror the glory of the Lord, are *progressively* being transformed into His image from [one degree of] glory to [even more] glory, which comes from the Lord, [who is] the Spirit" (2 Cor. 3:18, Amplified Bible, brackets and italics are part of quotation).

Christ gives to us a spirit of beloved children with their parents—the spirit of sonship (Rom. 8:14–17). As children of God, we then become daily imitators of him and his loving, sacrificial nature—"Therefore be imitators of God, as beloved children. And walk in love, as Christ loved us and gave himself up for us, a fragrant offering and sacrifice to God" (Eph. 5:1–2, English Standard Version).

God is Yahweh, the Great I Am, not the Great *I Do* (Exod. 3:14). Unlike how humans generally identify one another, God is not to be known chiefly by what he does or has done, but by who he is. After this age, we too will be known by who we are rather than being defined merely by what we do or have done. Jesus Christ, who was both God and man, was engaged in the human process while he lived here. He was birthed as a baby in the normal fashion. In fact, his birth is clearly documented as, at best, an inconvenient one. After his parents took him to Egypt for a while to escape Herod's attempt to kill the infant Messiah, he was apparently raised as any other boy in Israel at the time. And in human form, he surely dealt with many more life challenges.

As a boy and then a man, he had to be prepared for his redemptive work in humanity. Jesus had to learn, and he had to grow into the person he would have to be to face up to the incomparable burden of his death on the cross—"Although he was a son, he *learned* obedience through what he suffered. And being made perfect, he became the source of eternal salvation to all who obey him" (Heb. 5:8–9).

Because Jesus took on the task of God while in human form, he is our God-given role model of what we are to do and look like in order to become what we are to finally be eternally. He demonstrates once and for all who God really is and what the implications are to us in our walks with him—"Therefore, since we have a great high priest who has ascended into heaven, Jesus the Son of God, let us hold firmly to the faith we profess. For we do not have a high priest who is unable to empathize with our weaknesses, but we have one who has been tempted in every way, just as we are—yet he did not sin. Let us then approach God's throne of grace with confidence, so that we may receive mercy and find grace to help us in our time of need" (Heb. 4:14–16).

Among a vast array of God's attributes and nuances, Jesus has taught us that God is by nature incomparable love—"God *is* love" (1 John 4:8, italics added). He clearly demonstrated that God's love is for all humanity—"God so loved the world that he gave his one and only Son, that whoever believes in him shall not perish but have eternal life" (John 3:16). And thus Christ has similarly called us back to our original image of being incredibly loving, as he was loving—"A new command I give you: Love one another. As I have loved you, so you must love one another. By this everyone will know that you are my disciples, if you love one another" (John 13:34–35).

Also, unlike any other human conception of God up to his time, even among the Israelites, Jesus taught us that God is a humble, servant God, not a power-mongering, self-serving one as were the gods of the Romans, the Greeks, and the nations surrounding Israel—"Come to me, all you who are weary and burdened, and I will give you rest. Take my yoke upon you and learn from me, for *I am gentle and humble in heart*, and you will find rest for your souls. For my yoke is easy and my burden is light" (Matt. 11:28–30, italics added). God has likewise taught us to be humble servants, and most of all to the least among us, rather than seeking to control and trying to lord it over others—"Now that I, your Lord and Teacher, have washed your feet, you also should wash one another's feet" (John 13:14).

We are called to be imitators of our gracious and loving God because he lovingly made us in his image. He predestined us to be with him forever as his people in our final, finished form. And Jesus Christ showed us clearly what God's image looks like—what humanity-done-right-looks-like—so we could grow to be like him.

A Prayer:

Help me to be like Jesus,
Help me to follow him,
That my light grows ever brighter,
That it may never ever dim.

Help me to be like Jesus,
Who was the human form of God,
And not merely act like him,
Wearing a mere facade.

Make me like Jesus through and through,
His glory show through me,
That I may show the world around,
How life is supposed to be.

71
Looking Through a Dirty Lens

The whole world looks smudged and ugly to us when we are looking through the dirty lens of our fallen world. However, looking at creation, as well as ourselves, through the lens of our loving Savior affords us a completely new perspective.

To the pure, all things are pure, but to those who are corrupted and do not believe, nothing is pure (Titus 1:15).

THE EARLY GNOSTICS had a significant impact on early Christianity. They believed that the physical world is evil. Thus, they posited that Yahweh could not have created it. Gnostics believed variously that somehow the world had been created by a lesser being or by lesser beings. The earliest Christians were tasked with understanding, teaching, and handing down sound doctrine concerning Christ and scripture—"Watch your life and doctrine closely.

Persevere in them, because if you do, you will save both yourself and your hearers" (1 Tim. 4:16).

Such a great responsibility along with the encroaching views of Gnosticism likely played roles in the early development of and attitudes toward the doctrine of total depravity. Total depravity is the doctrine that claims all of us are born enslaved to or with at least a predisposition toward sin, because of the pervasive human nature stemming from the original sin itself—"Surely I was sinful at birth, sinful from the time my mother conceived me" (Ps. 51:5).

However, wrong assumptions and conclusions always imply wrong premises. Even a slight misdirection of early views can cause drastic misperceptions in later generations. Such then is the responsibility we also bear, individually and collectively, to watch our own lives and doctrines closely, as any slight error in ours can ultimately produce even more dangerous heresies later.

Whatever we conclude concerning the origin of sin and the human lust for it, one must realize that the paradigms we construct form the lens through which we look at the world. Our lenses are all already smudged by our sinful, carnal natures, which likely too, affect the very doctrines we accept as true. But human imperfection will not in the end impede God's truth and righteous judgment—"What if some were unfaithful? Will their unfaithfulness nullify God's faithfulness? Not at all! *Let God be true, and every human being a liar.* As it is written: 'So that you may be proved right when you speak and prevail when you judge'" (Rom. 3:3–4, Ps. 51:4, italics added).

When God created the world, he knew in advance what was to come, both for good and bad. God looks with eternal eyes. Nothing is hidden from him, past, present, or future. Thus, even knowing that the creation would fall under the curse of sin, when he looked on his creation, with humanity as its capstone, he declared it to be quite good—"God saw all that he had made, and it was very good" (Gen. 1:31). Humanity was created to be God's image bearer in creation, and it would be through us that God would carry out his will for creation—"He made known to us the mystery of his will according to his good pleasure, which he purposed in Christ, to be put into effect when the times reach their fulfillment—to bring unity to all things in heaven and on earth under Christ" (Eph. 1:9–10).

God, through Christ, designed and created the world for his divine purposes—"All things have been created through him and for him" (Col. 1:16). He predestined from creation itself that in spite of the impending curse of sin, he would see us in Christ through a clean or at least a filtered lens, and not the dirty lens of sin—"He chose us in him before the creation of the world *to be holy and blameless in his sight*" (Eph. 1:4, italics added). And he determined to create a new humanity for a new heaven and a new earth—"His purpose was to create in himself one new humanity" (Eph. 2:15), and "See, I will create new heavens and a new earth. The former things will not be remembered, nor will they come to mind" (Isa. 65:17).

Instead of condemning those who would trust in him, God would condemn sin itself through those who believe in him and live according to his Spirit—"And so he condemned sin in the flesh" (Rom. 8:3). Thus, God sees a new humanity, created in Christ, as already holy and blameless. And he is preparing new heavens and a new earth for his new humanity, as he planned from the beginning—"I am going there to prepare a place for you? And if I go and prepare a place for you, I will come back and take you to be with me that you also may be where I am" (John 14:2–3).

Most of what goes on even today is good. Most moms and dads get up every day and try very hard to do a good job. Most pastors do not intentionally mislead or abuse their churches. Most law-enforcement officers simply try to protect us and enforce the laws. Most people who drive the roads are just trying to get to their destinations and seek to be courteous and helpful to others.

However, Satan wants us to see and focus on the exceptions brought about by the pervasive evil that has spread over creation, casting over it an ugly pall. He wants us to see ourselves as sinners even after God has declared us saints! The Evil One wants us to see the rust on the metal, so to speak, rather than the otherwise strong and beautiful metal underneath. Satan wants to rub our faces in our own refuse and in the refuse of others.

But we must not allow it, even though we alone cannot prevent it. But Christ working through us can—"The one who is in you is greater than the one who is in the world" (1 John 4:4). It is Christ in whom we place all our trust and hope!

Christ opens our spiritual eyes through rebirth to see the kingdom of heaven, not merely the kingdoms of the fallen ones—"No one can see the kingdom of God unless they are born again" (John 3:3). In him and through him, we, the new humanity, can see clearly again through a clean lens, filtered only through the love and grace of God—"Then will the eyes of the blind be opened and the ears of the deaf unstopped" (Isa. 35:5).

Through God's eyes, we can look on creation—the new creation—and see it as "very good"! We have a new perspective, because we have a new point of view, because we have a clean lens to look through—"So from now on we regard no one from a worldly point of view. Though we once regarded Christ in this way, we do so no longer" (2 Cor. 5:16).

A Prayer:

> Lord, give me new eyes to see as you see.
> Give me a clean heart and mind that I can feel and think as you do.
> Filter what I see and hear through your love, grace, and goodness.
> Take Satan's hands from the back of my neck that he may no longer rub my face in the world's refuse.
> Allow me to see through what is heavenly and not what is earthly.

Help me to see beyond this present creation to the new creation.
Enable me to see emerging from this present humanity your new humanity.
Help me to live by faith and not by distrust.
Empower me to live by hope and not by dread.
Purify me so that I can see all things as pure.
Amen.

72
Love

If we *get* love, we *get* God. And too, if we love enough people, we will always have enough people to love us.

God is love. Whoever lives in love lives in God, and God in them (1 John 4:16).

MOST OF ALL, we humans need to feel our worth or value. Many would say our most basic need is for love, and we are indeed desperate for it. But we are desperate for it for a good reason. Our desperation for love comes because it is through our sensing and feeling love from those we deem important, whether God or others, that we assess and sense our own self-worth.

Self-worth and popularity found in the human social orders are dangerous things, because deep inside we all know that we, as well as everybody else around us, are deeply flawed and incapable of determining or understanding worth, either our own or that of others. Even the most loving and affectionate among us can be unreliable in consistently giving and expressing love, even to those we love the most. Therefore, reliance on human love above the love of God sets us up for spiritual trouble and possibly disaster!

Thus, we must never determine our worth by anything human but only by God's assessment. God's ultimate expression of his love for us, and thus our value to him, is by the giving of himself, his only Son, for us in his death on the cross—"Greater love has no one than this: to lay down one's life for one's friends" (John 15:13). He is indeed our greatest friend!

The gospel calls us to turn away from assessing our worth through humanity—our contribution to society or the love and respect we receive from our social order. The gospel calls us to a complete change of mind and heart—"The kingdom of God has come near. Repent and believe the good news!" (Mark 1:15).

To repent literally means to "change one's mind," implying, of course, a change in one's course of life. In the case of the gospel, we change our mind from assessing our worth and value by the social order, rather to believing the worth that God ascribes to us—that we are to him priceless! God clearly manifested and demonstrated his unconditional love for us—"God so loved the world that he gave his one and only Son, that whoever believes in him shall not perish but have eternal life" (John 3:16), and "God demonstrates his own love for us in this: While we were still sinners, Christ died for us" (Rom. 5:8). Christ calls us to change our mind about all this and determine the gospel of God to be patently true—to believe it!

The gospel is not first and foremost about what God did for us; it is first about who God really is. Evil deceives humanity into believing God is someone other than who he is. Satan would have us to believe that God is actually like him! He seeks to convince us that God is harsh, haughty, self-elevating, and self-serving. He would have us believe that God's love for us is conditioned on our near-perfect performance and good works. He would convince us that God's mercy is but meager. However, Christ clearly reveals otherwise.

God is in reality humble and kind—"I am gentle and humble in heart" (Matt. 11:29). God's love is incomparable and unconditional—"Whoever does not love does not know God, because *God is love*. This is how God showed his love among us: He sent his one and only Son into the world that we might live through him" (1 John 4:8–9). And God lavishes grace on us and is rich in mercy—"He [God] predestined us for adoption to sonship through Jesus Christ, in accordance with his pleasure and will—to the praise of his *glorious grace, which he has freely given us* in the One he loves" (Eph. 1:5–6, italics added), and "But because of his great love for us, God, who is *rich in mercy*, made us alive with Christ even when we were dead in transgressions—it is by grace you have been saved" (Eph. 2:4–5, italics added).

When we accept the essence of the gospel of God—of who God actually is—our life paradigm completely shifts—"So from now on we regard no one from a worldly point of view. Though we once regarded Christ in this way, we do so no longer. Therefore, if anyone is in Christ, the new creation has come: The old has gone, the new is here!" (2 Cor. 5:16–17). His love becomes powerful and compelling in our lives; it becomes the prime mover within us—"For Christ's love compels us, because we are convinced that one died for all, and therefore all died. And he died for all, that those who live should no longer live for themselves but for him who died for them and was raised again" (2 Cor. 5:14–15).

No longer must we feed at the slop trough of the world to try to nourish our very real need to feel and experience our true intrinsic worth and value. No longer must we compete with others living in Satan's pigsty for a sense of value and dignity. In our acceptance of the gospel, our worth is transfixed on our hearts through our faith in the gospel! Ours is but to daily believe the gospel. It may require repenting (changing our minds) multiple times some days, but our belief in it is what only can connect us to God!

When we discover and believe in the love of God, we find too an endless source of love to give to others—"We love because he first loved us. Whoever claims to love God yet hates a brother or sister is a liar. For whoever does not love their brother and sister, whom they have seen, cannot love God, whom they have not seen" (1 John

4:19–20). Love is the greatest gift one can give to another human, and since it is, "more blessed to give than to receive" (Acts 20:35), we are most blessed when we graciously extend to others the love God has given to us!

As it is with God in regard to humanity, we will certainly not always receive back love in kind and degree equal to the love we give to others, especially from those not of the faith. However, we can be assured that whether anyone else ever loves us, there is more than enough love flowing from God to nourish our hearts, souls, and spirits. And also, we can be assured if we love enough people, we will always have enough people to love us.

"Love never fails…now these three remain: faith, hope and love. But the greatest of these is love" (1 Cor. 13:8, 13).

A Prayer:

> Lord, help me to believe your love that I may be freed from a slavish reliance on the world.
> Open the doors of my heart that I can drink deeply of your love.
> Open the shutters of my heart that you love may radiate richly from me.
> Help me to grasp your love that I may clearly communicate it to others.
> Help me to experience your love that I may graciously manifest it to others.
> May I never be only a selfish reservoir of your love, but may I be a river of your rich love that flows out to others.
> And as your love flows through me, may I absorb and internalize at least enough to feed my hungry spirit, empowering me to be a living letter of your love to the world.
> Amen.

73
Love for Others

Our love for others, in actuality, can never exceed our love for God.

A new command I give you: Love one another. As I have loved you, so you must love one another. By this everyone will know that you are my disciples, if you love one another (John 13:34–35).

CHRIST LOVE IS a dynamic love, not an inert one—"For Christ's love compels us, because we are convinced that one died for all, and therefore all died. And he died for all, that those who live should no longer live for themselves but for him who died for them and was raised again (2 Cor. 5:14–15). And we can never love others beyond our comprehension of God's love for us.

God doesn't only love others, as in expressing loving behaviors toward us; love defines him! God *is* love—"Whoever does not love does not know God, because God is love" (1 John 4:8). And accordingly, our love for others reveals the measure of our own actual love God.

Our belief in God arises from an honest assessment of the incontrovertible evidence for his existence. Our faith or trust in him arises from a fair appraisal of his faithfulness and love. Our love for him arises from our faith experience of him—"The only thing that counts is faith expressing itself through love" (Gal. 5:6). The ultimately and only real, eternal love is the love of God, and we can first experience it through our faith experience of him. All such love among humans is in reaction to God's love—"We love because he first loved us" (1 John 4:19).

God's love (*agape*, Greek) is not a sentiment but rather is a definition of the all-encompassing character of God—"Love is patient, love is kind. It does not envy, it does not boast, it is not proud. It does not dishonor others, it is not self-seeking, it is not easily angered, it keeps no record of wrongs. Love does not delight in evil but rejoices with the truth. It always protects, always trusts, always hopes, always perseveres" (1 Cor. 13:4–7). It is not to be felt in the same way as mere human affection, rather it must be comprehended mentally, emotionally, and experientially at a spiritual level.

In fact, it rises above all that is human. Before it is anything else, it originates in the will. It is based on something completely outside of us. It is based on truth and right. Agape is a love that simply wills what is right based on the character and truth of God. Although it is to be expressed in the physical realm in various ways, agape is wholly spiritually. Therefore, it is unconditional and not based on situations and human personalities.

Brotherly or friendship love (*phileo*, Greek) is what we often think of when we think of loving others, and so on. Phileo is a love that involves not just goodwill but also affection, brotherhood, and friendship. It includes sentiments and feelings toward others. It involves more of the physical parts of us. Thus, it can grow or diminish over time. It is affected by personality and situation. Expressed according to God's will, it indeed flows naturally from agape.

Family love (*storge*, Greek) is even more of this physical world. It is the love we experience growing up around family members or the love we otherwise feel because of the commonalities of kinship even among those of our family we may not know well.

Sexual or romantic love (*eros*, Greek) is even more of this world. It has a strong, chemical component of our physical being. Thus, it apparently will not exist in the next age—"At the resurrection people will neither marry nor be given in marriage; they will be like the angels in heaven" (Matt. 22:3).

When brotherly love (phileo), family love (storge), and romantic love (eros) are under the rule of the love of God (agape), they become beautiful expressions of it. When they are not, they become base tools of our more prurient human desires.

The one who has truly discovered and experienced the love of God is the one who can and will, in actuality, express such love to others—"By this everyone will know that you are My disciples, if you have love *and* unselfish concern for one another" (John 13:35, Amplified Bible). The presence of the love of God (agape) is proof positive of the hand of God in a life. Unselfishness and "unconditionality" can only be experienced and expressed by ones living in him.

Such can only be learned in this age by following the life, character, and example of Jesus Christ, for he alone is the consummate expression of God's love—"Greater love has no one than this..." (John 15:13).

A Prayer:

> Lord, fill me to the measure with all your fullness.
> Inspire within me a grasp of the magnitude of your love for humanity.
> Strengthen me within by your Spirit that Christ may operate freely within me and from me.

Help my experience of the full degree of your love to be fully expressed to others.
Defeat those sins within me that would rob me of your love and rob others of the love you would otherwise express to them through me.
Help my love for you to grow to the full extent that I may love others fully!
Amen.

74
Motivation and Maslow

Love for Christ turns all human motivations upside down. The mind without the Spirit of God cannot begin to grasp the motivations of God.

These who have turned the world upside down have come here too (Acts 17:6, New King James Version).

THE EARLY DISCIPLES "turned *the* world upside down" because Jesus had turned *their* worlds upside down. Or in reality, right side up again. In the minds of unbelievers, however, turning their world upside down meant they were causing them trouble—"These men…have caused trouble all over the world" (Acts 17:6, New International Version).

The kingdom of God is the exact opposite, internally, to the kingdom of the world. This is precisely the reason most people stumble over Jesus rather than follow him. God designed it that way in advance so that only honest souls that seek truth, accept truth, and align with truth will find it. Those who refuse to accept Christ will only trip over the gospel and fall—"He will be a holy place; for both Israel and Judah *he will be a stone that causes people to stumble and a rock that makes them fall.* And for the people of Jerusalem he will be a trap and a snare" (Isa. 8:14, italics added).

As Abraham Maslow, the humanist psychologist, observed, the basic human motivations form a pyramid of needs from the most basic to those of the highest order, with individuals meeting these needs in ascending order. In order from bottom to top, they are identified variously as (1) survival needs, (2) safety needs, (3) social needs, (4) self-esteem needs, and (5) self-actualization needs. Although many in the psychology and humanism worlds dispute this hierarchy of needs, that basic human motivations begin and end with self is hardly disputable at all!

Humanity apart from divinity is self-centered and self-seeking. Apart from God, in our natural selves, we will seek to first survive at all cost, unless of course we decide to simply take our own life rather than face what we see as difficulties we are unwilling to face. We will even risk our safety in order to provide our most basic biological survival needs. However, once those needs are reasonably met to our relative satisfaction, we will then seek to secure our safety. If we will feel safe, then we will move outward to meet our social needs. Humans apart from God then determine their worth and meet their self-esteem needs from their interactions with their social orders, and by navigating those waters the best way possible, we try to esteem ourselves as highly as possible in others' eyes.

If all those seem reasonably met, the human soul will then seek to "self-actualize," defined as realizing our fullest potential as a person. The world has been sorely disappointed at the reality that very few humans seem to ever get to the pinnacle of the humanistic motivation pyramid and actually "self-actualize!" Even the Maslow himself was apparently disappointed in this regard.

And no wonder. The hopes of the natural world always disappoint in the end. The world, left to its own devices, is a one-way, dead-end street. On the other hand, the world connected to God leads to eternal life. Thus, our hope in the eternal does not disappoint us—"Such hope [in God's promises] never disappoints *us*, because God's love has been abundantly poured out within our hearts through the Holy Spirit who was given to us" (Rom. 5:5, Amplified Bible, the brackets and italics are part of the original paraphrased text).

In Christ, the Holy Spirit turns the pyramid of needs upside down in us. Our needs become the exact opposite of those of the world!

Because the eternal life that we receive from Christ at rebirth is not of this world, our inner motivations are inverted from those of the world. We come first to identify with Jesus. Thus our "self-actualization" is actually a "Christ realization." That is, we believe identifying with and becoming like Christ is our fullest potential! That is where it all derives from the Christian heart. He is our motivation—"For to me, to live is Christ" (Phil. 1:21).

In identifying with Christ, we repent and believe the gospel, knowing that our worth to God is endless and unconditional. We are priceless to him. Thus our "self-esteem" is rather our "God-esteem," therefore it is fixed, unconditional, and fully attested to by the cross of Christ—"But God demonstrates his own love for us in this: While we were still sinners, Christ died for us" (Rom. 5:8).

Believers are able, then, to operate in the social order not to gain esteem through the acceptance, approval, or accolades of others. Rather, we live to present to the world the living gospel of God so that others too can experience the unchanging "God-esteem" that we experience, and no longer be held hostage to the evil designs of Satan himself. Satan brings humanity only shame, disdain, rejection, and eternal destruction, as he has done from the original sin in the Garden of Eden. He wants us to join him in his own fate.

However, the believer need not have a death wish. We too seek reasonable safety and to meet our basic biological survival needs. But because our motivations are inverted from those of the worldly order, deriving rather from our identification with Christ, we will risk the more basic fleshly needs in favor of the higher order ones of Christ—"Rather, as servants of God we commend ourselves in every way: in great endurance; in troubles, hardships and distresses;

in beatings, imprisonments and riots; in hard work, sleepless nights and hunger; in purity, understanding, patience and kindness; in the Holy Spirit and in sincere love; in truthful speech and in the power of God; with weapons of righteousness in the right hand and in the left; through glory and dishonor, bad report and good report; genuine, yet regarded as impostors; known, yet regarded as unknown; dying, and yet we live on; beaten, and yet not killed; sorrowful, yet always rejoicing; poor, yet making many rich; having nothing, and yet possessing everything" (2 Cor. 6:4–10). As believing servants of God we will behave differently. Often the exact opposite of the world.

The gospel of Christ turns the humanistic motivation pyramid upside down for us. And the Holy Spirit within us balances this crazy world we live in on the point of the pyramid turned upside down. Our identifying with Christ helps us realize our fullest potential and allows us to meet our natural human needs legitimately while we live out the purposes of God for our existence in this present age.

A Prayer:

> Father, help me to be holy as you are holy.
> Infuse within me the substance of your existence and being.
> Strengthen my faltering faith that I may fully live out the life you alone give.
> Help me to be fully in the world as your servant, but not of the world, serving myself.
> Lift my spirit to function fully in the heavenly realm in which you give me life.
> May the weapons with which I fight not be the weapons of this present world.
> Transform me to the image of Christ that I no longer live as simply a higher order animal, but live fully as an image bearer of you.
> Amen.

75
Motives

With God, it is generally better for us to do the wrong thing for the right reason than to do the right thing for the wrong reason, if either are even possible

After removing Saul, he made David their king. God testified concerning him: "I have found David son of Jesse, a man after my own heart; he will do everything I want him to do" (Acts 13:22).

IT MAY BE said that, in the spiritual realm at least, motive is everything, mostly—"The Lord does not look at the things people look at. People look at the outward appearance, but *the Lord looks at the heart*" (1 Sam. 16:7, italics added). Because God connects with us inwardly, he desires sincerity from within us, that is, in our hearts and minds—"You desire [God desires] truth in the innermost being" (Ps. 51:6, Amplified Bible, brackets included in quotation). God, in fact, seeks out those who will approach him and worship him with sincere motives—"A time is coming and is already here when the true worshipers will worship the Father in spirit [from the heart, the inner self] and in truth; for the Father seeks such people to be His worshipers" (John 3:23, Amplified Bible, brackets included).

Thus, those things we may do in God's name that are being done for wrong motives profit us nothing—"Be careful not to practice your righteousness in front of others to be seen by them. If you do, you will have no reward from your Father in heaven" (Matt. 6:1). The ultimate motive in God's mind is love (*agape*, Greek), and without it, nothing we do will bring God's blessing—"If I give all I possess to the poor and give over my body to hardship that I may boast, but do not have love, I gain nothing" (1 Cor. 13:3).

Many among even the believers will be shocked in judgment to find that their religious doings were not only not pleasing to God but in actuality counter to his will—"Many will say to me on that day, 'Lord, Lord, did we not prophesy in your name and in your name drive out demons and in your name perform many miracles?' Then I will tell them plainly, '*I never knew you. Away from me, you evildoers*!'" (Matt. 7:22–23, italics added). There will be no greater disappointment than for those among us who find their alleged service to God to be useless because of condemning motives.

God sees our thoughts and feelings as behavior—"I the Lord search the heart and examine the mind, to reward each person according to their conduct, according to what their deeds deserve" (Jer. 17:10). Thus we are commanded to actively love God with both our heart and mind—"Love the Lord your God with all your heart and with all your soul and with all your mind" (Matt. 22:37). We are to obey God with all our thoughts, both mental and emotional—"We take captive every thought to make it obedient to Christ" (2 Cor. 10:5).

Even though we may outwardly appear obedient to God, our disobedience within can nullify any positive effect of our religion without—"These people honor me with their lips, but their hearts are far from me. They worship me in vain; their teachings are merely human rules" (Matt. 22:8–9). God gives command to our whole person—heart, mind, and body—and searches our inner behavior concerning all three.

Our prayers too can remain unanswered because of bad motives—"You do not have because you do not ask God. When you ask, you do not receive, because you ask with wrong motives, that you may spend what you get on your pleasures" (James 4:2–3). And it is those with singleness and sincerity of heart who will see God—"Blessed are the pure in heart, for they will see God" (Matt. 5:8).

In the Sermon on the Mount (Matt. 5–7), beginning with the beatitudes (Matt. 5:1–12) and ending with the cautionary warning about false prophets and disobedience (Matt. 7:15–27), Jesus aims his message squarely at our hearts and our character. The one to be blessed is the one poor in spirit rather than one full of self, the mourner who grieves over sin and its curse, the meek and humble one who sees himself or herself not at the top but at the bottom, the one hungering and thirsting for God's righteousness over self-will, the one merciful to others as God has been merciful to us, the one pure and single in heart toward God, the one who serves as peacemaker between God and humanity as well as between people, and the one who rejoices rather than curses when persecuted for God's sake.

Each of us must take special care toward God. Carelessness in regard to God reveals an inner malignancy of heart. Just because one's conscience is clear concerning a thing does not mean we are therefore innocent—"My conscience is clear, but that does not make me innocent. It is the Lord who judges me" (1 Cor. 4:4). I may indeed deem my motives as good and pure, but that does not necessarily make it so—"All a person's ways seem pure to them, but motives are weighed by the LORD" (Prov. 16:2).

God's first agent of testing our hearts and minds and convicting of sin within and without is the word of God—"For the word of God is alive and active. Sharper than any double-edged sword, it penetrates even to dividing soul and spirit, joints and marrow;

it judges the thoughts and attitudes of the heart. Nothing in all creation is hidden from God's sight. Everything is uncovered and laid bare before the eyes of him to whom we must give account" (Heb. 4:12–13, italics added).

The Holy Spirit as well works within us in conjunction with the word to bring about conviction about sin and righteousness—"He [The Holy Spirit] will convict the world concerning sin and righteousness and judgment" (John 16:8). The Holy Spirit knows that as we groan under the weight of sin's curse, we are often weak. And he is here to help us rather than to condemn us—"Likewise the Spirit helps us in our weakness. For we do not know what to pray for as we ought, but the Spirit himself intercedes for us with groanings too deep for words. And he who searches hearts knows what is the mind of the Spirit, because the Spirit intercedes for the saints according to the will of God" (Rom. 8:26–27), and "God did not send his Son into the world to condemn the world, but in order that the world might be saved through him" (John 3:17).

Thus, we must listen to the inner voices of our own heart and mind, the echoes of God's word working within, and the guidance of the precious Holy Spirit in order for our motives to be purified by the redeeming work of God!

Motive matters most.

A Prayer of David (Ps. 51:1–17):

> Have mercy on me, O God, according to your steadfast love; according to your abundant mercy blot out my transgressions. Wash me thoroughly from my iniquity, and cleanse me from my sin!
>
> For I know my transgressions, and my sin is ever before me.
> Against you, you only, have I sinned and done what is evil in your sight, so that you may be justified in your words and blameless in your judgment.

Behold, I was brought forth in iniquity, and in sin did my mother conceive me.
Behold, you delight in truth in the inward being, and you teach me wisdom in the secret heart.

Purge me with hyssop, and I shall be clean; wash me, and I shall be whiter than snow.
Let me hear joy and gladness; let the bones that you have broken rejoice.
Hide your face from my sins, and blot out all my iniquities.
Create in me a clean heart, O God, and renew a right spirit within me.
Cast me not away from your presence, and take not your Holy Spirit from me.
Restore to me the joy of your salvation, and uphold me with a willing spirit.

Then I will teach transgressors your ways, and sinners will return to you.
Deliver me from bloodguiltiness, O God, O God of my salvation, and my tongue will sing aloud of your righteousness.
O Lord, open my lips, and my mouth will declare your praise.
For you will not delight in sacrifice, or I would give it; you will not be pleased with a burnt offering.
The sacrifices of God are a broken spirit; a broken and contrite heart, O God, you will not despise.

76
Mustard Seed Faith

Just as the sun doesn't cease to shine and energize the earth when clouds obscure it, so God does not cease to exist, and even work within us, when our faith—our ability to "see" the invisible—is weak.

Truly I tell you, if you have faith as small as a mustard seed, you can say to this mountain, 'Move from here to there,' and it will move. Nothing will be impossible for you (Matt. 17:20).

ALL HUMAN LIFE is lived by faith, whether we like it or not, whether we are willing to admit it or not. The things we assume to "know" are simply those things we have reason to believe with the greatest conviction. Relative to the more vague and obscure, we consider such things as being "known." However, it can easily be argued that we cannot absolutely know anything, for we are finite, prone to be mistaken, and at any given moment we cannot know what we might *not* know. Nor can we ever be absolutely certain of our reasoning.

Knowledge and reason require faith. And, likewise, biblical faith requires reason. Good reason and biblical faith are not in conflict; rather they are essential components of each other. Both reason and faith alike are subject to being skewed by subjectivity, fallacy, illogic, misinformation, and closed-mindedness.

Since knowledge is never absolute, the things we consider to be known—the things we hold to be true with the most conviction—are simply the things we have the greatest faith in and thus are what affect our lives to the greatest degrees. It is the faith that we generally live by—"For we live by faith, not by sight" (2 Cor. 5:7).

Although there will always be some incongruity between what we believe and how we actually live, due to our fleshly nature, still our faith is in what we hold to be most true and reliable. These things we hold to be most certain are what determine our life paradigms, perspectives, opinions, and feelings. They are rooted in our traditions, cultures, and heritages. They are the "truths" we rely on to set our life courses. These are what we use to make our most important decisions.

But they are all most assuredly imperfect and can even be woefully misguided.

There are certain things in life that we must *believe in greatly* in order to believe in them at all and especially for them to affect us, or others, very much. To be very successful and effective in the most important endeavors, apart from God, requires a lot of faith and fortitude. However, there is one thing—one person—in the universe that we only have to believe in just a little in order for it—for him—to revolutionize our lives and the life of the world around us. That one thing is Jesus—"Truly I tell you, if you have faith as small as a mustard seed, you can say to this mountain, 'Move from here to there,' and it will move. Nothing will be impossible for you" (Matt. 17:20).

A little bit of faith in God can change everything. It only takes a mustard seed amount—just enough to cause us to turn to God. Just enough to make us trust him a little.

Contrary to the necessities of faith in the things of this material realm, the reality is that our spiritual success is not as much a function of possessing a great faith as it is in possessing at least a little faith in our great God. The effects of our faith in someone or something other than God are limited by either the extent of their power and influence or by the measure of our willingness to tap into (believe in) and sync up with (follow) their power or influence. Although our faith clearly has limits, God's power and influence are unlimited.

Faith in anything or anyone finite is clearly limited by time and space. Thus, it is also limited by power, scope, and influence. Even Jesus faced certain limits while in human form here. Faith within the infinite realm has no such bounds or limits, however. And only God is infinite! And since he is boundless, our trust in him connects us to the unlimited—"With God all things are possible" (Matt. 19:26).

Although God is infinite and therefore limitless, we are neither of those, and our ability to believe in him is therefore subjected to the ravages of our finite, fallen experiences. Our knowledge and spiritual vision is clouded and obscured by the limitations and deceptions of this present age.

And, *to live beyond ourselves, we must see beyond ourselves*. To live beyond this present age, we must reach beyond it—"So we fix our eyes not on what is seen, but on what is unseen, since what is seen is temporary, but what is unseen is eternal" (2 Cor. 4:18). This ability to "see" beyond the finite into the infinite realm of the God of the universe is an ability that we have had formed in us by the hand of God himself—"He has also set eternity in the human heart; yet no one can fathom what God has done from beginning to end" (Eccles. 3:11).

If we open our eyes objectively to see, we can see the Creator through the creation—"For since the creation of the world God's invisible qualities—his eternal power and divine nature—have been clearly seen, being understood from what has been made, so that people are without excuse" (Rom. 1:20). To not believe in ourselves specifically or in humanity in general is to be weak in this world. To not believe in God is tragic—"The fool says in his heart, 'There is no God'" (Ps. 14:1).

God's handprint can be seen simply by beholding this unbelievably enormous universe in the night sky—"The heavens declare the glory of God; the skies proclaim the work of his hands. Day after day they pour forth speech; night after night they reveal knowledge. They have no speech, they use no words; no sound is heard from them. Yet their voice goes out into all the earth, their words to the ends of the world" (Ps. 19:1–4). That such a limitless God could even be aware of, let alone care for, such limited creatures is itself unbelievable—"When I consider your heavens, the work of your fingers, the moon and the stars, which you have set in place, what is mankind that you are mindful of them, human beings that you care for them?" (Ps. 8:3–4).

Although our ability to believe in God is universal, our faith in Jesus Christ is not—"No one can come to me unless the Father who sent me draws them, and I will raise them up at the last day" (John 6:44). Our faith in Christ and our calling by God are gifts of God's grace and are contingent on our willingness to humbly seek him out and surrender to him—"For many are invited, but few are chosen" (Matt. 22:14).

Our faith is not only a gift of God, the measure we have is also determined by him—"For by the grace given to me I say to everyone among you not to think of himself more highly than he ought to think, but to think with sober judgment, each *according to the measure of faith that God has assigned*" (Rom. 12:3, English Standard Version, italics added). Through his divine interaction with us, God gifts to us measures of faith in accordance with his will and righteous judgment.

And it is through our seeking him and through prayer that our inner eyes can be opened to his infinite power—"I pray that the eyes of your heart may be enlightened in order that you may know the hope to which he has called you, the riches of his glorious inheritance in his holy people, and his incomparably great power for us who believe" (Eph. 1:18–19). At any given moment, there is always more ahead that God can do for us and through us.

So, it is through our awareness of the incredible nature of his work *through* us, our realization of his generosity *to* us, and our recognition of the power he wields *in* us that we can finally begin to believe—to see within ourselves—the magnitude of what he can do *for* us—"Now to him who is able to do immeasurably more than all we ask or imagine, according to his power that is at work within us, to him be glory in the church and in Christ Jesus throughout all generations, for ever and ever! Amen" (Eph. 3:20–21).

Thus, we can surely believe that through our miniscule faith in him that God can do magnificent things in us.

A Prayer:

> I believe, Lord, help me with my unbelief.
> Grant me a measure of faith beyond my capacity that I may be a reflection of your infinite power and glory.
> Grow from my small seed of faith a tree others can find fruit on and under which they find restful shade.
> Help my faith to be an unobstructed conduit of your goodness flowing to others.

77
Objectivity

Objectivity is a truth within itself and is possibly the most difficult one to discover. The whole of the Bible is designed to bring us to the conclusion that Jesus is the truth, the objective reality of God. Jesus Christ then is the ultimate standard of objectivity and truth and the Bible, along with creation's revelation, is our pathway to him.

Jesus answered, "I am the way and the truth and the life. No one comes to the Father except through me" (John 14:6).

OBJECTIVITY AND SUBJECTIVITY are within themselves difficult to define. But we all seemingly somehow know they both exist. Subjectivity can feel within us as objectivity. And as well, objectivity can *appear* quite subjective. Jesus, as God's exact earthly representation, is the greatest example of objectivity. But, because he is "the truth" and therefore all his thoughts and opinions are correct, he can seem to us, from our personal perches, as awfully self-absorbed and subjective.

We all live by faith, both in general ways and in particular ways—faith expressed simply as belief in the existence of certain things or people and faith as trust in their reliability. Since the absolute "knowing" of things is, within itself, at best questionable, faith is inevitable in this finite, changing world. We can all too easily be deceived.

We also all must live by reason. Reason and logic are a part of our sensibility. We must rely on our logic and reason, even though they can prove to be flawed. The reality is that faith requires reason and reason requires faith. They are not mutually exclusive; rather they are mutually inclusive. When we seek to cause one to indiscriminately overrule the other, or even exclude the other, we err greatly.

God is completely objective—"You can trust this: Every word that God speaks is true" (Prov. 30:5, Easy-to-Read Version). *Objectivity is the ability to see and understand things without being overly influenced by our own personal feelings, preferences, and prejudices.* It is the ability to see what is true without any personal skew based on feelings and opinions alone.

Every word God speaks is true, because God is truth. It defines him and he defines it! There is a discipline called "hermeneutics" that attempts to bring logic and reason to the interpretation of God's word, as well as other writings, in order to allow objective interpretation. However, hermeneutics can itself be wrought with human subjectivity. But in principle, objectivity first demands logic and reason in thinking, communicating, and interpreting others' communications. We must seek even to be objective about those things that are otherwise subjective and personal to us and others.

Contrary to objectivity, *subjectivity is interpreting and communicating based on feelings, opinions, and personal points of view rather than on evidence and external facts.* Too many times, unfortunately, humanity tends first toward subjectivity rather than objectivity and thereby can be oh-so wrong in regard to even the most important things—"There is a way that appears to be right, but in the end it leads to death" (Prov. 14:12).

Some forms of humanism even argue that there is no objective, absolute truth however and that truth is therefore inherently subjective. And the reality is that what I think or feel, when understood and communicated accurately, is indeed an objective truth within itself. *That* I think or feel a certain way can indeed be true and real *when* what I think or feel is emphatically incorrect or otherwise out of touch with reality!

If there is objective truth, and the believer vehemently affirms by faith in God that to be a reality, then although it is a truth that I think or feel a certain way, but since such thoughts are based on untruths or inaccuracies, the conclusions reached will therefore be baseless and ultimately only subjective. The subjective however is not inherently bad. In fact it is necessary to our existence. But subjectivity must follow objectivity and never be allowed to come before it.

The scripture teaches us to first be objective and says objectivity begins with Jesus—"The Word became flesh and made his dwelling among us. We have seen his glory, the glory of the one and only Son, who came from the Father, full of grace and truth" (John 1:14). Christ is the ultimate revelation of the truth of God, and it is through our seeking out and following what he has taught us that we discover objective truth—"To the Jews who had believed him, Jesus said, 'If you hold to my teaching, you are really my disciples. Then you will know the truth, and the truth will set you free'" (John 8:31–32).

Jesus confidently asserted that all who are seeking the truth would ultimately become followers of him—"Everyone on the side of truth listens to me" (John 18:37). Indeed, if Jesus is the consummate revelation of objective, absolute truth, then those who diligently seek truth will in the end come to believe in Jesus. If that is not the case, then we, as believers in Christ, define futility—"If

Christ has not been raised, our preaching is useless and so is your faith…*If only for this life* we have hope in Christ, we are of all people most to be pitied" (1 Cor. 15:14, 19, italics added).

But Christ was indeed raised from the dead, as attested to by eyewitnesses who were willing to, and did, die standing up for what they had seen and heard—"We cannot help speaking about what we have seen and heard" (Acts 4:20). They repeatedly attested to their personal witness of Jesus's miracle-filled life, his unparalleled teaching, his unjust execution, and finally his miraculous resurrection and ascension—"That which was from the beginning, which we have heard, which we have seen with our eyes, which we have looked at and our hands have touched—this we proclaim concerning the Word of life" (1 John 1:1), and "We did not follow cleverly devised stories when we told you about the coming of our Lord Jesus Christ in power, but we were eyewitnesses of his majesty" (2 Pet. 1:16). History clearly records the impact of their testimony on humankind.

Thus, the apostles and prophets taught that all thoughts must be surrendered to the truth of Christ—"We take captive every thought to make it obedient to Christ" (2 Cor. 10:5). They pointed out that it is the living, breathing word of God that judges the objectivity and truth of our inner thoughts, feelings, and opinions—"The word of God is alive and active. Sharper than any double-edged sword, it penetrates even to dividing soul and spirit, joints and marrow; *it judges the thoughts and attitudes of the heart*" (Heb. 4:12, italics added).

The whole of the Old Testament story is designed to bring us to a reasoned, objective faith in Christ as the fullness of truth and reality—"The law was our tutor to bring us to Christ, that we might be justified by faith. But now that faith has come, we are no longer under a tutor" (Gal. 3:24–25, Modern English Version), and "Everything that was written in the past was written to teach us, so that through the endurance taught in the Scriptures and the encouragement they provide we might have hope" (Rom. 15:4). The whole of the New Testament reveals Christ, confirms Christ as the Son of God, and explains what it means to live in and follow him.

The truth equation is this: objectivity and truth equals Christ—"I am the way and the truth and the life. No one comes to the Father except through me" (John 14:6). He is the universal standard of truth. He is reality revealed in human form. He is the eternal benchmark and the ultimate lens of all objective interpretation. If Christ is not all that, then he is nothing, or even worse. The whole argument of the Bible falls apart. But we believe that Jesus Christ was indeed raised from the dead and that what we confidently assert is true!

A Prayer:

> Lord, I seek only truth, and I come to you because I believe that you are the truth.
> Thus, I seek only you, Lord Jesus.
> Holy Spirit, continue to purify my heart that what I believe is less and less skewed by my own preferences, prejudices, feelings, and opinions.
> Lead me, Divine Father, into the pure truth, as your word is truth.
> May in you and through you I experience the fullness of God.
> Amen.

78
Our Unique Life Sermon

Every life is a unique story and a sermon all its own. Early on, God hands us each a pen and our own piece of paper, and allows us to write much of the story, whether it is by his inspiration or against his will for us. The essence of our faith will be the determinant of the sermon and its underlying message.

Remember your leaders, who spoke the word of God to you. Consider the outcome of their way of life and imitate their faith (Heb. 13:7).

WHILE ALL OF us as humans share a common nature and heritage from God, we are each given a uniqueness and an identity all our own. No matter the similarities that may exist, no other human will ever be exactly like us or live the life we live. Regardless of the diversity that has developed among humanity as we have lived and overseen the earth through the ages, from the beginning there has only been one primary race of image-bearers of God—the human race. The DNA of God is in each of us, and we all derive from that same source. Thus we are in the broadest sense all one big family biologically, and the new humanity, the church, is a family within the family—"For this reason I kneel before the Father, from whom every family in heaven and on earth derives its name" (Eph. 3:14–15).

Although our natural adaptations and diversification as well as our existence under the curse of sin has changed us in both wonderful and troubling ways, we were originally made in the two genders, together reflecting the image of the Creator God himself—"God created mankind in his own image, in the image of God he created them; male and female he created them" (Gen. 1:27). Humanity is the image bearer, inside and out, of God in all creation.

God gave all life forms the germs of regeneration—each kind procreating in unique and wonderful ways. However, in humanity, God breathed his own special spiritual breath of life, such that our procreation itself became a beautiful expression of God's relationship with us. Through love, mating, and intimacy among men and women, God wills that we can not only experience deep inner physical satisfaction but also deep inner spiritual satisfaction in our humanly love bonds.

And too, God gave humans the unique ability to procreate spiritually—to bear his children. God designed for his kingdom children to collectively be his bride and to bear his children—the children of God. The seed of God is implanted in the heart of his church, his bride, and newly born children of God emerge from the living womb of his people—"The Lord added to their number daily those who were being saved" (Acts 2:47). We as believers are each a part of the collective bride of Christ!

Each new person, no matter the circumstances of his or her natural birth be it seen as good or bad, is given God's precious gift of life, both physical and spiritual. God blesses what we do in this regard, whether our exercise of our sexuality is in bounds or out of bounds. Each of us, no matter our human origin, is a wonderfully braided chord from the strands of divinity and humanity. We are each a unique, living tapestry designed by God and woven by acts of our own will as well as the will of others all under the umbrella of God's will. Each of our lives is a unique version of the God and humanity story.

Who we are outwardly is but an expression of what we are inwardly—"Watch out for false prophets. They come to you in sheep's clothing, but inwardly they are ferocious wolves. *By their fruit you will recognize them*" (Matt. 7:15–16, italics added). It is by one's manner and conduct of life that the true inner faith may be known—"Consider the outcome of their way of life and imitate their faith" (Heb. 13:7).

As humans we are prone to being deceived and deceiving—"The heart is deceitful above all things and beyond cure" (Jer. 17:9). It is because of the original deception perpetrated on Adam and Eve. Satan, the perpetrator of the deception, is the original and ultimate liar, and he continues his attempted subversion of God's plan in each of us—"When he lies, he speaks his native language, for he is a liar and the father of lies" (John 8:44), and "We are not unaware of his [Satan's] schemes" (2 Cor. 2:11, brackets added).

Thus we cannot always accept what we may *believe* is the truth about our lives, nor can we accept as certain the seemingly right motives of our moment-to-moment behaviors—"My conscience is clear, but that does not make me innocent" (1 Cor. 4:4). However, what we can know to be true is the outcome of our overall way of life. This cannot be faked—"Show me your faith without deeds, and I will show you my faith by my deeds" (James 2:18). Others cannot (really they should not) always believe what we *say*, but they can, and generally will, believe what we *do*.

Our real life story—our life sermon—is first written on our hearts, either with the wasted ink of futile thinking and living or by the hand of God—"You show that you are a letter from Christ, the result of our ministry, *written not with ink but with the Spirit of the living God,* not on tablets of stone but on tablets of human hearts" (2 Cor. 3:3, italics added).

Our life in general—our gifts, our opportunities, and our challenges and obstacles—reveals our calling. How we utilize our specific gifts and opportunities tells how we have responded to our calling. Thus it might be said that God provides the outline and structure of our lives, and we determine what is said by it.

A Prayer:

> Father, help my life to be a living sermon of praise to you.
> Let each day of my life, each moment of my life, tell the story of your love and goodness to me.
> Inspire me from within, O God, that your praise be in my heart and on my lips.
> Use each unique gift and all my experiences, both good and bad, of my every day to show your wonders.
> May my life be your paper and my will be your ink to write the story you have willed for me.
> Let my strengths and accomplishments be examples of your power.
> Let my failures and sins be examples of your grace expressed in your kindness for me.
> Reveal to me your nature and show me your ways that I may follow you closely.
> Overrule me when my wrong words overwrite your right ones.
> Correct me when my life chords become disharmonic with you.
> And when the final story of me is completed, may every line tell the story of your power, compassion, and mercy in me, and may others be drawn to experience the immeasurable grace, the incomparable goodness, the indescribable joy, and the unbelievable eternal life that I have found in you!
> Amen!

79
Pain and Hardship

In the love of God, pain finds its meaning. Without choice there can be no love. In this life, with choice comes pain.

Not only so, but we also glory in our sufferings, because we know that suffering produces perseverance; perseverance, character; and character, hope (Rom. 5:3).

ONE OF THE greatest causes or excuses for doubt and unbelief is the existence of pain and suffering. It is ironic then that pain and suffering is one of the greatest producers of faith and blessings in us, and that it is also, in fact, one of the greatest manifestations of God's love for us! Times of pain and hardship are, then, a precipice of choice on which we all stand occasionally, and some seemingly often. On it there is, of course, great peril as to which way we will choose to go, or perhaps even fall. Will we choose *to grow* our faith, or will we choose *to let go* of our faith?

God made us beings with choice so we could be *like him*, and thus, *freely love him*. He is a being with choice, and he is love. He gave us choice so that we could *love him*, because godly love must be willed, or it is no love at all. In giving us a choice *for* him, he by necessity had to give us a choice *against* him. Pain and hardship are now not only results of humanity's choices against God, they are, in this fallen world, essential to our coming to, growing in, and becoming like him—"Jesus was the Son of God, but he still suffered, and through his sufferings he learned to obey whatever God says" (Heb. 5:8, Easy-to-Read Version). Thus pain, while not to be sought out, is not inherently bad but often helpful, and it will find you often enough. We ultimately choose whether to let it bring good or bad in us by either getting better because of it or bitter through it. It is our choice. It is fallen humanity that has seemingly and arbitrarily decided that, generally speaking, what is pleasurable to us is somehow good and what is painful to us is bad.

Job is the classic book of the Bible that explores in dramatic fashion the problem of pain and suffering in the human experience. Job's story is humanity's ideal history, given our current fallen state, in that as Job was at the outset seen as "good" by God, as was humanity at our inception. Satan was allowed by God to attack Job—"The Lord said to Satan, 'Very well, then, everything he [Job] has is in your power, but on the man himself do not lay a finger" (Job 1:12). Similarly, he has been allowed to strike humanity—"Woe to the earth and the sea, because the devil has gone down to you! He is filled with fury, because he knows that his time is short" (Rev. 12:12). Job's story is humanity's ideal story in that just as Job stayed faithful to God through trial, that we stay faithful during our time of testing, and in the end just as Job was blessed even more than before, that in the end after our testing is complete, the faithful among humanity will be blessed even more, as well.

In one day, Job lost his ten children, and all his wealth. Then Satan asked and was given permission to afflict Job with a terrible skin disease. Job however did not lose his faith; rather his faith in God was summed up in his brief but profound testimony and its accompanying comment—"'Naked I came from my mother's womb, and naked I will depart. The Lord gave and the Lord has taken away; may the name of the Lord be praised.' In all this, Job did not sin by charging God with wrongdoing" (Job. 1:21–22). Yes, Job's story is quite a testimony to the power of faith. And so can ours be!

Further, Job's painful dilemma apparently lasted for a considerable length of time—"Like a slave longing for the evening shadows, or a hired laborer waiting to be paid, so *I have been allotted months of futility*, and *nights of misery* have been assigned to me" (Job 7:2–3, italics added). Job repeatedly sought from God the reason for his pain and losses, but without forthcoming explanation. At least until his questions for God became a questioning of God. That did not go so well for Job when God did finally answer Job. Job was soundly rebuked from out of a storm for his ignorant questioning—"Who is this that obscures my plans with words without knowledge? Brace yourself like a man; I will question you, and you shall answer me" (Job 38:2–3).

As with Job's, humanity's faith has, no doubt, from our beginning been challenged by the problem of suffering, especially acute or prolonged suffering and hardships faced by those generally deemed more innocent or vulnerable. Each of us must daily reconcile the hardship we see and experience to the validity of faith in a good, loving God. We must understand that God is not like us and he does not see things merely from a short-term, shortsighted human perspective—"As the heavens are higher than the earth, so are my ways higher than your ways and my thoughts than your thoughts" (Isa. 55:9).

There is a fairly simple, albeit difficult, way given to us in the Bible to look at trouble and hardship—"Endure hardship as discipline; God is treating you as his children" (Heb. 12:7). In the existential moment of reckoning, a child cannot for one second appreciate the purpose and good that can come from a painful polio vaccination shot. She may, and likely will, see mom, dad, the doctor, or the nurse as cruel. However, those same adults, with their broader perspective, see and understand that the child's momentary pain is nothing compared to the polio or other disease that vaccination might prevent! Thus, their forcing it upon her. A digital rectal exam for a man or a mammogram for a woman may be painful in the moment, but the purpose is well worth the pain. So it is with our pain before God; in the end it will prove well worth it to those who in both their pains and hardships still trusted him—"I consider that our present sufferings are not worth comparing with the glory that will be revealed in us" (Rom. 8:18), and "For our light and momentary troubles are achieving for us an eternal glory that far outweighs them all" (2 Cor. 4:17).

It comes down to this: do we believe God is good or not? As a child will ultimately come to understand, with his godly, doting parents, that their love and provision far surpasses the hardships they may be forced to allow upon him. Do we not have even more reason to trust God's faithfulness and goodness in spite of our momentary pain? As reasoning adults, can we not make the connection of the disciplines and pains our good earthly parents may need to allow upon us to those of an even better heavenly Father?

There is, then, a twofold question that we must all answer for ourselves otherwise doubt will always swirl around, haunting our faith. Will we discern the purpose of pain and suffering through our belief in a good and loving God, or will we presume upon ourselves, with our temporal, limited perspectives, to judge God somehow guilty because of the existence of pain and suffering? Said another way, will we see the pain, hardship, and testing we endure here as a part of God's love or will we see it as a testimony that he does not love us or perhaps that he does not exist at all?

The Bible gives, as its testimony of God's goodness, the fact that he allowed himself through Jesus to be subjected physically, emotionally, and spiritually, to something worse than any other human has or will ever experience. No other human will ever be as brutalized, unjustly convicted, and cruelly executed for the sins of so many others as was God's only son! He allowed himself to be unjustly tortured and executed on the cross for each and every act of sin committed by every human who will ever live, as if he had committed each sin himself—"For the joy set before him he endured the cross, scorning its shame, and sat down at the right hand of the throne of God. Consider him who endured such opposition from sinners, so that you will not grow weary and lose heart" (Heb. 12:2–3).

Just as God's sacrifice grew out of his tremendous love for us, so the suffering and sacrifices to which he calls us grow out of that same love—"For *God so loved the world that he gave his one and only Son*, that whoever believes in him shall not perish but have eternal life. For God did not send his Son into the world to condemn the world, but to save the world through him" (John 3:16–17, italics added), and "*The Lord disciplines the one he loves*, and he chastens everyone he accepts as his son" (Heb. 12:6, italics added).

Whether our faith matures through or withers in hardship depends wholly on the perspective we take in regard to it. Will we choose to perceive hardship, pain, and suffering as God's loving discipline designed into creation, or will we see it a design flaw of creation? Or might we see pain through a deistic view of God and therefore as an otherwise mere unfortunate happenstance of human existence?

In spite of our idyllic view of early man, as depicted in the Garden of Eden, there was most assuredly an earthly life cycle that involved challenges—"There was evening, and there was morning—the first day" (Gen. 1:5), and "I command lights to appear in the sky and to separate day from night and to show the time for seasons, special days, and years" (Gen. 1:14, Common English Version). Humanity had a responsibility to his home planet—"God gave them his blessing and said: Have a lot of children! Fill the earth with people and bring it under your control. Rule over the fish in the ocean, the birds in the sky, and every animal on the earth" (Gen. 1:28, Common English Version). A definition of "Edenic perfection" is likely as flawed as the rest of us.

But, indeed, our responsibility and work was not a curse but a blessing! There was important work for humanity to do, and thus, there were challenges to be faced—"The Lord God put the man in the Garden of Eden to take care of it and to look after it" (Gen. 2:15, Common English Version). Work itself is not part of the curse; rather work is a blessing. Plant life surely had life cycles. Animal predation surely occurred; therefore, there was death. However literally one might interpret Genesis, it is a sweeping, poetic expression of creation, not a myopic, historical, or scientific explanation of it.

The curse on humanity, because man chose to depend on himself and not God, was that our "care of the Garden" (or the earth) would become much more difficult because of "weeds"—"The ground will be under a curse because of what you did. As long as you live, you will have to struggle to grow enough food. Your food will be plants, but the ground will produce thorns and thistles. You will have to sweat to earn a living; you were made out of soil, and you will once again turn into soil" (Gen. 3:17–19). Food crops must generally be planted and carefully cultivated, and still they are vulnerable to drought, disease, and yes, weeds. Weeds don't have to be planted or cultivated and they seemingly spring up out of nowhere, thriving in the harshest conditions. They often easily choke out more desirable crops. Weeds' existence is clearly also allegorical for sin in the world at large.

The curse that also came on humanity, because of the original bad choice of self-dependence, was that death came over the world—"Dust you are and to dust you will return" (Gen. 3:19), and "Everyone must die once. Then they are judged" (Heb. 9:27, Easy-to-Read Version). Both physical and spiritual death must now be the fate of all humans. Life however is not meant to be lived by fate, rather it is meant to be lived by faith!

In the Bible narrative, hardship, struggle, and death, above and beyond our natural work and responsibilities, came on as a part of the curse. They even became an important part of our survival, physically as well as spiritually. Thus, the believer's take on hardship and trial is to be counter to that of a doubter or unbeliever—"*Consider it pure joy, my brothers and sisters, whenever you face trials of many kinds*, because you know that the testing of your faith produces perseverance. Let perseverance finish its work so that you may be mature and complete, not lacking anything" (James 2:2–4, italics added).

Hardship, pain, suffering, and trial are not to be seen in this present world as a curse but rather as a result of the curse. They are not to be seen as a testimony to the lack of God's existence but rather as a proof of his existence. They are not an expression of God's failures or of his lack of love for us, rather they must be seen as an expression of his love for us.

Get bitter in trial or get better in trial; those are the two choices on either side of the pain and suffering's precipice. The Bible says the "better" choice is indeed immeasurably better—"I consider that our present sufferings are not worth comparing with the glory that will be revealed in us" (Rom. 8:18).

A Prayer:

> Through pleasure or through pain, through serenity or through tumult, may your love flow in and through me.
> In trial, help me to trust you, because of what you've already done, for what you will ultimately do for me.
> May my life always be a humble expression to your love and goodness.
> Let me be a living sermon of your grace expressed in your kindness to me in Christ Jesus.
> Amen.

80
Perseverance

Never ever quit on God, no matter what.

You need to persevere so that when you have done the will of God, you will receive what he has promised. For, "In just a little while, he who is coming will come and will not delay." And, "But my righteous one will live by faith. And I take no pleasure in the one who shrinks back." But we do not belong to those who shrink back and are destroyed, but to those who have faith and are saved (Heb. 10:36–39).

MANY ARE THEY who start; far fewer are those who finish—"For many are invited, but few are chosen" (Matt. 22:14). It is because the journey to finding the life of God is narrow and difficult to maintain—"For wide is the gate and broad is the road that leads to destruction, and many enter through it. But small is the gate and narrow the road that leads to life, and only a few find it" (Matt. 7:13–14).

The seed—the word of God—has been planted worldwide—"The gospel that you heard...has been proclaimed to every creature under heaven" (Col. 1:23). Still today, after the waxing and waning of the faith over the last two millennia, only in a few places in the world is God's gospel still easily avoided. And regardless, God has promised himself to all who seek him—"Seek and you will find" (Matt. 7:7).

Jesus gave a parable of a man sowing crops to show the categories we fall into according to our receptivity to his message—"A farmer went out to sow his seed. As he was scattering the seed, some fell along the path, and the birds came and ate it up. Some fell on rocky places, where it did not have much soil. It sprang up quickly, because the soil was shallow. But when the sun came up, the plants were scorched, and they withered because they had no root. Other seed fell among thorns, which grew up and choked the plants. Still other seed fell on good soil, where it produced a crop—a hundred, sixty or thirty times what was sown" (Matt. 13:3–8).

Jesus explained his parable (Matt. 13:18–23). He said that there are many whose hearts are hardened; therefore, Satan finds it easy to snatch away God's word from them. These are as the seeds on the hardened ground of the walking path. That there are many who are shallow, and although they outwardly appear willing to accept God, inwardly they are hard and closed-minded. Hence, God's word can take no root inside of them. Their seeming acceptance of Christ withers quickly under the heat of life, as with the seed on rocky places. Further, there are many who are willing to accept Christ, but because they are also willing to accept far too many other things in their lives, their life clutter chokes God's word out, as with the seeds falling among thorns and weeds. Finally, there are the few who will not only commit to God but will also remain committed to God for life. These are as the seeds on the good soil. The faithful are those who hear God's word, carefully examine it studiously, and when convinced of its veracity, eagerly internalize it—"They received the message with great eagerness and examined the Scriptures every day" (Acts 17:11).

Only one category of hearers—those who are like seed on the good soil—perseveres to growth and fruitfulness. These are the few who find the life of God. Unfortunately, the other three categories line the road that leads to destruction.

Living the life of God takes patience, persistence, consistency, and yes, perseverance! One must begin the journey with the end in mind, that is, the blessed hope that God gives us—"Therefore, since we have such a hope, we are very bold" (2 Cor. 3:13), and "Therefore, since through God's mercy we have this ministry, *we do not lose heart*" (2 Cor. 4:1, italics added). Discouragement in such an endeavor as seeking and serving God is inevitable; giving up, however, is not!

The one who has never wanted to give up is the one who has never really tried anything difficult. The one who has never wanted to give up is the one who has never suffered badly. The one who has never wanted to quit something is the one who has not yet actually faced up to the faith crises that are inevitable in this present life!

But there are many who have gone before us in this walk of faith that can attest to not only our own ability to walk this walk, but also to the worth of doing so—"Therefore, since *we are surrounded by such a great cloud of witnesses*, let us throw off everything that hinders and the sin that so easily entangles. And let us run with perseverance the race marked out for us, fixing our eyes on Jesus, the pioneer and perfecter of faith. For the joy set before him he endured the cross, scorning its shame, and sat down at the right hand of the throne of God. Consider him who endured such opposition from sinners, so that you will not grow weary and lose heart" (Heb. 12:1–3, italics added).

We too then must be resolute that we will not only strive to forge ahead, never giving up, but also will determine to thrive during the journey itself, anticipating the rich rewards that lie ahead—"But as for you, be strong and do not give up, for your work will be rewarded" (2 Chron. 15:7). Even in the direst of circumstances, as with the ancient Jews of the dispersal, in God, great hope lies ahead—"'For I know the plans I have for you,' declares the LORD, 'plans to prosper you and not to harm you, plans to give you hope and a future'" (Jer. 29:11). As we face such challenges, God wills us to be bold, strong, and full of courage—"Have I not commanded you? Be strong and courageous. Do not be afraid; do not be discouraged, for the LORD your God will be with you wherever you go" (Josh. 1:9).

Though dark days seem long in facing them, they will seem but a wisp in our redeemed eternity—"But do not forget this one thing, dear friends: With the Lord a day is like a thousand years, and a thousand years are like a day. The Lord is not slow in keeping his promise, as some understand slowness. Instead he is patient with you, not wanting anyone to perish, but everyone to come to repentance" (2 Pet. 3:8–9). Thus in this brief moment of what is our present life, we must never ever, for any reason or under any circumstance, quit in our hot pursuit of God—"Let us not become weary in doing good, for at the proper time we will reap a harvest if we do not give up" (Gal. 6:9). A rich harvest is in store for those who do not give up.

And, the greater the sacrifices we must make or the suffering we must endure for the kingdom's sake, the greater the reward that God has for us—"Anyone who has left house, husband, wife, brothers, sisters, parents, or children because of God's kingdom will receive many times more in this age and eternal life in the coming age" (Luke 18:29–30). Thus, although we will indeed tire physically, we must never allow ourselves to succumb to that fatigue spiritually, mentally, or emotionally—"And as for you, brothers and sisters, never tire of doing what is good" (2 Thess. 3:13). For there is great blessing and promise to the one who sticks with it—"Blessed is the one who perseveres under trial because, having stood the test, that person will receive the crown of life that the Lord has promised to those who love him" (James 1:12).

To truly love God is to persevere with him; to love others is to persevere with them—“Love *bears all things* [regardless of what comes], believes all things [looking for the best in each one], hopes all things [remaining steadfast during difficult times], *endures all things* [*without weakening*]” (1 Cor. 13:7, Amplified Bible, italics added). Although apart from God the strongest among us weaken and even fall, those who live in and stick with God will ultimately grow stronger through trial and suffering—“Even youths grow tired and weary, and young men stumble and fall; but those who hope in the Lord will renew their strength. They will soar on wings like eagles; they will run and not grow weary, they will walk and not be faint” (Isa. 40:30–31).

Our endurance is because through Christ we have learned the secret to patience and persistence in this present life. He is our hope. He is our “secret” to not only enduring but also to thriving in all circumstances—“I have learned to be content whatever the circumstances. I know what it is to be in need, and I know what it is to have plenty. I have learned the secret of being content in any and every situation, whether well fed or hungry, whether living in plenty or in want. I can do all this through him who gives me strength” (Phil. 4:10–13).

Although we cannot yet in this present life experience the glorious finality of our faith, we can indeed experience the glorious determination of it—“Not that I have already obtained all this, or have already arrived at my goal, but I press on to take hold of that for which Christ Jesus took hold of me. Brothers and sisters, I do not consider myself yet to have taken hold of it. But one thing I do: Forgetting what is behind and straining toward what is ahead, I press on toward the goal to win the prize for which God has called me heavenward in Christ Jesus” (Phil. 3:12–14).

And our God promised us in his own voice from heaven that our efforts will all be well worth it—“Then I heard a voice from heaven say, ‘Write this: Blessed are the dead who die in the Lord from now on.' 'Yes,' says the Spirit, 'they will rest from their labor, for their deeds will follow them'" (Rev. 14:13).

A Prayer:

> O Lord, measure out to me a determined heart of faith.
> May I be undeterred in my seeking of you.
> May I be unyielding in my devotion to you.
> May I be unfettered in my service for you.
> In you I find hope, Lord.
> In you I find strength, Lord.
> In you I find resoluteness, Lord.
> You are my only lot and in you I place all my hope.
> Complete me, my Savior, that I may finish this race in you
> and for you.
> Amen.

81
Prayer, Part 1

Prayer is not about informing God of anything or daring to instruct him on what is needed. Nor is it even so much about overly influencing him. Prayer, purely and simply, is about surrendering to him.

My Father, if it is possible, may this cup be taken from me. Yet not as I will, but as you will (Matt. 26:39).

JESUS TAUGHT US the significance of prayer by praying himself—"Jesus often withdrew to lonely places and prayed" (Luke 5:16). He not only prayed often but also, because of the rigors of his daily challenge, he prayed early, most assuredly in order to be unbothered by others for a bit—"Very early in the morning, while it was still dark, Jesus got up, left the house and went off to a solitary place, where he prayed" (Mark 1:35). His prayers seemed mostly, in various ways, to be prayers of surrender. The disciples noticed his prayers and wanted to learn from Jesus how to connect with God through prayer—"Lord, teach us to pray" (Luke 11:1).

His teaching on prayer was really quite simple—"Pray, then, in this way: 'Our Father, who is in heaven, Hallowed be Your name...'"

(Matt. 6:9). Prayer is not about informing an omniscient God about things he needs to know—"Your Father knows what you need before you ask him" (Matt. 6:8). Prayer is not about impressing an eager, spectating God with our powers of oratory or needs enumeration and explanation—"And when you pray, do not keep on babbling like pagans, for they think they will be heard because of their many words" (Matt. 6:7).

Neither is prayer about impressing others around us—"And when you pray, do not be like the hypocrites, for *they love to pray standing in the synagogues and on the street corners to be seen by others*. Truly I tell you, they have received their reward in full. But when you pray, go into your room, close the door and pray to your Father, who is unseen. Then your Father, who sees what is done in secret, will reward you" (Matt. 6:5–6, italics added). In order for prayers to be prayers of surrender to him, they must be sincerely and worshipfully meant for him—"God is spirit, and his worshipers must worship in the Spirit and in truth" (John 4:24).

Prayer is about worship and surrender. Prayer is about humbling our self in order to seek God in truth and sincerity—"But the tax collector stood at a distance. He wouldn't even lift his eyes to look toward heaven. Rather he struck his chest and said, 'God, show mercy to me, a sinner'" (Luke 18:13, Common English Bible). Prayer is all about changing us and not at all about changing God. It is about calling God's attention to us by giving all our attention to him.

Because it is in our surrender to him that we find help from him! It is in conforming our will to his that we find peace in him. Likely, this is why our prayer forms, postures, and positions—kneeling, bowing, standing, lying prostate, lifting hands, speaking loudly, whispering, singing, praying silently, and so forth—matter. They matter most to us because our body postures affect how we see and feel in respect to God and others as we speak to them. They matter most to God because they matter so much to us—how we open ourselves up to him to both give the communications of our hearts and minds and receive spiritual communication from him.

But prayer must not be allowed to be a source of guilt in us for not praying often enough, long enough, or as thoroughly as we might desire. Prayer must not be seen as merely a meritorious act to gain favor from the God who offers his mercy for free. Prayers through Jesus are a recognition and reception of God's grace. Therefore prayer must never be seen as some ascetic discipline designed to cause us pain and to abase us in order to placate a fearsome God.

Prayer must be seen as a blessed activity where we find respite and peace—"Come to me, all of you who are struggling and burdened, and I will give you rest" (Matt. 11:28). Prayer is where we realign ourselves with God, recognizing him as God rather than trying to play such a daunting and impossible role ourselves! Prayer is at the cutting edge of worship, where, in our hearts, the kingdom of God ultimately rules and resides—"But in your hearts set Christ apart [as holy—acknowledging Him, giving Him first place in your lives] as Lord" (1 Pet. 3:15, Amplified Bible). Through prayer, all is reset to as it should be, with Jesus on the throne of our heart and us at his feet, how it was in the beginning, and as it will be in the eternity.

Jesus obviously found consolation through prayer in experiencing closeness to God, such that he prayed sustained prayers, certainly not of constant chattering to God (see the minimal content of his lengthy prayer times as depicted in Gethsemane), but in the sustained, conscious, spiritual presence of God—"One of those days Jesus went out to a mountainside to pray, and spent the night praying to God" (Luke 6:12). He demonstrated that there is a powerful presence of God that comes on us through our prayers to him—"Therefore I tell you, whatever you ask for in prayer, believe that you have received it, and it will be yours" (Mark 11:24).

Jesus teaches us that prayer should bring us to an earnestness concerning what we seek—"Then Jesus told his disciples a parable to show them that they should always pray and not give up" (Luke 18:1). It is this earnestness that brings us confidence—"This is the confidence we have in approaching God: that if we ask anything according to his will, he hears us" (1 John 5:14). Such prayer produces in us strength to face trial and temptation—"Watch and pray so that you will not fall into temptation. The spirit is willing, but the flesh is weak" (Matt. 26:41). Even in our trials and despair, such prayers of broken heartedness draw God near to us—"The Lord is close to the brokenhearted and saves those who are crushed in spirit" (Ps. 34:18).

When we get ourselves right before him, he is finally able to do what is right for us—"If my people, who are called by my name, will humble themselves and pray and seek my face and turn from their wicked ways, then I will hear from heaven, and I will forgive their sin and will heal their land" (2 Chron. 7:14). As we position ourselves aright in relationship to him, he is able to position himself aright in regard to us—"God opposes the proud but shows favor to the humble" (James 4:6). When we bear our own fruit of humility and trust toward him, he bears his fruit of peace and blessing within us—"Rejoice in the Lord always. I will say it again: Rejoice! Let your gentleness be evident to all. The Lord is near. Do not be anxious about anything, but in every situation, by prayer and petition, with thanksgiving, present your requests to God. And the peace of God, which transcends all understanding, will guard your hearts and your minds in Christ Jesus" (Phil. 4:4–7).

Thus, our nonburdensome objective toward him is to pray early, pray often, and pray always—"And pray in the Spirit on all occasions with all kinds of prayers and requests. With this in mind, be alert and always keep on praying for all the Lord's people" (Eph. 6:18).

Just do it—pray.

A Prayer:

> Father, teach us to pray as you taught the men and women of old.
> Teach us to pray as you showed us to pray.

Give us hearts *to* pray as you have the heart *for* us to pray.
Help us to find consolation in prayer and not guilt.
Help us to find freedom in prayer and not bondage.
Help us to find confidence in prayer and not shame and fear.
Help us to find peace in prayer and not troubling tumult of heart.
Be our refuge, be our guide, be our consoler, O gracious Lord!
I surrender it all to you, Lord, and humbly receive back as generous and precious gifts all the good that comes from you.
Amen.

82
Prayer, Part 2

Prayer is not about me changing God; it's about God changing me.

But when you pray, go into your room, close the door and pray to your Father, who is unseen. Then your Father, who sees what is done in secret, will reward you (Matt. 6:6).

PRAYER IS DIFFICULT, as faith is difficult. Am I merely speaking to the wind? Am I simply speaking to the walls? One who has not experienced difficulty in prayer is the one who has not encountered, or at least not recognized, the realities of faith challenges—"Stay awake and pray for strength against temptation. Your spirit wants to do what is right, but your body is weak" (Matt. 26:41, Easy-to-Read Version).

Faith calls us beyond our present existence. It forces us to believe beyond our own borders. There are of course the all the stories, biblical and otherwise, from "beyond" our present realm. There are the unexplained realities within the present that can be explained only from outside of it. Our borders themselves—the walls of the present—clearly reveal a greater reality beyond them—"Since the creation of the world God's invisible qualities—his eternal power and divine nature—have been clearly seen, being understood from what has been made" (Rom. 1:20).

Those who have come before us were restricted by the same boundaries; those who come after us will be as well. These were set up by God—"From one man he made all the nations, that they should inhabit the whole earth; and he marked out their appointed times in history and the boundaries of their lands" (Acts 17:26). They were set up with great purpose—"God did this so that they would seek him and perhaps reach out for him and find him, though he is not far from any one of us" (Acts 17:27).

This present finite existence emanates from God's infinite one. Ours is not apart *from* his; ours is a part *of* his. God is not somewhere else; he is near each of us, because while his realm is not easily experientially accessible from ours, ours is from his—"In him we live and move and have our being" (Acts 17:28).

God is unchanging in nature. He is not to be defined by any human desires or notions. Nothing we do changes him. We do not define him; he defines us. He does not need to find us; we need to find him. He desires to interact with and responds to the prayers of his people. He has designed it that way. In prayer, we connect with him so that he will engage us, and thus, better us and our situations. We also intercede for others with him similarly.

God's immutability—his unchanging nature—is clearly affirmed by scripture—"I the LORD do not change" (Mal. 3:6), and "Jesus Christ is the same yesterday and today and forever" (Heb. 13:8). Further, his eternal, invisible qualities are observable in and through creation—"The invisible things about Him—His eternal power and deity—have been clearly seen since the creation of the world and are understood by the things that are made" (Rom. 1:20, Modern English Version).

While his immutability is affirmed as a part of Christian orthodoxy, it is not so easily understood, and any shallow acceptance and interpretation of it can prove most prohibitive to a meaningful relationship with him. A naïve, thoughtless view of God will be very detrimental to productive prayer.

When we pray, we are speaking out of our finiteness into his infiniteness. His reality comprehends ours; ours presently can only scratch the surface in relating to his. And yet in Christ we have been given access to and existence in the heavenly realms—"God raised us up with Christ and seated us with him in the heavenly realms in Christ Jesus" (Eph. 2:6).

In that our operational capabilities in this present realm are limited inside the heavenly realm, the Holy Spirit within us serves as the link and as our enabler—"Also, the Spirit helps us. We are very weak, but the Spirit helps us with our weakness. We don't know how to pray as we should, but the Spirit himself speaks to God for us. He begs God for us, speaking to him with feelings too deep for words. God already knows our deepest thoughts. And he understands what the Spirit is saying, because the Spirit speaks for his people in the way that agrees with what God wants." (Rom. 8:26–27).

By his design, God engages us when we engage him through how he has made us and what he has given us. And his transformative power regenerates within us powers lost from the fall. His power energizes capabilities in us that, due to the original "power failure," were left silent in this present dark existence—"If my people, who are called by my name, will humble themselves and pray and seek my face and turn from their wicked ways, then I will hear from heaven, and I will forgive their sin and will heal their land" (2 Chron. 7:14).

When we behold and contemplate his immutable and perfect nature, revealed in human form through Christ Jesus, and we seek him experientially through prayerful engagement, he transforms us to be more like him—"And we all, who with unveiled faces contemplate the Lord's glory, are being transformed into his image with ever-increasing glory, which comes from the Lord, who is the Spirit" (2 Cor. 3:18). He is not to be changed by us; we are to be changed by him. Our prayers are not telling him something he doesn't already know. Rather our prayers are helping us access what he knows that we do not. Our prayers are not helping him become something he is not already. They are helping us become something we are not but can and should be. And our prayers to him prepare us for what he will do to and for us.

However, the older, orthodox understanding of his unchanging nature, that seems to have crept into parts of the church over the ages, can cause a view of God as somehow unalive, static, and even benign. It can be quite deistic, really, implying God is emotionless and unmoved by our concerns. Such an arcane view can only mute dynamic and hopeful prayer.

"Let us then approach God's throne of grace with confidence, so that we may receive mercy and find grace to help us in our time of need" (Heb. 4:16).

Prayer makes a difference, with both God and with us!

A Prayer:

> O Lord, as we observe and experience your unchanging nature, let us believe that it is a part of your nature to be dynamic, active, and transformative.
>
> Help us to see you as alive and active and to believe that out of your unchanging, infinite nature, you respond and engage us in our ever-changing nature and world.
>
> Help us, Holy Spirit, through revelation and creation to understand more and more about God.
>
> Strengthen us in our present mortal nature that we may engage you in your eternal immortal one.
>
> Change, grow, and transform us in our present form as we contemplate and behold your already glorious existence.
>
> Amen.

83
Pride

Pride is at the root of all evil. It is the prime motive of sin. It is the great divider of people and the ultimate destroyer of humankind. Pride always leads to failure. Pride is the essence of evil itself.

Pride goes before destruction, a haughty spirit before a fall (Prov. 16:18).

PRIDE WEARS MANY masks. Pride in fact always wears masks. It hides. It deceives both the one who dares wear it and the one who looks on—"Anyone who listens to the word but does not do what it says is like someone who looks at his face in a mirror and, after looking at himself, goes away and immediately forgets what he looks like" (James 1:23–24).

Pride is the great divider of humankind, including the church. Pride is in fact the prime motive of evil. Pride's greatest weapon still, even in modern Christianity, is the fruit of the "Tree of the Knowledge of Good and Evil." It represents the principle of knowing right and wrong, good and evil, and living it out on our own—living by the principle of law and the basic principles of the world. It was manifested in Israel in the Law of Moses, the requirements God placed on the children of Israel as their part of their covenant with him, which they found impossible to keep in toto—"For whoever keeps the whole law and yet stumbles at just one point is guilty of breaking all of it" (James 2:10). The law principle manifests itself in Christianity through the approach to the Bible often used by Protestants and Evangelicals alike—believing we are *right* with God because we are *right* in certain things about God. Unfortunately, we find this most deadly tree with its toxic fruit planted squarely in the middle of our sanctuaries. Bowls of its fruit are served at our fellowships. We share it in our living rooms and at mealtimes.

We bask in its glorious shade—seemingly often blocking out the light himself. Our presumptive, self-righteous, narrow-minded, self-centered, and ultimately misguided attempts to somehow gain monopolies on God and his kingdom by being biblically "right" have led us to the greatest of wrongs. That wrong is to, in the name of Christ, subvert the very plan of God to, through Christ, finally unite heaven and earth. We have dared use God's revelation to gain presumed power and prestige for ourselves, and in doing so divided his people at our very faith core. A right faith in Jesus should unite; it is a flawed faith that tears us apart.

Jesus is the Bond of Peace through whom the Unity of the Spirit can be maintained—"Make every effort to keep the unity of the Spirit through the bond of peace" (Eph. 4:3), and "For he himself is our peace" (Eph. 2:14). In fact, only Jesus can fully unify us, the new humanity. It is a tragedy, and it is surely a huge disappointment to God, that we have used the revelation of Jesus, who is in fact the Tree of Life and the Bond of Peace, to be to us the Tree of the Knowledge of Good and Evil, dividing us from one another and even from God. And thus it has prompted us to murder our own brothers and sisters, as Cain did to his brother Abel, in the cause of our alleged service to God. The likely purpose being the same—to boast in our own knowledge and righteousness rather than trusting in God's. There is nothing new in this sin; it is in fact a reenactment of the original one.

Pride is seen in the secular world through the displacement of God in individuals and societies. We take pride in ourselves, and we boldly deny God and the truths about God—"In the pride of his face the wicked does not seek him; all his thoughts are, 'There is no God'" (Ps. 10:4, English Standard Version). We become humanistic, centering our view of the world around ourselves, rather than our creator—"They exchanged the truth about God for a lie, and worshiped and served created things rather than the Creator" (Rom. 1:25). However, by the very nature of the secular argument itself, it is denied that humans have any real value beyond the present.

Still, we would rather believe nothing created something and go on pretending we are our own "gods," than to discover the reality of the one who created everything—Yahweh, the Ever Existent One. To admit that God is the Tree of Life means to admit that we are not. To admit that we must eat of him to truly live, we must admit that we have no life without him. To admit we must rely on God, we must admit that we, apart from him, are unreliable. None of which is desirable to us in our prideful, fallen, sinful condition. Secularism prefers the bitter taste of the fruit of the Tree of the Knowledge of Good and Evil over that of the Tree of Life because it allows us to feel important *apart from God*, rather than *because of God*. Secularism prefers the forbidden fruit even though, in denying God, it denies the Tree's very existence. And even though the fruit continues to wreak havoc on humanity, secularism prefers to blame faith for the world's problems.

Pride in the religious world at large is seen in the displacement of the true God by our historical religions and human-derived god paradigms. Our religion is *right* because it is ours! It is our heritage. It connects us with our past and with our ancestors. It makes us feel unique and special. Because it feeds our egos, we are willing to ignore blatant ignorance, proven unreliability, and obvious human origins. Let nothing get in the way of what we want to believe! Religion at large, and even Christianity, when it is reduced to mere religion, is the cause of vast amounts human destruction and social havoc. This is not however caused by sincere faith in the one God; it is caused by insincere faith in us and our religions under the *guise* of faith in God!

Pride in the church at large is seen in our displacement of God by our doctrinal egos. Although we would deny it, we too often, rather than priding ourselves only in knowing the true God and Jesus Christ his Son, pride ourselves in the rightness of our doctrines, believing *we* are right because *we* are right. We often mistakenly believe that we prove ourselves right when we prove others wrong. We compete with our sister churches over relatively minor points of doctrine, ignoring what Jesus said were more important doctrines, such as love and unity, which he said were to be the distinguishing marks of our genuineness—"A new command I give you: Love one another. As I have loved you, so you must love one another. By this everyone will know that you are my disciples, if you love one another" (John 13:34–35). Sadly, rare is the church known first by its love. Perhaps even rarely do churches try to do so!

The problem is not in seeking what is true and right, for that is a good thing. The problem is in taking pride in thinking we always *are* right. All while reluctantly admitting that we are never perfectly right about anything, and certainly not everything, and that our willingness to do so is essential to our continued growing and learning. We simply too often make concrete what is biblically not, and we even turn positions on arguable doctrines into alleged conditions of salvation and Christian fellowship. And to support our egotism, we seemingly often pay large salaries to those individuals and institutions that most consistently make us feel "right"—"They will gather around them a great number of teachers to say what their itching ears want to hear" (2 Tim. 4:3). However, believing *in* God should come before we settle in on too many specifics concerning what we believe *about* God.

Any confidence in ourselves or in anything human that supersedes confidence in God is of pride. And, "Pride goes before destruction, a haughty spirit before a fall" (Prov. 16:18). God finds pride in us repulsive and simply will not bide too much of it—"The Lord detests all the proud of heart. Be sure of this: They will not go unpunished" (Prov. 16:5). He not only rejects our pride but also resists us in it—"He mocks proud mockers but shows favor to the humble and oppressed" (Prov. 3:34). Human pride is simply not from God or of God; it is of the evil of this present age—"For everything in the world—the lust of the flesh, the lust of the eyes, and the pride of life—comes not from the Father but from the world" (1 John 2:16). The child of God is to do nothing out of prideful, self-centered motives—"Do nothing out of selfish ambition or vain conceit. Rather in humility value others above yourselves" (Phil. 2:3).

Our pride turns us from the wisdom of God and to the ways of humanity. And thus, "There is more hope for a fool than for them" (Prov. 26:12).

A Prayer:

> O Holy God, turn me from my pride and self-reliance.
> Defeat within me any of illusion of independence from you.
> Show me your way and your wisdom that I might find you and rely on you.
> Grant me a humble spirit and call me to you.
> Wash me of the filth and grime that is my ugly pride!
> O Holy Spirit, conform me to the image of the true meek and lowly one, Jesus Christ!
> Amen.

84
Questions versus Questioning

In seeking truth, the hardest thing to get at is the right question.

Ask and it will be given to you; seek and you will find; knock and the door will be opened to you. For everyone who asks receives; the one who seeks finds; and to the one who knocks, the door will be opened (Matt. 7:7–8).

THERE IS A vast difference between asking God questions and actually questioning God. The right questions can be the gateways to truth, the keys to understanding, and the mineshaft to the mother lode. A question can serve mentally as a file folder for learning and holding onto truth! A questioning thought inside our head becomes a safe repository for storing what we are learning along the way and a place to draw insights and thoughts from to begin processing more complex ideas. We should, in fact, open a question file folder, so to speak, on truths to be more fully understood, and never consider the file closed until God's final revelation in redemption. We must never staple it closed or allow it to be sealed by anyone else but God.

The difference between asking an honest, open question and questioning God lies in the intent. Asking God questions represents seeking to grow and understand. Questioning God, on the other hand, represents lack of trust in him or doubting his intent—"But who are you, a human being, to talk back to God? Shall what is formed say to the one who formed it, 'Why did you make me like this?'" (Rom. 9:20).

Outwardly, a question may appear to be humble and sincere when, in fact, inwardly it is prideful and even accusatory. And what may at first appear to be questioning God may actually represent honest, searching questions. We must search our own hearts in the matter. We may not always know for sure, but God's grace is for sure—"My conscience is clear, but that does not make me innocent. It is the Lord who judges me" (1 Cor. 4:4). However, God always knows our intent—"The Lord searches all hearts *and* minds, and understands every intent *and* inclination of the thoughts" (1 Chron. 28:9, Amplified Bible). And he will expose our inner yearnings back to us, if indeed we seek him through his word—"For the word of God is alive and active. Sharper than any double-edged sword, it penetrates even to dividing soul and spirit, joints and marrow; *it judges the thoughts and attitudes of the heart*" (Heb. 4:12, italics added).

Honest questions flow out of humble hearts seeking to learn at the feet of our all-knowing God. Questioning God flows out of the prideful hearts of those who would dare doubt or even accuse him. Asking humble questions of God in order for us to learn is good and desirable. Any prideful questioning of God will not bring us a desirable outcome—"God opposes the proud but shows favor to the humble" (1 Pet. 5:5). If we dare seek to indict him on any account,

God will most definitely rather indict us on every account—"Then the Lord spoke to Job out of the storm. He said: 'Who is this that obscures my plans with words without knowledge? Brace yourself like a man; I will question you, and you shall answer me'" (Job 38:1–3). And we are indeed guilty; he is certainly not—"Let God be true, and every human being a liar" (Rom. 3:4).

Mere fairness demands that we assume others innocent until proven guilty. How much more should we examine God with such fairness? Because God is just, he is fair. And because he is just, he wants us to be just and therefore fair—"He has shown you, O mortal, what is good. And *what does the Lord require of you*? *To act justly* and to love mercy and to walk humbly with your God" (Mic. 6:8, italics added). Especially toward him! And he wants us to be fair to others—"For in the same way you judge others, you will be judged, and with the measure you use, it will be measured to you" (Matt. 7:2).

Good relationships require trust. Trust must be built through observing the deeper and more important aspects of another person that are observable and knowable, so that in the things that are not so easily known or observed, trust can otherwise be extended. And in our relationship with him, God has given us all the observable and objective reasons we need to have faith in him, so that in those things that are not observable and are difficult to understand, we can still trust him.

Creation declares that God is good. Humanity has been blessed with wonderful things. The basic fiber of creation is beautiful and good—"God saw all that he had made, and it was very good" (Gen. 1:31). Evil and bad are corruptions of the good, not some other things coexistent with it. And scripture clearly demonstrates the goodness of God, the pinnacle of its demonstration being his sacrifice on the cross—"In your relationships with one another, have the same mind-set as Christ Jesus: Who, being in very nature God, did not consider equality with God something to be used to his own advantage; rather *he made himself nothing* by taking the very nature of a servant, being made in human likeness. And being found in appearance as a man, he humbled himself by becoming obedient to death—even death on a cross!" (Phil. 2:5–8, italics added).

God promises us as his people that he will work out everything for our good—"And we know that in all things God works for the good of those who love him, who have been called according to his purpose" (Rom. 8:28). He clearly and definitively demonstrated his all-surpassing love for us, once and for all—"You see, at just the right time, when we were still powerless, Christ died for the ungodly. Very rarely will anyone die for a righteous person, though for a good person someone might possibly dare to die. But *God demonstrates his own love for us in this: While we were still sinners, Christ died for us*" (Rom. 5:6–8, italics added).

If that is so, then what should be our honest response to God in the matter: humble sincere questions of clarification and understanding or interrogative, accusatory questions?—"*What, then, shall we say in response to these things*? If God is for us, who can be against us? He who did not spare his own Son, but gave him up for us all—how will he not also, along with him, graciously give us all things? Who will bring any charge against those whom God has chosen? It is God who justifies. Who then is the one who condemns? No one. Christ Jesus who died—more than that, who was raised to life—is at the right hand of God and is also interceding for us. Who shall separate us from the love of Christ? Shall trouble or hardship or persecution or famine or nakedness or danger or sword?" (Rom. 8:31–35, italics added).

God has more than proven himself loving and faithful, and thus, worthy of our trust. We should by all means extend trust to him. We have not and cannot earn his trust of us, and yet he has freely extended it to us, because he is indeed the definition of love itself, and the love of God is trusting—"It [Love] always protects, *always trusts*, always hopes, always perseveres" (1 Cor. 13:7). Because he loves us, he even trust us with his mission—"All this is from God, who has reconciled us to Himself through Jesus Christ and has given to us the ministry of reconciliation, that is, that God was in Christ reconciling the world to Himself, not counting their sins against them, and *has entrusted to us the message of reconciliation*. So we are ambassadors for Christ, as though God were pleading through us. We implore you in Christ's stead: Be reconciled to God" (2 Cor. 5:18–20, Modern English Version, italics added).

Certainly, we should take all our questions to God—"If any of you lacks wisdom, you should ask God, who gives generously to all without finding fault, and it will be given to you" (James 1:5). But for countless very good reasons, we should not doubt him or question his goodness and judgments—"But when you ask, you must believe and not doubt, because the one who doubts is like a wave of the sea, blown and tossed by the wind. That person should not expect to receive anything from the Lord. *Such a person is double-minded and unstable in all they do*" (James 1:6–8, italics added).

God has all the answers, and he is completely trustworthy. We will do well to behave similarly.

A Prayer:

Lord, teach me to believe,
Because of all that you have done,
Teach me e'er to trust,
Your one and only Son.

Open my eyes to the good,
You've shown in every way;
Teach me love and trust,
In all I do and say.

Give me a humble heart,
Fully open to all of you,

Make my faith in you complete—
The trust that you are due.

Defeat in me all doubt,
To question your intent,
Make all my prayers to you "Amens,"
With ne'er hint of doubtful dissent!

85
Reasonable Faith

There is no real faith without reason, and there is no reason without faith.

The fool says in his heart, "There is no God" (Ps. 14:1).

FAITH AND REASON are only in conflict when faith is bad and poorly construed or when reasoning is poor or illogical. Both faith and reason are essential to a meaningful human experience. One *must* live by faith; it is not optional in this present age. In fact, one cannot *not* live by faith in something or someone. The only real question can be: in what or in whom does our faith lie?

Similarly, one must also live by reason. Whether or not we can see it or understand it, there is a reason for everything human. Insanity and illogic are reasons within themselves for certain seemingly insane, illogical human behaviors.

Biblical faith, by definition, is based on reason—"Now faith is the assurance (title deed, confirmation) of things hoped for (divinely guaranteed), and the evidence of things not seen [the conviction of their reality—faith comprehends as fact what cannot be experienced by the physical senses]" (Heb. 11:1, Amplified Bible). Faith is about confidence based on reasonable evidence. Faith is a decision based on some reasonable assurance. Biblical hope is a confident expectation, not merely a faint wish. Faith without sensibility and valid reason is only superstition. Alleged reason apart from faith is clearly "reason" that is in denial.

The one who cannot believe in the unseen is the blindest person of all!—"So we fix our eyes not on what is seen, but on what is unseen, since what is seen is temporary, but what is unseen is eternal" (2 Cor. 4:18). The unseen and seen are parts of the whole, not wholly separates. They are integrated. And what is seen emanates from the unseen—not the other way around—"For since the creation of the world God's invisible qualities—his eternal power and divine nature—have been clearly seen, being understood from what has been made, so that people are without excuse" (Rom. 1:20). The world is the artwork and engineering of God, and as humanity—male and female—we bear his actual image.

There is infinitely more to know than can be seen with human eyes—"What no eye has seen, what no ear has heard, and what no human mind has conceived—the things God has prepared for those who love him—these are the things God has revealed to us by his Spirit" (1 Cor. 2:9–10). Humanity has from the beginning been given a spiritual antenna by which to tune into the eternal and invisible. We must however seek it out and train this faculty within us—"You will seek me and find me when you seek me with all your heart" (Jer. 29:13). We must pray for the development of these inner eyes of ours—"I keep asking that the God of our Lord Jesus Christ, the glorious Father, may give you the Spirit of wisdom and revelation, so that you may know him better. I pray that the eyes of your heart may be enlightened…" (Eph. 1:17–18).

Reason requires reasonable faith, and faith requires faithful reason. Honesty and objectivity are essential to the fair pursuit of each. Sanctimoniousness on the part of theology, science, and philosophy alike is driven by arrogance and insecurity rather than reason and trust. None should worship at fabricated altars of any of them. Rather we must see the whole of the knowledge and wisdom of God through both creation and through revelation and serve only at his holy altar.

A Praise:

> Beholding towering rocky peaks draped with snow,
> Mountains and valleys painted with trees,
> It's your sweet whisper that I hear in the pines,
> Strummed by the cool, gentle mountain breeze,
>
> White wispy clouds dance over me,
> As if to grand music of angelic chorus,
> Singing praises to its beautiful creator,
> Yahweh, God, that made all this before us.
>
> Father, with tears of speechless joy I give thanks,
> For all the ways creation reveals you,
> In mind's eye I sit atop a mountain in unspeakable peace,
> An enormous boulder as my worship pew.

86
Revelation from God

Jesus Christ was never merely about speaking words *from* God; he is in fact the word *of* God. He is not just *a* truth; he is *the* truth.

We have seen his glory, the glory of the one and only Son, who came from the Father, full of grace and truth (John 1:14).

GOD COMMUNICATES HIS ever-existent nature through creation and words (scripture). Both the creation of God and the words *from* God lead us to the ultimate reality—*the* Word *of* God, Jesus Christ—"In the beginning was the Word, and the Word was with God, and the Word was God" (John 1:1). The creation as well as the scriptures are designed to lead us to one ultimate reality—that Jesus is Lord of the Universe—"All authority in heaven and on earth has been given to me" (Matt. 28:18).

God gets us if we "get" God. And we get God the Father by "getting" Jesus the Son—"Anyone who has seen me has seen the Father" (John 14:9), and "The Son is the radiance of God's glory and the exact representation of his being" (Heb. 1:3). Jesus Christ is the singular, one-way road to God—"I am the way and the truth and the life. No one comes to the Father except through me" (John 14:6).

The road to the life he offers is straight and narrow and only a few find it, not because God desires to make it difficult, but because the true and simple reality is that it is straight and narrow and restrained, whether we approve of it or not—"But small is the gate and narrow the road that leads to life, and only a few find it" (Matt. 7:14). The clear and validated truth is that, "Salvation is found in no one else, for there is no other name under heaven given to mankind by which we must be saved" (Acts 4:12).

Jesus is not just words *from* God; he is the word *of* God. Jesus is not just a truth; he is *the* truth. Jesus is *the* Word and *the* truth because he is in fact the manifestation and presence on earth of *the one and only* God—"Don't you know me, Philip, even after I have been among you such a long time? Anyone who has seen me has seen the Father" (John 14:9). And, "No one has ever seen God, but the one and only Son, who is himself God and is in closest relationship with the Father, has made him known" (John 1:18).

It is in our mind's and heart's eyes and the subsequent experiences that follow, derived from the testimony of the writings and lives of those who walked with him here, that we behold the glory of God in human form, in our own human "language"—"We have seen his glory, the glory of the one and only Son, who came from the Father, full of grace and truth" (John 1:14). And it is from such revelation that we discover the existential reality that Jesus is ever-present still with those who believe—"And surely I am with you always, to the very end of the age" (Matt. 28:20). Paul experienced Christ's presence in his own life till the very end—"But the Lord stood at my side" (2 Tim. 4:17). And so each of us can experience his presence daily.

So we too, as surely as we believe Christ was present in the past, can fully believe that he is still present and with us today. Through our faith, we can experience him fully and in reality. If we are in him, he is in us. If we are standing by his side, he is standing right by ours.

God, as the great designer, architect, engineer, and artist of the creation, has revealed and is daily revealing himself to us—"For ever since the creation of the world His invisible attributes, His eternal power and divine nature, have been clearly seen, being understood through His workmanship [all His creation, the wonderful things that He has made], so that they [who fail to believe and trust in Him] are without excuse *and* without defense" (Rom. 1:20, Amplified Bible). He made humanity in his image, an image that was blurred and distorted due to our fall into sin's grip.

However, in Christ, God is restoring back to his image those who place their faith in him. He transforms those who by faith receive the gift of the Holy Spirit—"Repent and be baptized, every one of you, in the name of Jesus Christ for the forgiveness of your sins. And *you will receive the gift of the Holy Spirit*" (Acts 2:38, italics added). It is through his Spirit that he gives the believer the power to understand his revelation—"What we have received is not the spirit of the world, but the Spirit who is from God, so that we may understand what God has freely given us. This is what we speak, not in words taught us by human wisdom but in words taught by the Spirit, explaining spiritual realities with Spirit-taught words" (1 Cor. 2:12–13).

Thus, the revelation of God, through creation and through scripture, comes clear to us through the Holy Spirit God places in us—"You have an anointing from the Holy One, and all of you know the truth" (1 John 2:20). It is his Spirit then that gives us the revelation of how to ultimately rely on God to show us how to live by faith wholly in the reality of who Jesus is—our Lord and Savior. For this we are not reliant solely on the leadership and teaching of others, but only on God—"As for you, the anointing you received from him remains in you, and you do not need anyone to teach you. But as his anointing teaches you about all things and as that anointing is real, not counterfeit—just as it has taught you, remain in him" (1 John 2:27).

The Spirit reveals God to us, explains God to us, and empowers us to hear and know God, as well as to live out our lives for him in this present world in preparation for the eternal age to come. Also, he reveals us to God.

A Prayer:

> By the power of your Holy Spirit, open the eyes of my heart, Lord, that I can hear you, understand you, and know you.
>
> Give my heart and mind wings to fly higher and farther in my seeking of you.
>
> May you be to me the pearl of great price and the field with the buried treasure.
>
> Hide not your face from me, Lord, but reveal yourself to me.

87
Self-Discipline

Biblically, self-discipline is not about organization and self-management; it is about sound judgment and mental balance.

The Spirit God gave us does not make us timid, but gives us power, love and self-discipline (2 Tim. 1:7, New International Version).

For God did not give us a spirit of timidity or cowardice or fear, but [He has given us a spirit] of power and of love and of sound judgment and personal discipline [abilities that result in a calm, well-balanced mind and self-control] (2 Tim. 1:7, Amplified Bible).

BIBLICALLY, TO BE self-disciplined or self-controlled is to be of sound mind—"For God has not given us a spirit of fear, but of power and of love and of *a sound mind*" (2 Tim. 1:7, New King James Version, italics added). To be self-disciplined means to be logical and sensible. The word the apostle Paul uses for self-discipline in 2

Timothy 1:7 (*sóphronismos*, Greek) is used only this once in the New Testament. But, it was a common word used to make a spiritual point—"This is what we speak, not in words taught us by human wisdom but in words taught by the Spirit, explaining spiritual realities with Spirit-taught words" (1 Cor. 2:13). It means having disciplined thinking, act out of a sound mind, and live out God's will through good mental reasoning. As if to say, "think!"

The Spirit transforms us through renewing and regenerating our mental capacity—"be transformed by the renewing of your mind" (Rom. 12:2). He helps us to be of a sound mind and to take captive our thoughts for Christ (2 Cor. 10:5).

To live in the world apart from the Holy Spirit is to live by our fleshly nature, doing what we feel, what we want, and what seems wise by worldly standards of thought and judgment—"A person's selfish desires are set against the Spirit, and the Spirit is set against one's selfish desires. They are opposed to each other, so you shouldn't do whatever you want to do" (Gal. 5:17, Common English Bible). Apart from life in the Spirit, we become intoxicated with our worldly senses and therefore drunk in sensuality—"They have given themselves over to sensuality so as to indulge in every kind of impurity" (Eph. 4:19).

But God calls us back to truth—to his sensibility and wisdom. He calls us to a sound mind rather than to an unsound one. He calls us to Spirit-inspired soberness rather than worldly intoxication—"Therefore do not be foolish, but understand what the Lord's will is. Do not get drunk on wine, which leads to debauchery. Instead, be filled with the Spirit" (Eph. 5:17–18).

In a world caught up with its own happiness, pleasure, and selfish purposes, we are taught by its humanistic philosophy that we should do as we "feel." We are told to follow our hearts! How foolish! In reality, the human heart, apart from a reasoning mind, is, in fact, not generally logical but rather subjective, emotional, fickle, and illogical, and thus unreliable—"The heart is deceitful above all things and beyond cure" (Jer. 17:9). Even among Christians, our feelings are often equated with God's Spirit within us! This misunderstanding seems embedded in much Christian teaching. The word of God empowered by the Holy Spirit must be the objective metric by which we discern our thinking as right or wrong.

As God's children, we are taught to think wisely rather than simply trusting our feelings and intuitions apart from sound reasoning. We are instructed to bring our whole inner being into conformity with God and to make our thoughts obedient to Christ—"We take captive every thought to make it obedient to Christ" (2 Cor. 10:5). It is his word that discerns the rightness or wrongness of our mind and heart thoughts rather than our inner feelings—"The word of God…judges the thoughts and attitudes of the heart" (Heb. 4:12).

Most of us as Christians wish we could always do what is right and good. However, we find very early on that *willing* to do right and actually *doing* it can be vastly different propositions—"The spirit is willing, but the flesh is weak" (Matt. 26:41). Because of our nagging sinful nature, we regularly find ourselves conflicted between the tug of the Spirit and the tug of the world—"I do not understand what I do. For what I want to do I do not do, but what I hate I do" (Rom. 7:15). Our deliverance is not to be found in our being good or even just getting better. It is not found first in external self-discipline and personal organization. True deliverance from our worldly intoxication and conflicted-ness is found only in God's goodness and grace extended to us in Christ—"Wretched *and* miserable man that I am! Who will [rescue me and] set me free from this body of death [this corrupt, mortal existence]? Thanks be to God [for my deliverance] through Jesus Christ our Lord!" (Rom. 7:24–25, Amplified Bible).

The Holy Spirit gives us an inward, spiritual sensibility that alone is able to defy the outward insanity of this present darkness—"But we have the mind of Christ" (1 Cor. 2:16). In the world we are deceived and "drunk" with the desires and sensuality of our fleshly nature. In Christ we find blessed sobriety of mind and heart—"But **you**, be sober in all *things*, suffer-hardship, do *the* work *of an* evangelist, fulfill your ministry" (Disciples' Literal New Testament, italics and bold letters are part of quote). This sobriety allows us to do the work of God in the midst of this present sin-cursed world. Through the Holy Spirit, we think differently, and thus, we behave and live differently—"Do everything without grumbling or arguing, so that you may become blameless and pure, *'children of God without fault in a warped and crooked generation.'* Then you will shine among them like stars in the sky as you hold firmly to the word of life" (Phil. 2:14–16, italics added).

Ours is a self-discipline beginning and ending with the objective revelation and guidance of the word of God and work of the Holy Spirit in us. It is planted in our mind, flows out into our heart, and manifests itself in our lives. As children of the Light, the admonition of the word is clear—"But since we belong to the day, let us be sober, putting on faith and love as a breastplate, and the hope of salvation as a helmet" (1 Thess. 5:8). Rather than being lulled to sleep by the droning worldly drumbeat, we maintain our alertness, as a gazelle grazing in a meadow surrounded by a jungle full of predators—"Therefore, with minds that are alert and fully sober, set your hope on the grace to be brought to you when Jesus Christ is revealed at his coming" (1 Pet. 1:13). It is in this God-given, spiritual clarity of mind that we are able to connect and trust in our protector and savior, Jesus Christ—"Therefore be alert and of sober mind so that you may pray" (1 Pet. 4:7).

Either we will let the world discipline, train, and mold us in its way of feeling and thinking or we will submit to the Holy Spirit's discipline, training, and molding. The only "self" that is actually involved in it is in the choice we must make in what or whom we allow to discipline us.

A Prayer:

Holy Spirit of all that is good and right, bring our minds into alignment with yours.
And thus, make our "self-discipline" in actuality "God-discipline."
Give us spiritual sobriety and soundness of mind.
Squelch within us the worldly intoxication of sensuality.
Give us reason, wisdom, and mental clarity.
Help us to take our mind and heart thoughts captive and obedient to you.
Make our minds of your mind.
Amen.

88
Simplicity

To live an overly complicated life is, for a Christian, to live a corrupted life.

But I fear, lest somehow, as the serpent deceived Eve by his craftiness, so your minds may be corrupted from the simplicity that is in Christ (2 Cor. 11:3, New King James Version).

ULTIMATELY, ONLY ONE thing will matter most—"Only one thing is important" (Luke 10:42, Easy-to-Read Version). Although it may appear there are many paths in life, there are in actuality only two—"Enter through the narrow gate. For wide is the gate and broad is the road that leads to destruction, and many enter through it. But small is the gate and narrow the road that leads to life, and only a few find it" (Matt. 7:13–14). True spirituality brings us to that reality and thus produces simplicity of choice.

The depth and vastness of God, within himself, is complex beyond human imagination. However, he communicates and connects with us in the purest and simplest way—"The simplicity that is in Christ" (2 Cor. 11:3, New King James Version). God takes the complexity that flows out of his own glory, wonder, and magnificence and connects with us in simple kindness and gentleness. In God's plan, being human is in reality supposed to be fairly simple. Our trying to play God is simply the wrong choice for us.

Jesus's friend Martha personifies the wrong, religious way of thinking, behaving, and living, while her sister Mary represents the making of the right choice—"While Jesus and his followers were traveling, he went into a town, and a woman named Martha let him stay at her house. She had a sister named Mary. *Mary was sitting at Jesus' feet and listening to him teach. But her sister Martha was busy doing all the work that had to be done.* Martha went in and said, 'Lord, don't you care that my sister has left me to do all the work by myself? Tell her to help me!'" (Luke 10:38–40, Easy-to-Read Version, italics added).

Martha was *doing things right*, it might be supposed. Mary, however, was definitively *doing the right thing*. Martha was serving people's purposes. Mary was serving God's. Martha was bogged down in the complexity of human personalities and social systems. Mary was simply focused on the God at hand. Martha was focused on herself, the other people present, and especially what she saw as Mary's failure to properly serve. Mary was focused on Jesus.

Jesus's answer to Martha is Jesus's answer to all of us in the confusion and complexity we all too often get bogged down in—"But the Lord answered her, 'Martha, Martha, you are getting worried and upset about too many things. *Only one thing is important. Mary has made the right choice*, and it will never be taken away from her'" (Luke 10:41–42, Easy-to-Read Version, italics added). God will never take away what is important and put in its place the trivial.

Martha's behavior reflects Israel's slavish focus on the minutia of the law—"Woe to you, teachers of the law and Pharisees, you hypocrites! You give a tenth of your spices—mint, dill and cumin. But *you have neglected the more important matters of the law—justice, mercy and faithfulness*. You should have practiced the latter, without neglecting the former. You blind guides! You strain out a gnat but swallow a camel" (Matt. 23:23–24, italics added). They got the law's "rules," but they missed its heart, that of loving and serving God's perfect and beautiful purposes—"One of them, an expert in the law, tested him with this question: 'Teacher, which is the greatest commandment in the Law?' Jesus replied: 'Love the Lord your God with all your heart and with all your soul and with all your mind.' This is the first and greatest commandment. And the second is like it: 'Love your neighbor as yourself'" (Matt. 22:35–39).

They were focused on what made them "look" good rather than focusing on God's goodness. Their self-focus—a focus on their own appearance—led them to an attempt at mere appeasement of God rather than a sincere effort at really pleasing him!

God had simplified his will for Israel some seven centuries earlier through the prophet Micah—"He has told you, human one, what is good and what the Lord requires from you: *to do justice, embrace faithful love, and walk humbly with your God*" (Mic. 6:8, Common English Bible, italics added). Many of them still had obviously not gotten the message. Many didn't get it when Jesus actually brought it to us, and not just in words, but in human form.

And by the time Jesus, Emmanuel, meaning "God with us," arrived on the scene, they were still bogged down in the "Martha way of thinking and acting." Jesus tells us that, sadly, it will still be the same way for many Christians at the end. But they will only realize it when it is already too late to do anything about it—"Many will say to me on that day, 'Lord, Lord, did we not prophesy in your name and in your name drive out demons and in your name perform many miracles?' Then I will tell them plainly, 'I never knew you. Away from me, you evildoers!'" (Matt. 7:22–23).

Christian busyness and humanity's pursuit of pleasure and comfort are corrupted, sad substitutes for true life—"A simple life in the Fear-of-God is better than a rich life with a ton of headaches (Prov.

15:16, The Message). They are the fruit of the original wrong choice of the Tree of the Knowledge of Good and Evil—humanism. They are human-focused and human-serving. The former is the pursuit of being *like* God, the original deceptive promise of the Evil One—"God knows that when you eat from it [the Tree of the Knowledge of Good and Evil] your eyes will be opened, and you will be *like God*, knowing good and evil" (Gen. 3:5, bracket and content added for clarification). The latter is the human pursuit of *being* God, serving our own purposes and seeking merely to pleasure our own selves.

Oh, it was indeed true that eating the fruit of the wrong tree would result in eyes open to the realities of good and evil, right and wrong. It was, however, not true that they would not die. It was patently false that merely pursuing good behavior and eschewing bad would make them like God. The world wasn't created that way. It wasn't created for that purpose!

The world God created was "very good"; it was not, however, yet perfected. That was the role humanity was to play in God's plan to perfect and complete it—"Be fruitful and increase in number; *fill the earth and subdue it*" (Gen. 1:28). Humanity was to continue creation by procreating and by leading in its perfecting by "subduing" it. At creation's inception, humans were a scant population and perfection was still only a distant destination. Much was still to be done, and God purposed to carry it out through humanity.

And, we are now nearer than ever to the ultimate destination, and yet, far too many still haven't gotten to a focus on the only important thing. Mary represents the right choice humanity needs to make in order to know God and for God to know us. Mary represents what God wills for his believers, the church.

We are called to the simple way of Christ—the one with the narrow gate that is Jesus himself, and the one with the narrow path, well worn down by his own repetitive footsteps on earth—"To this you were called, because Christ suffered for you, leaving you an example, that you should follow in his steps" (1 Pet. 2:21).

We are called to such simplicity—a pure and sincere devotion to Christ (2 Cor. 11:3).

Mary chose the good thing—the only important thing—and so should we.

A Prayer:

> Father, help me to be one who chooses the only important thing—Jesus.
> Help me to calm my inner striving and sit at his feet.
> Help me to see you in him and through him.
> Help me to see you, Father, through your manifestation in Christ Jesus, My Lord.
> May my focus be specific and my path to you simply Jesus.
> Amen.

89
Sin, Part 1

Sin will take you a lot deeper into it than you ever plan to go, it will keep you considerably longer than you ever plan to stay, and it will cause you to do things you never believed you would ever do. Sin—every single bit of it—is far more deadly and long-lasting than you could have ever imagined.

For the wages of sin is death (Rom. 6:23).

SIN IS NOT something to be toyed with. The only joking there is to be done concerning sin is that sin is ever joked about at all. Sin is no joke. As all of us too soon learn.

Sin has no existence apart from God. It is not a preexistent thing opposite of God, as Satan is not a preexistent thing opposite of God. Sin is simply all that is not of God. Sin in fact finds its existence in the freedom that comes from God—"Now the Lord is the Spirit, and where the Spirit of the Lord is, there is freedom" (2 Cor. 3:17). God wants us to be free because he is free, as Jesus demonstrated to us—"The Father loves me because I give my life. I give my life so that I can get it back again. No one takes my life away from me. *I give my own life freely.* I have the right to give my life, and I have the right to get it back again. This is what the Father told me" (John 10:17–18, Easy-to-Read Version, italics added).

Jesus made the choice to give his life for us. Of course that choice flowed easily from his essence and attitude, and we are called to have that same attitude and thus make the same choice—"In your relationships with one another, have the same mind-set as Christ Jesus: Who, being in very nature God, did not consider equality with God something to be used to his own advantage; rather, he made himself nothing by taking the very nature of a servant, being made in human likeness. And being found in appearance as a man, he humbled himself by becoming obedient to death—even death on a cross!" (Phil. 2:5–8).

God has choice, and Jesus, as God and God's earthly emanation, had choice. And so, we too have choice. Somehow God's predestination of us in no way precludes his freeing of us—"So if the Son makes you free, you are really free" (John 8:36, Easy-to-Read Version). As our Lord, our older brother, and our consummate model did, so we too have power to choose whether to lay our lives down for God or not. And in the end of this age, we will "get" what *we chose*.

We would, of course, have no choice unless God gave it to us. As a parent gives a child a choice between two things, either choice being an option allowed by the parent, so God gives us a choice between two things. Our freedom is not unlimited, however. God limits our freedom of choice for or against him. And our calling itself is by invitation only—"No one can come to me unless the Father who sent me draws them" (John 6:44).

God, by his own purpose and will, stipulates the conditions for our calling, and he compiles the invitation list by his own volition. He even desires that everyone be invited—"[God] wants all people to be saved and to come to a knowledge of the truth" (1 Tim. 2:4, bracket added). But not all will be invited because of their own choices. There are apparently certain conditions, set by God himself, for any one of us being invited to meet Christ in the first place, and there are clearly further conditions for being chosen by him and enabled to accept him by faith—"For many are invited, but few are chosen" (Matt. 22:14).

God is love, and God wants us to be free so that we can indeed love as he loves. The love of God (*agape*, Greek) is first a love of the will. Agape is a manifestation of the character of its giver. It cannot be faked or feigned. Its actions are always consistent with its essence. Agape means to will what is right. This kind of love does what is right because before it does it, it wills to do it. Agape's essence flows from God's essence—Yahweh, ("I AM WHO I AM," Exod. 3:14). Therefore, love *is* before it *does*. Doing what is right, and thus what is good for the other as well as for self, is its sole intent. And without freedom of choice, there is none of the love that is of God and in fact that defines God—"God is love" (1 John 4:8). For there to be agape at all, its desire and action must be chosen. Thus, God gives us choice so that we can be like him.

For purposes of understanding sin might be thought of in two ways: Sin with an uppercase "S" and sin with a lowercase "s." In the uppercase, it is the overarching thing—Sin in general. It is all that is opposed to the nature and will of God. It is the principle of sin. In the lowercase, "sins" are the specific offenses that flow from the principle of sin itself. Because the essence of sin—that which is against or opposite of God—came about through the first sin; specific violations (sins) flow from principle of it (Sin)—"Therefore, just as sin entered the world through one man, and death through sin, and in this way death came to all people, because all sinned" (Rom. 5:12). We commit "sins" because of "Sins" existence. Sin is a 100 percent contagion. Everyone catches it. And it has a 100 percent mortality rate.

Sin in general was a one-time option of humanity, as represented in the Garden of Eden. There was the choice to live by faith in God (the Tree of Life) or the choice to trust in our selves (the Tree of the Knowledge of Good and Evil)—humanism. Since that original choice, humanity has had no further say in the matter because humanity itself opted for it.

However, we do have a choice regarding any specific violations, or sins. Through the power of the word of God and the Holy Spirit of God, we can choose to be godly—"Train yourself to be godly" (1 Tim. 4:7). Through repetitively choosing God over self, we can learn to discern good from evil—"But solid food is for the [spiritually] mature, whose senses are trained by practice to distinguish between what is morally good and *what is* evil" (Heb. 5:14, Amplified Bible). We can successfully resist the tempter by determinedly choosing God—"Submit yourselves, then, to God. Resist the devil, and he will flee from you" (James 4:7).

We must first unchoose sin in principle before we can unchoose it in practice, for the practice of sin in us flows from the principle of sin all around us. We must intentionally opt out of sin in order to opt in to God. In fact, we opt out of sin *when* we opt in to God. To choose sin is to choose death—"The payment for sin is death, but the gift that God freely gives is everlasting life found in Christ Jesus our Lord" (Rom. 6:23, GOD'S WORD Translation). To choose life, we must choose Christ, for he is the only way to God and the life found in God—"I am the way and the truth and the life. No one comes to the Father except through me" (John 14:6).

Sin is pervasively powerful and overwhelmingly deadly. It is not to be toyed with. Period.

A Prayer:

> Help me, O Lord, to not be deceived by sin's attractiveness to my fleshly nature.
>
> Guide me, dear Savior, to grasp your saving, life-giving hands, and to never turn loose.

Heal me, God, of my sinful wanderlust and fleshly gravitation to pleasure and ease.
Enlighten me, Father, that the eyes of my heart may be ever aware of the deadliness of sin and all that is against you in your holiness, beauty, and magnificence.
Free me, Spirit, that I might be free indeed of all that would separate me from your glorious presence.
May I always and ever only glory in you, God!
Amen.

90
Sin, Part 2

A single sin is to the human spirit what one malignant cell is to the human body. As one mutated cancer cell can ultimately lead to the death of the whole body, so one sinful aberration of thought or behavior can lead to the destruction of our entire spirit.

You are tempted by the evil things you want. Your own desire leads you away and traps you. Your desire grows inside you until it results in sin. Then the sin grows bigger and bigger and finally ends in death (James 1:14–15, Easy-to-Read Version).

WE QUICKLY AND easily become numb to sin. Since we literally "wake up" in it and grow up in it as a child, as we move into adulthood, we have to be made aware of what has gone awry within us. We are sinners before we even know it—"I was born to do wrong, a sinner before I left my mother's womb (Ps. 51:5, Easy-to-Read Version). The sinful progression started at our onset, at the fall of humankind into sin in Eden, and it has progressed and reached to the very core of each of us. No one escapes its grasp. Only Christ's redemptive work in us can arrest it.

Although none of us is personally to blame for sin's entry into the world, each of us is personally responsible to God for our part in it—"Just as through one human being sin came into the world, and death came through sin, so death has come to everyone, since everyone has sinned" (Rom. 5:12, Common English Bible).

And lest we dare try to blame God for it, he is not to blame for our own progression into sin. Humanity is first responsible, and then as we mature, we become personally responsible—"When tempted, no one should say, 'God is tempting me.' For God cannot be tempted by evil, nor does he tempt anyone; but each person is tempted when they are dragged away by their own evil desire and enticed. Then, after desire has conceived, it gives birth to sin; and sin, when it is full-grown, gives birth to death" (James 1:13–15).

Just as we inherit our genetic imprint through the DNA we receive from our parents and these genes will both bless us and also lead to various problems, so it is with sin. Genetic diseases and problems, once they are there, come from the inside of us. Some germ we catch along the way does not likely cause them. They are caused by our own inherent inner nature. Although our genetic nature is "imposed" on us through humanity's progression, once it is there, it is there. And we have to deal with the weaknesses and unhelpful propensities that come with our bodies.

Our sinful, or fleshly, nature comes to us first through the human lineage via our parents. And then, it seemingly is breathed into us socially through our culture and all those around us. No one has to teach us as children to sin. As we grow up though, our sin is not at first insidious and consciously malicious; however, it is still sin. But thankfully, God apparently does not hold us accountable for it—"Blessed is the one whose sin the Lord does not count against them" (Ps. 32:2), and "Let the little children come to me, and do not hinder them, for the kingdom of heaven belongs to such as these" (Matt. 19:14).

A large part of the church believes that babies and children are indeed separated from God because of this inherited sinfulness. However, since salvation requires an individual to turn to God in faith, infants would be disqualified for salvation until they were of sufficient age to come to faith. But Jesus clearly did not look at children through sin's lens. On the contrary, he sees them as the models of kingdom citizenship—"Truly I tell you, unless you change and become like little children, you will never enter the kingdom of heaven" (Matt. 18:3).

Even though, sins that are common to children, such as lying, hitting, hating, and being selfish, are still sins. As we grow and mature and become more conscious of ourselves and our world, these sins do indeed become more and more willful and insidious. As we take willful ownership over them, they begin to own us. Only Jesus can remit our sin and renew us as a person, canceling our sin account balance. That is why the only answer to our sin problem is to trust Jesus—"For it is by grace [God's remarkable compassion and favor drawing you to Christ] that you have been saved [actually delivered from judgment and given eternal life] through faith. And this [salvation] is not of yourselves [not through your own effort], but it is the [undeserved, gracious] gift of God; not as a result of [your] works [nor your attempts to keep the Law], so that no one will [be able to] boast *or* take credit in any way [for his salvation]" (Eph. 2:8–9, Amplified Bible, brackets and italics are part of quote).

The sinful nature is rooted deeply within us, all the way to our physical and spiritual core. Thus we must recognize that our innate desire to sin does not come from somewhere outside of us; it gurgles up from within—"It's what comes out of a person that contaminates someone in God's sight…It's from the inside, from the human heart, that evil thoughts come: sexual sins, thefts, murders, adultery, greed, evil actions, deceit, unrestrained immorality, envy, insults, arrogance, and foolishness. All these evil things come from the inside and contaminate a person in God's sight" (Mark 7:20–23).

And while our sin can be somewhat hidden from others, it cannot at all be hidden from God. God knows and examines not only our behavior but also our thoughts and our feelings, counting them as behavior as well—"I the Lord search the heart and examine the mind, to reward each person according to their conduct, according to what their deeds deserve" (Jer. 17:10). Not even the slightest evil thought or motive can be hidden from him—"Nothing in all creation is hidden from God's sight. Everything is uncovered and laid bare before the eyes of him to whom we must give account" (Heb. 4:13).

Thus our deliverance is not to be found in attempting to hide our sin or hide from God or others with our sin, but on the contrary, God wants us to come out of our proverbial "Edenic underbrush" (as Adam and Eve hid in the trees from God after their sin, Genesis 3:8) and to come into his glorious light—"If we claim to be without sin, we deceive ourselves and the truth is not in us. If we confess our sins, he is faithful and just and will forgive us our sins and purify us from all unrighteousness" (1 John 1:8–9), and "Therefore confess your sins to each other and pray for each other so that you may be healed" (James 4:16). If we hide in our sin, it will destroy us; if we bring our sin out into the open to God, he will heal it—"Those who hide their sins won't succeed, but those who confess and give them up will receive mercy" (Prov. 28:13, Common English Bible).

Every single sin we commit is the very tip of a gargantuan iceberg lurking beneath the waters of humanity as a whole. Every individual sin is to be taken seriously because of what underlies it and because of the nature of sin itself. We must not discount it; rather we must confidently confess it to God through Christ and submit it to him for his forgiveness of it—"In Christ we come before God with freedom and without fear. We can do this because of our faith in Christ" (Eph. 3:12, Easy-to-Read Version).

Christ has made provision for the forgiveness of our sins and thus the removal of all our guilt for it. He has done this to free us so that we can get on with the process of being healed from and transformed away of it. Jesus deals not first with the mere exposures of the iceberg that appear in our lives; he deals first with the enormous iceberg beneath the surface. He melts our sinful hearts and renews within us the original heart he gave us—"I will also put a new spirit in you to change your way of thinking. I will take out the heart of stone from your body and give you a tender, human heart" (Ezek. 36:26, Easy-to-Read Version).

We must submit the entirety of our sin to Jesus. We must conceal none of it. Nor should we live for a minute in guilt and shame for it. We must not delay our going to him with it. For while we cannot handle our sin alone for one moment, he can indeed handle it in one moment!

A Prayer:

> Holy Father, in Jesus name, I submit my sin—all of it—to you for your cleansing.
> I cannot handle it for one more moment; you can handle it all in a moment.
> Although I cannot fully comprehend it, I trust what you have shown me about your love for me and about your eternal goodness and mercy by dying for me, as well as the rest of the world, on the cross.
> There is no claim of merit on my part in this request, because I only deserve death.
> My bold request is solely through the gracious promise and call of the Lord Jesus Christ—your Son and my Savior.
> Make me clean from my sin and make me resolute in my determination to be rid of it.
> Amen.

91
Spirituality

The real external witness to genuine spirituality in our lives is not as much prayer and piety as in the ability to love, live, and sacrifice beyond ourselves into times, places, and people we will never ourselves experience, see, or directly interact with.

By faith Moses, when he had grown up, refused to be known as the son of Pharaoh's daughter. He chose to be mistreated along with the people of God rather than to enjoy the fleeting pleasures of sin. He regarded disgrace for the sake of Christ as of greater value than the treasures of Egypt, because he was looking ahead to his reward (Heb. 11:24–26).

PIETY AND REVERENCE, in fulfilling obligations to God, are good, but they are only a means to the end. Works are good, but good works in their right and proper context are only a result of faith in God. The end or outcome that all seekers must desire, however, is a right relationship with God. This is what true righteousness is at its core—"What is more, I consider everything a loss because of the surpassing worth of knowing Christ Jesus my Lord, for whose sake I have lost all things. I consider them garbage, that I may gain Christ and be found in him, not having a righteousness of my own that comes from the law, but that which is through faith in Christ—the righteousness that comes from God on the basis of faith" (Phil. 3:8–9).

The reality is that one can have good works while having little to no faith in God. Other less-than-noble motives exist for doing good deeds other than doing them for God. However, one cannot have faith without the commensurate good works—"As the body without the spirit is dead, so faith without deeds is dead" (James 2:26). But we cannot discern with any certainty another's motive. Nor can we be totally confident of our own motives in the good we do. A clear conscience does not totally eliminate the possibility of impure motives—"My conscience is clear, but that does not make me innocent. It is the Lord who judges me" (1 Cor. 4:4).

There are two undeniable witnesses to genuine faith, however: (1) completely others-centered, sacrificial love, as exhibited by Jesus and (2) sacrificial living that extends beyond ourselves into a future that we will not personally experience, as well as into places, present and future, that we likely will remain personally unaffected by. The selfish and self-centered ultimately live their lives on a barter basis—only giving when expecting something in return. Only the truly God-centered can live outside themselves, giving on behalf of God expecting nothing personally in return and sacrificing for the worst among us because of the One within us. And doing it all solely for the reward of heaven—"But love your enemies, do good to them, and *lend to them without expecting to get anything back*. Then your reward will be great, and you will be children of the Most High, because he is kind to the ungrateful and wicked" (Luke 6:35, italics added).

Jesus said that our love (*agape*, Greek, the sacrificial love of God) is what will bear external witness to our truly following him—"By this everyone will know that you are my disciples, if you love one another" (John 13:35). This kind of love is not the love of mere affection, friendship, affinity, fellowship, or socialization. This is the unmitigated love of God willing when called, to give all, including one's life, for those otherwise completely undeserving of it. It is not love that only reacts; it is a love that preacts out of its sincere love for, devotion to, and attachment with God. The love *of* God in a person can only come from a sincere love *for* God!

It is the person possessing this love who gives freely to the poor (even if they seem undeserving of help), honestly prays for blessings and help for their enemies, endures mistreatment without retribution, is hated but never hates, and spends himself or herself in service to deeds and causes with only the expectation of serving and pleasing God. Only those given over to complete faith in God, and its genuine spirituality, can truly live strategically for people and places faraway and for future generations to come, who will most assuredly know or care little or nothing about us and our sacrifices. True spirituality is being able to act and live for purposes outside of the here-and-now physical realm and one's personal interests in it.

Abram, who became the "father of our faith," left his home and everything he knew to go to a place he had never seen, and not even to take possession of it but only live there in preparation for the generations to follow to finally take possession of it—"By faith Abraham, when called to go to a place he would later receive as his inheritance, obeyed and went, even though he did not know where he was going" (Heb. 11:8). Noah spent decades building a ship on dry land in preparation for a coming flood in a world where rain purportedly had never fallen—"By faith Noah, when warned about things not yet seen, in holy fear built an ark to save his family" (Heb. 11:7). Daniel bore witness to, risked his life for, and sacrificed for a vision of a coming kingdom that he would not live to help usher in (Dan. 2). Moses gave up safety and security for an undesired calling back to an uninviting place to lead an unappreciative people—"By faith Moses, when he had grown up, refused to be known as the son of Pharaoh's daughter. He chose to be mistreated along with the people of God rather than to enjoy the fleeting pleasures of sin. He regarded disgrace for the sake of Christ as of greater value than the treasures of Egypt, because he was looking ahead to his reward" (Heb. 11:24–26).

Our faithful predecessors endured what they endured in their own times for what they believed would come to future generations—"Some faced jeers and flogging, and even chains and imprisonment. They were put to death by stoning; they were sawed in two; they were killed by the sword. They went about in sheepskins and goatskins, destitute, persecuted and mistreated—the world was not worthy of them. They wandered in deserts and mountains, living in caves and in holes in the ground" (Heb. 11:36–38).

Thus, "These were all commended for their faith, yet none of them received what had been promised, since God had planned something better for us so that only together with us would they be made perfect" (Heb. 11:39–40).

Our attachment to the truly divine, spiritual, and eternal is most witnessed in our willing detachment from and sacrifice of things that are human, physical, temporal, and in the present for purposes that extend beyond them—"So we fix our eyes not on what is seen, but on what is unseen, since what is seen is temporary, but what is unseen is eternal" (2 Cor. 4:18). Only the love of God, which is the truly eternal spiritual gift, allows us to extend ourselves beyond our physical boundaries into the spiritual—"Love knows no limit to its endurance, no end to its trust, no fading of its hope; it can outlast anything. It is, in fact, the one thing that still stands when all else has fallen…In this life we have three great lasting qualities—faith, hope and love. But the greatest of them is love" (1 Cor. 13:7-8, 13, J. B. Phillips New Testament).

Love outlasts time because it transcends it. And thus it stands at the pinnacle of true spirituality.

A Prayer:

> Father, help me to be truly spiritual in this life.
> Open my eyes to the unseen, that I may see the present as you see it.
> Let my perspective be yours, my vision from you, and my light be you.
> Help me to find life as you know it—eternal life.
> And may I experience your life here so that I can have it forever with you in the age to come.
> Amen.

92
Standing on the Side of Truth

Stand on the side of truth and move forward without fear.

Everyone on the side of truth listens to me (John 18:37).

CASTING ASIDE A priori judgments and conclusions, it can be argued that the most basic human endeavor is not first to seek God, in whatever form or fashion we might otherwise perceive him; rather the most basic human endeavor should simply be to seek the pure, unadulterated *truth*. Any unnecessary assumptions or preconceptions can only inhibit our finding the truth—reality—as it actually is. Finding truth and reality is the philosophical, and thus the theological, underpinning of what it means to be human. What do we know and how do we know we know it—epistemology? What is existence, and what does it mean to exist—ontology? We must perceive reality aright in order to deal with it aright.

And the biblical proposition on the matter of seeking and finding truth is clear: if individuals are really seeking the unadulterated truth, they will come to Jesus—"Everyone on the side of truth listens to me" (John 18:37). Jesus and therefore the Bible make the bold assertion that Jesus *is* the truth and that the authentic truth is revealed in him—"But you did not learn Christ in this way! If in fact you have [really] heard Him and have been taught by Him, just as truth is in Jesus [revealed in His life and personified in Him]" (Eph. 4:20–21). There is no equivocation in scripture about Jesus and truth—"I am…the truth…" (John 14:6).

The adage, "perception is reality," may indeed be a truism in human behavior; however, how we perceive things in no way alters anything but our own responses and actions concerning them. Humanity's early perception of the earth as the center of the universe in no way changed the universe's order! At any given moment, reality is fixed, and any misperception we might have of it can only skew our own experience of it. But in no way do our misperceptions alter the transcendent realities outside of us. Such misperceptions only drive us as humans to senseless thoughts and actions—"So I tell you this, and insist on it in the Lord, that you must no longer live as the Gentiles do, in the futility of their thinking" (Eph. 4:17).

In actuality, God's reality is what defines us, not the inverse of it, and with him the eons of time are but a single moment—"With the Lord a day is like a thousand years, and a thousand years are like a day" (2 Pet. 3:8). We must, then, see reality—epistemology and ontology—through God's eyes, or we will see no reality at all—"So from now on we regard no one [*nothing*] from a worldly point of view" (2 Cor. 5:16, bracket and italics added). God does not think or act as a human, in the same way but to a much greater degree than a mature adult does not think or behave as a two-year-old. To fail to realize this will continue to lead to the ongoing and collective insanity witnessed in and among humankind on a daily basis.

The creation—the universe—is the primary revelation of God—"From the creation of the world, *God's invisible qualities, his eternal power and divine nature, have been clearly observed in what he made.* As a result, people have no excuse" (Rom. 1:20, GOD'S WORD Translation, italics added). Also, the scripture has also been handed down from God, first through Israel and then through the church, to further explain what had not already been revealed through creation itself. The scripture makes the broad sweeping revelations of creation ever more specific, clarifying and explaining God's work through humanity and the world he made, as well as giving a vision for what lies in store for the creation and God's people in the age to come.

And God continues to communicate with his people, deepening our understanding of creation and the word through our meditations and observations, through the church, through prayer and the Holy Spirit, and through whatever other means he may choose. Although still, all avenues of his communication to us now are a function of and under the reign of Jesus Christ as Lord—"In the past God spoke to our ancestors through the prophets at many times and in various ways, but in these last days he has spoken to us by his Son, whom he appointed heir of all things, and through whom also he made the universe. The Son is the radiance of God's glory and the exact representation of his being, sustaining all things by his powerful word" (Heb. 1:1–3).

Truth is defined by and emanates from God. But humanity, in our desire to serve ourselves and have dominance at least equal to that of God, rejected the reality of God in favor of contriving our own version of truth, which was no truth at all—"They exchanged the truth about God for a lie, and worshiped and served created things rather than the Creator" (Rom. 1:25). In our fallen state, because we want to define and control our own destiny, humanity generally does not deem it of personal expedience to remember some if not *all* the truth God has already shown and revealed to us—"They did not think it worthwhile to retain the knowledge of God, so God gave them over to a depraved mind, so that they do what ought not to be done" (Rom. 1:28). Oh, in order to justify ourselves to ourselves, we will remember the parts we like and can work into our own overarching, self-serving versions of it. But this is of grave concern because our doing so causes us great pain and futility by blocking us from finding truth.

But we prefer not the whole truth; rather we like to pick and choose certain "truths" we prefer and ignore others that may be seem "distasteful" to us. We like to define God as we want him to be and put our self-styled "Gods" in our safe little boxes, marked with our own contrived names and personal logos, which in fact often contain only mental images of us rather than containing much of God at all! Then we refuse to think outside these little boxes—"Although they [humanity] claimed to be wise, they became fools" (Rom. 1:22, brackets added).

Jesus came to show us, in human form and language, the truth of God—"The Word became flesh and made his dwelling among us. We have seen his glory, the glory of the one and only Son, who came from the Father, full of grace and truth" (John 1:14). Because he is God come in the flesh, Jesus Christ is himself truth—"I am the way and *the truth* and the life" (John 14:6, italics added).

Many of us, and arguably most of us, cannot seek pure, unadulterated truth though, because of our fears—fears of the reactions of family, friends, churches, other religions, coworkers, sociopolitical blocs, and so forth. However, who among us doesn't realize that our own social and cultural situations are surely wrought with flaws, misperceptions, and perhaps even deceptions? And yet all-too-often, because of fear, we remain in our same, "safe" status quo ruts. Our fears run the gamut from the fear of losing things to fears about not getting other things. Often, it simply comes down to our eschewing seeking truth and its transforming power because of our fear of rejection and our often seemingly overpowering desire for the respect and adulation of people—"Yet at the same time many even among the leaders believed in him. But because of the Pharisees they would not openly acknowledge their faith for fear they would be put out of the synagogue; for *they loved human praise more than praise from God*" (John 12:42–43, italics added).

Social and peer pressure are most reliant on fear. Sometimes our fear is based on the threat of physical harm, but most of the time, it is based on psychological and emotional pressure—the fear of rejection, alienation, embarrassment, or humiliation. Often we base our assurance of being right on the norms of and the acceptance by our "group," and we lack confidence in our ability to find truth outside of it. However, unless we find the truth about who God really is and thus who we really are, fear will otherwise relationally be the chief control and manipulation mechanism of what can become deceptive and debilitating groupthink!

Jesus warned us however concerning the essentiality of overcoming fears that keep us adhered to society as we have known it and therefore can keep us alienated from God—"If anyone comes to Me, and does not hate his own father and mother and wife and children and brothers and sisters, yes, and even his own life [in the sense of indifference to or relative disregard for them in comparison with his attitude toward God]—he cannot be My disciple. Whoever does not carry his own cross [expressing a willingness to endure whatever may come] and follow after Me [believing in Me, conforming to My example in living and, if need be, suffering or perhaps dying because of faith in Me] cannot be My disciple" (Luke 14:26–27, Amplified Bible).

Thus, rather than succumbing to the pressures of a world fallen, we must stand on the side truth and move forward without fear.

A Prayer:

> Make me a person of truth, My Lord,
> Show me the paths that you've trod,
> Lead me to see you through all you've made and said,
> Help me to know you, O God!

93
Thankfulness and Gratitude

To truly believe is to be genuinely and blessedly thankful.

Give thanks in all circumstances; for this is God's will for you in Christ Jesus (1 Thess. 5:18).

THANKFULNESS AND GRATITUDE are basically the same ideas in the scriptures, often translated from the variations of the same Greek word, *eucharistia*. It can mean *being* thankful or grateful, and it can mean *giving* thanks. Jesus gave thanks (*eucharista*) to God in breaking the bread at his institution of the Lord Supper—"The Lord Jesus, on the night he was betrayed, took bread, and when he had given thanks, he broke it and said, 'This is my body, which is for you; do this in remembrance of me'" (1 Cor. 11:23–24). Thus the early church began calling the Lord's Supper or Holy Communion the "Eucharist"—the Christian Thanksgiving Meal.

Sincere thankfulness and gratitude are reflective of a truly converted life—"Therefore, if anyone is in Christ, the new creation has come: The old has gone, the new is here!" (2 Cor. 5:17). Lack of gratitude and thankfulness reflect an unconverted one, still operating from an old, untransformed perspective of self and God—"They know about God, but they don't honor him *or even thank him*" (Rom. 1:21, Common English Version, italics added).

There is situational thankfulness, and then there is pervasive thankfulness. Situational thankfulness is merely momentary and reactive. Since it is only momentary, it often does not really sink into our heart. It may even reflect an inner selfishness when I am happy only because of getting my way or getting what I want. In this state of mind, we will of course, conversely, be unhappy when things don't go our way or when we don't get what we want. Pervasive thankfulness though is a gift of God in conversion when God causes us to see the world aright, from his perspective, and not from the point of view of a selfish, sinful soul—"So from now on we regard no one from a worldly point of view. Though we once regarded Christ in this way, we do so no longer" (2 Cor. 5:16).

The heart of gratitude "gets it"; it sees the world as it has been from inception—"very good." The world is presently not perfect but only "very good" though; and is therefore still being made perfect. It is not yet perfect, as we are not yet perfect. The heart of gratitude recognizes the supreme good that lies beneath the fallen world's presently corrupted exterior. It does not interpret from its fleshly perspective what is and is not a blessing but rather discerns it from a godly one. No longer are pleasure, ease, and prosperity seen as the standards of blessing, and pain, discomfort, and austerity seen as curses. The great martyrs of our faith, beginning with Jesus himself, can give testimony to the great blessings that God can produce from our pain.

The converted person knows that the world as God originally made it capsized and overturned in the first garden of God, Eden. The present world is fallen from its original state and will be righted only by God, first in the converted individual, then in the collective of all those ever converted, the church, the stirrings of the kingdom of God on earth. Thus, the kingdom of God is simply the world through Christ actually turned right side up again. Therefore, pain is not to be seen as necessarily bad and pleasure as not necessarily good. Through the eyes of Christ both pain and pleasure can be seen as blessings, because we know God will work them all out for the good of us, as well as the world—"We know that God works all things together for good for the ones who love God, for those who are called according to his purpose" (Rom. 8:28, Common English Bible).

God reigns not only over his kingdom, he is the ultimate ruler of heaven and earth, and his will supersedes that even of the kingdom of darkness in this present world. Hence, he is able to work everything out for his ultimate purposes—"In him we were also chosen, having been predestined according to the plan of him who *works out everything in conformity with the purpose of his will*" (Eph. 1:11, italics added). Seeing the world from God's perspective, we are able to be equally thankful for pain or pleasure—"Consider it pure joy, my brothers and sisters, whenever you face trials of many kinds, because you know that the testing of your faith produces perseverance" (James 1:2–3). In fact we know better than to think that all that seems pleasurable as blessings.

Thankfulness and gratitude produce within the believer those deepest and most priceless conditions of joy, peace, and contentment. Joy (*chara*, Greek) is the experience of deep inner delight growing out of a heart that is converted and therefore thankful. Peace (*eiréné*, Greek) describes the heart that is calm and at rest. Contentment (*autarkeia*, Greek) describes the heart that is fully supplied; thus not wanting. By trusting God and being thankful, the believer finds joy, peace, and utter contentment—"Do not be anxious about anything, but in every situation, by prayer and petition, *with thanksgiving*, present your requests to God. And the peace of God, which transcends all understanding, will guard your hearts and your minds in Christ Jesus" (Phil. 4:6–7, italics added).

Joy, peace, and contentment are the ultimate inner delights the world so slavishly pursues, but, absent of God's ongoing blessing, only in futility and always at great price. The "preacher" in Ecclesiastes exposes the utter uselessness of seeking these priceless gifts through worthless pursuit—"Vanity of vanities, says the Preacher, vanity of vanities! All is vanity. What does man gain by all the toil at which he toils under the sun?" (Eccles. 1:2–3, English Standard Version). As well, the prophet Isaiah admonished God's people concerning their useless worldly strivings for the things only God can give—"Why do you spend your money for that which is not bread, and your labor for that which does not satisfy? Listen diligently to me, and eat what is good, and delight yourselves in rich food" (Isa. 55:2).

Only in the serendipity of faithfully serving Christ, both in pain and pleasure, will we discover joy, peace, and contentment as gifts of Christ simply left by him on our doorsteps when we faithfully serve him without conditions. They are discovered in the kingdom paradoxes: those who are poor will be rich; those who mourn will be comforted; those who are humble will be exalted; those who are starving will be sated; those who are merciful will find mercy; those who are purely God's will see God; those who bring peace for God, not war on man, will be God's true children; and those who are persecuted, not pleasured, will find themselves a part of his eternal kingdom (Matt. 5:2–10).

The one who has come to see the world aright, through the eyes of God, has learned the secret of contentment—thankfulness and reliance on God. This reality leads to the inner celebration and strength drawn from knowing the nearness of the all-surpassing, all-knowing, ever-loving God who reigns supreme, in control of all—"Rejoice in the Lord always. I will say it again: Rejoice! Let your gentleness be evident to all. The Lord is near" (Phil. 4:4–5).

God calls his followers to stillness and calmness before him so that we can be witnesses to the world of his power and blessing—"He says, 'Be still, and know that I am God; I will be exalted among the nations, I will be exalted in the earth'" (Ps. 46:10), or "Cease *striving* and know that I am God; I will be exalted among the nations, I will be exalted in the earth" (Ps. 46:10, New American Standard Version). Our frenetic, faithless struggling and strivings do not serve his purposes and do not enrich our lives.

On the other hand, trusting God produces a calmness and gentleness in believers rather than the fearful and frenzied condition common to unbelievers. Simple trust in God is the key to peace, joy, and contentment—"I have learned to be content whatever the circumstances" (Phil. 4:11). It brings the inner strength the Christian needs to not just survive in the fallen world with its abundance of pain, hardship, and suffering but also to actually thrive in it with the kind of strength that can only be found in God—"I can do all this through him who gives me strength" (Phil. 4:13).

Thus, comes the summary command to us—"Rejoice always, pray continually, give thanks in all circumstances; for this is God's will for you in Christ Jesus. Do not quench the Spirit" (1 Thess. 5:16–19). If we will place our joy in the reality of who God is and what all that implies to us, if we will confidently avail ourselves of coming into his supreme presence with all our needs and desires, and if we will be ever thankful and see all we face as ultimately being blessings from God, then we will not quench the all-powerful Holy Spirit within us who emboldens and empowers us to triumphantly face whatever we might encounter in our lives for God.

On the other hand, thanklessness and lack of gratitude lead to the malignant maladies of complaining, negativity, envy, jealousy, greed, loneliness, and selfishness. The gracious hand of God on our hearts only can cure these. Thankfulness is more powerful than antidepressants. Gratitude is more calming than antianxiety medicines. To finally calm our troubled spirits, thankfulness and gratitude must underlie any and all other treatments for our inner emotional struggles that otherwise might be physiologically generated—"Sing and make music from your heart to the Lord, *always giving thanks to God the Father for everything*, in the name of our Lord Jesus Christ" (Eph. 5:19–20, italics added).

In our hearts we give reign to his peace when we recognize that he is in control of the world and that he turns all things into blessings for his people—"Let the peace of Christ rule in your hearts, since as members of one body you were called to peace. And *be thankful*" (Col. 3:15, italics added). So, we always live in thankfulness, worshiping him with thanksgiving in our hearts—"Enter his gates with thanksgiving and his courts with praise; give thanks to him and praise his name" (Ps. 100:4).

Simply put, God gives us his joy, peace, and contentment when we give him our trust, service, reliance, and, yes, thanksgiving.

A Prayer:

> Make mine a heart of great thankfulness, Lord,
> Give me always a heart of praise,
> May my life be a testimony to your goodness and grace,
> Let your joy be the song of my days!
>
> Let me trust you in pleasure or pain, Lord,
> Make me know it all works for your plan,
> Help me never to waver in my trust in you,
> Let me be a thankful woman or man!

94
Two Trees, Part 1

There are only two life choices available for us to pick from—two ways, two roads, two foundations. We must live on the foundation we build on, and we will end up where the road we choose leads.

The tree of life was in the midst of the garden, and the tree of the knowledge of good and evil…And the LORD God commanded the man, saying, "You may surely eat of every tree of the garden, but of the tree of the knowledge of good and evil you shall not eat, for in the day that you eat of it you shall surely die" (Gen. 2:16–17).

GENESIS TELLS AN ancient Biblical story of our beginning. Our story. An account told and retold over the ages. It has various parallels in other extra Biblical retellings of human beginnings. It is an oh-so-brief look into God's creation and humanity's role in it. It is clear and concise, it is meaningful, it is insightful, it is intriguing, it is frustrating, and it is hopeful.

The participants: God, man, woman, and the serpent. Its scene: a garden with many delightful trees and two trees in particular—the Tree of Life and the Tree of the Knowledge of Good and Evil. Humanity could eat from the fruit of all the trees; however, the fruit of the Tree of the Knowledge of Good and Evil would prove most deadly to humankind. To all of us. Theirs for the picking. Their choice, given to them by God. Given to them through the gift of the creation itself.

Our choice. The fruit that brings life was there and is still here. The fruit that brings death was there and is still here. Each person, each generation, each people group, and even each church must choose anew.

The Bible reveals there are two choices, but we must pick only one. Each takes us down a road or way in this life. They have very different destinations however. There are, in fact, not many roads to God or otherwise; there are, in reality, only two roads. There are not many ways to God; there is only one way to the one God—"I am the way and the truth and the life. No one comes to the Father except through me" (John 14:6). And that way is Jesus himself. Jesus made his point very clear.

Jesus Christ is the right choice. He is the right way. He is the right foundation. He is the Tree of Life. His is the right fruit. The fruit from no other tree can bring eternal life, life as God knows it.

Legalism and humanism, knowing and doing right by human contriving, are the wrong choices. Legalism is the deadly fruit in religious form. It is living by law—the knowledge and way of right and wrong. Not relationship, but religion. Legalism and religious "rightness" constitute its belief system. On the other hand, humanism is the deadly choice of unbelief. Its constitution consists of the basic principles of the world. Legalism and humanism are both the wrong ways because they are not the way to God. They are the wrong foundations. They are the fruit of the Tree of the Knowledge of Good and Evil. They are both of the ilk of thinking one can be *right*, however, it might be defined, by being *right*. Which is wrong! A deadly mistake.

It all started out very good—"And God saw everything that he had made, and behold, it was very good" (Gen. 1:31). None of it was an accident. Nothing to do with God is by accident. Chance itself, as a part of God's creation, is no accident. Choice itself, as a part of creation, is no accident.

God has in this present age given humanity, individually and collectively, an existential choice. We receive the finality of our choice in the age to come. Humanity chose wrong very early on. Tragically, most of humanity still chooses wrong. Prompted by the serpent, identified later as Satan, man and woman—humankind—decided to eat the deadly fruit—"When the woman saw that the fruit of the tree was good for food and pleasing to the eye, and also desirable for gaining wisdom, she took some and ate it. She also gave some to her husband, who was with her, and he ate it" (Gen. 3:6). And death fell on humanity in every way. Creation groans still because of it—"We know that the whole creation has been groaning as in the pains of childbirth right up to the present time" (Rom. 8:22).

Choosing the fruit of the Tree of the Knowledge of Good and Evil, for any of us, is thinking we can live without God—humanism! And, just any old faith is not the answer either, because not all faiths are equal, for sure. Only one faith—faith in Yahweh, the LORD, God of Heaven and Earth, as revealed in Jesus Christ, is the right choice. The only good choice. All other choices involve trusting in what is human-created, not God-created. All other choices, other than that of choosing Jesus, require trusting in human knowledge apart from God, human ingenuity void of God, and human endeavor opposed to God, whether it be religious or nonreligious, and whether it involves faith of some sort or it involves no faith at all.

As Christians, we are not *right* because we are *right*; we are right because we believe God is! We are not believers in our own good; we are believers that God is good! We are not the devisers of a better way; we are believers in God's way!

We have chosen the blessed fruit of the Tree of Life, offered again to humanity through Christ. In him and in him alone, we trust.

A Prayer:

Father, teach me to eat from your Tree of Life,
And all other fruit to eschew,
Help me choose not what is human,
Help me to choose what is of you.

Let me never be drawn again,
In lust to the Tree that deceives,
Draw me to the Tree that is you, Lord,
Help me be one who believes.

95
Two Trees, Part 2

Human choice is God's ultimate act of grace. In order for grace to be revealed, a need must be established. We need God more than we need food, more than we need water, and more than we need air itself.

No one can come to me unless the Father who sent me draws them, and I will raise them up at the last day (John 6:44).

OUR FINAL FATE is wrapped up in the ultimate choice we make. Not the choice we might *say* we make. But the choice we actually make! And, the choice itself is God's greatest act of grace—his calling, the opportunity he gives us to come to him. However, we must be drawn to him and then we must present ourselves before God as truly choosing him, from the inside out. Because of our faith in him. And he judges our choice, not from our words, or even from actions, but from the reality of what is inside of our minds and our hearts and based on what we really choose—"I the Lord search the heart and examine the mind, to reward each person according to their conduct, according to what their deeds deserve" (Jer. 17:10). But still, the reality is that, "Many are invited [called], but few are chosen" (Matt. 22:14).

God's calling through the gospel triggers our choice, which determines his final choice for or against us. That is he chooses [elects] whom to call based on his own principles and righteous judgment—"For the eyes of the LORD range throughout the earth to strengthen those whose hearts are fully committed to him" (2 Chron. 16:9), and "I will have mercy on whom I have mercy, and I will have compassion on whom I have compassion" (Rom. 9:15). Thus, he judges the hearts of the ones called to determine their election or choosing. He offers grace to whomever he chooses—"The Lord is not slow in keeping his promise, as some understand slowness. Instead he is patient with you, not wanting anyone to perish, but everyone to come to repentance" (2 Pet. 3:9). He calls some; he chooses fewer—"But small is the gate and narrow the road that leads to life, and only a few find it" (Matt. 7:14).

None of it is an accident. God predetermined and predestined outcomes before he created anything. Nothing with God is an accident, including our calling, our choice, and our election—"For he chose us in him before the creation of the world to be holy and blameless in his sight. In love he predestined us for adoption to sonship through Jesus Christ, in accordance with his pleasure and will—to the praise of his glorious grace, which he has freely given us in the One he loves" (Eph. 1:3–6). Further, "In him we were also chosen, having been predestined according to the plan of him who works out everything in conformity with the purpose of his will, in order that we, who were the first to put our hope in Christ, might be for the praise of his glory" (Eph. 1:11–12).

God works out everything in conformity with his will; therefore, it all works out well for those who trust in him, both in this age and in the age to come—"And we know that in all things God works for the good of those who love him, who have been called according to his purpose. For those God foreknew he also predestined to be conformed to the image of his Son, that he might be the firstborn among many brothers and sisters. And those he predestined, he also called; those he called, he also justified; those he justified, he also glorified" (Rom. 8:28–30).

Foreknown—predestined—called—chosen—justified—glorified. An origination. A progression. A destination—God's final glory for the saved.

Humanity's first choice, that is, the fruit of the wrong tree, was to believe the big lie and commit the ultimate sin, trusting in humankind over the divine. To trust in "me" rather than "Him." We are never right with God because we are right within ourselves. We have no identity apart from God. We can have no life apart from God. We exist by him and for him. There is no other right choice. Thus if we are to live at all, really live, we must relate to him out of our faith in him. If we will *get* him "right," he will *make* us right. Anything we do that is not out of faith in him is wrong—"Everything that does not come from faith is sin" (Rom. 14:23).

The two trees still stand in the midst of this plain upon which we presently abide. The fruit of mere human knowledge, apart from God, destroys the masses. Not only is it the main fare of the unbelieving and the ungodly but also it is often planted in Christian sanctuaries with our bold standards of self-proclaimed rightness. Nonetheless, within the garden of God standing proudly and eternally is the Tree of Life—Jesus himself. The Tree that is Jesus towers over and will ultimately fell the cursed, forbidden tree. God through Christ is offering himself freely to those who would believe solely in him and his goodness and his rightness—"Come to me, all you who are weary and burdened, and I will give you rest. Take my yoke upon you and learn from me, for I am gentle and humble in heart, and you will find rest for your souls. For my yoke is easy and my burden is light" (Matt. 11:28-30). It is offered to all. But only some are called to it. And it is given to few.

God is sovereign, and all his judgments are good and righteous—"I am God, and there is no other; I am God, and there is none like me, declaring the end from the beginning and from ancient times things not yet done, saying, 'My counsel shall stand, and I will accomplish all my purpose…'" (Isa. 46:9–10). His is the right way, the good way, the only way! Any choices, all choices, derive from him and only him.

His way is a matter of hearing and obeying. Not obeying what humans may say he says, but obeying what Jesus actually says—"Therefore everyone who hears these words of mine and puts them into practice is like a wise man who built his house on the rock…But everyone who hears these words of mine and does not put them into practice is like a foolish man who built his house on sand" (Matt. 7:24, 26).

Choose wisely. Choose God. Only God. Let all other choices fall under that choice. And be undeterred and undistracted from the divine by what is merely human.

A Prayer:

> Help me, Lord, to choose wisely—to choose you.
> Call me to you in my brokenness and humility.
> Choose me out of your goodness and grace.
> Give me your new life and help me to drink only from your cup.
> I thank you for all you are and all you do for me and those I love.
> To you alone be all honor and glory and praise forever and ever!
> Amen.

96
Vision

To have *vision* means to be able to see well in the present and foresee into the future, literally or figuratively. To have *a vision from* God means to see, as shown to you by God, what is indeed to come.

Where there is no vision, the people perish (Prov. 9:18, King James Version).

OUR VISION—WHAT WE see with our eyes—is one of the greatest gifts that God has given to humanity. Only those who have been able to see and then lost that ability can fully grasp its impact on and its blessing to our lives. Human vision is being able to see with our eyes what is presently before us. But in this age, there is much we cannot see, that is currently invisible to us, thus we must live by faith—"For we live by faith, not by sight" (2 Cor. 5:7). Because there is much about the world that we cannot see with our eyes, we must be ever aware of the presence and work of that which we cannot see—"So *we fix our eyes not on what is seen*, but on what is unseen, since what is seen is temporary, but what is unseen is eternal" (2 Cor. 4:18, italics added).

Then, there are *visions*—mental and emotional images of a future time—either those generated by the work of our own minds or those given to us by God foretelling of things unknown but yet to come. There are, of course, also hallucinations—those mental images and thoughts which are generated by malfunctioning brains; therefore not to be regarded as real.

There are plenty of accounts of regular breakdowns between what our eyes actually behold and how our mind interprets it all or perhaps even fails to interpret it at all. We can, as well, "see" things visually and not perceive them at all. We can see things in their many parts and still not understand at all how the parts fit together or what it may mean, that is, see the "big picture."

God has made himself known to humanity from the beginning through his creative ingenuity—"For since the creation of the world God's invisible qualities—his eternal power and divine nature—*have been clearly seen*, being understood from what has been made, so that people are without excuse" (Rom. 1:20, italics added). The creation tells of the wonders of God without uttering an actual word—"The heavens declare the glory of God; the skies proclaim the work of his hands. Day after day *they pour forth speech*; night after night they reveal knowledge. They have no speech, they use no words; no sound is heard from them. *Yet their voice goes out into all the earth, their words to the ends of the world*" (Ps. 19:1–4, italics added).

Even though the creation clearly reveals God, many never "see" or hear it, thus they never "get" God! When we deny God's existence, we must act as though we are God! When we don't see God's light and face reflecting back to us in creation's mirror, all we will see is our own face. This is no new thing; it is the original sin itself reinventing itself over and over in the generations of humanity. It was triggered by Satan's original ruse at our inception—"The snake was the most clever of all the wild animals that the Lord God had made. The snake spoke to the woman and said, 'Woman, did God really tell you that you must not eat from any tree in the garden?' The woman answered the snake, 'No, we can eat fruit from the trees in the garden. But there is one tree we must not eat from. God told us, You must not eat fruit from the tree that is in the middle of the garden. You must not even touch that tree, or you will die.' But the snake said to the woman, 'You will not die. God knows that if you eat the fruit from that tree you will learn about good and evil, and then you will be like God!'" (Gen. 3:1-5, Easy-to-Read Version).

There was admittedly tremendous freedom of choice in what humans could partake of in creation. And it had all been declared by God to be very good. Yet there was a hook in Satan's deceptive bait—that eating the forbidden fruit would supposedly *make them like God*! Aha! What a tremendous, albeit deceptive, discovery for the original naïve, ego-vulnerable humanity. However, surely Eve and Adam did not in reality eat the fruit because it was good for food or because it was visually inviting. They ate it because, in their pride, they believed it would make them equal to God and therefore not in need of him—"They did not think it worthwhile to retain the knowledge of God" (Rom. 1:28).

Satan has always used a threefold attack in tempting us. He of course uses appearances and looks to attract us. And he uses the anticipation of how good things might *feel* (taste) to our senses to further lure us into disobedience and harmful behavior. However, the hook in the bait is always our pride—"For all that is in the world—the lust *and* sensual craving of the flesh and the lust *and* longing of the eyes and the boastful pride of life [pretentious confidence in one's resources or in the stability of earthly things]—these do not come from the Father, but are from the world" (1 John 2:16, Amplified Bible). Ultimately, our pride is how he always gets to us and how he keeps us on his line.

Thus was born humanism—worshiping and serving ourselves based on our own presumed knowledge of what is good and bad—"For although they knew God, they neither glorified him as God nor gave thanks to him, but *their thinking became futile and their foolish hearts were darkened*" (Rom. 1:21, italics added). When all we can see is our flesh, then we will never see God. Not really. What we will call "God" in our spiritual blindness will be just ourselves, masquerading as God, no matter what "ism" such misbelief masquerades as—atheism, agnosticism, deism, humanism, or so forth. It is all still merely worship of ourselves as God. In our fallen-ness, we can perceive ourselves as intelligent, wise, and insightful, when we are in actuality blind and foolish—"Claiming to be wise, they became fools, and exchanged the glory *and* majesty *and* excellence of the immortal God for an image [worthless idols] in the shape of mortal man and birds and four-footed animals and reptiles" (Rom. 1:22–23, Amplified Bible).

Failing to see God is failing to really see at all—"The fool says in his heart, 'There is no God'" (Ps. 14:1). It's as if we see the train track in front of us and see its trail through the terrain, noting that someone designed and constructed it. Yet, when we are looking far down the train tracks in the wrong direction, marveling at human ingenuity, we fail to see the train barreling down those same tracks from behind us, destined to run over and crush us in our error—"For the foolishness of God is wiser than human wisdom, and the weakness of God is stronger than human strength" (1 Cor. 1:28). Denial of God—the failure to see him—not the ongoing distortion and abuse of belief in God, is the greatest human failure!

And religion, whether it originates from God or man, can prove just as blind, or even blinder, than unbelief itself—"Though seeing, they do not see; though hearing, they do not hear or understand" (Matt. 13:13). Denying God's existence or despising his way because of the misbehavior of humanity in his name is as illogical as denying that science or scientists exist because of misuse or abuse of science. That others get a thing wrong does not make whatever they misinterpret or misuse wrong any more than finding an exception to a rule disproves the rule itself. It's merely a philosophical case of the modern concept of "victim-blaming." But such is the illogic—the "foolishness"—of unbelief. Just because humanity cannot fully understand or is not able to clearly explain something does not make that thing nonexistent or belief in it illogical.

Science asserts that we cannot see or even detect some 95 percent of what comprises the universe, labeling it "dark matter and energy." But based on science's own evidence and calculations, we have reason to *believe* they exist. Is it possible that the unseen 95 percent that is presumed to exist but that seems invisible to us now is in fact what we call the "spiritual" or "heavenly" realms? Isn't it perfectly feasible, since there is much that exists that remains unseen to us? Isn't it a reality that most of the universe remains unexplained by human minds? If that is then the case, what is the basis of the barrage that comes against faith in the first place?

It should be lost on no one that we do not see things themselves with our eyes, but what we in fact see is light reflecting back to us off things. Similarly, by our spiritual vision, we do not see those things we otherwise believe in and call spiritual but we only see the spiritual light of God reflecting off them. Christ came to show us, and in fact to be, the ultimate light of God—"*I am the light of the world.* Whoever follows me will never walk in darkness, but will have the light of life" (John 8:12, italics added).

Thus it is only through God that we can *see* what is presently unseen—"Very truly I tell you, *no one can see the kingdom of God* unless they are born again" (John 3:3). And when we are born again, we are only beginning to see, as with a newborn baby. As in our physical births, we must learn as we grow up to see and mentally interpret the images reflecting back at us, so it is with our spiritual rebirths. We must have our "inner eyes" opened in order to learn to see and interpret the spiritual images of the presently unseen world that are being reflected back to us by God—"I pray that the eyes of your heart may be enlightened in order that you may know the hope to which he has called you, the riches of his glorious inheritance in his holy people, and his incomparably great power for us who believe" (Eph. 1:18–19).

As we grow then in our new life in Christ, we develop spiritual vision to see things that exist but that we have not otherwise yet been able to see. The prophet Elisha once prayed for God to open the eyes of his assistant so he would be able to see the armies of God operating unseen all around them—"Then Elisha prayed and said, 'O LORD, I pray, open his eyes that he may see.' And the LORD opened the servant's eyes and he saw; and behold, the mountain was full of horses and chariots of fire all around Elisha" (2 Ki. 6:17). There was much more happening under the circumstances than the servant could behold with his mortal eyes. As it is at any given moment with each of us.

Further, we must have the eyes of hearts opened to be able to *see* any special revelations of God that may be giving to each or all of us. Just as it is believed that dark matter and energy likely are always traveling through us and the matter around us but that we simply cannot perceive or detect it, so it is with the unseen things of God. God and his spiritual agents, as well as Satan and the evil spirits, are always operating around us, and perhaps even in us, but we do not have the faculties in our physical bodies to directly perceive them—"For our struggle is not against flesh and blood, but against the rulers, against the authorities, against the powers of this dark world and against the spiritual forces of evil in the heavenly realms" (Eph. 6:12).

When we are born again, we are given life in the presently unseen spiritual realms and even the ability to operate there—"And God raised us up with Christ and seated us with him in the heavenly realms in Christ Jesus" (Eph. 2:6). The Holy Spirit gives us the inner faculties that we need to perceive and operate in these heavenly, or spiritual, realms—"This is what we speak, not in words taught us by human wisdom but in words taught by the Spirit, explaining spiritual realities with Spirit-taught words. The person without the Spirit does not accept the things that come from the Spirit of God but considers them foolishness, and cannot understand them because they are discerned only through the Spirit" (1 Cor. 2:13–15).

Thus, through the Holy Spirit and the word of God, we are able to see and sense those things that are presently unseen to our mortal eyes and we are able to see any revelations of future things to come that God might give us—"So we fix our eyes not on what is seen, but on what is unseen" (2 Cor. 4:18. We therefore become people of vision.

Persons of vision have developed their mental and physical capacities to the fullest in order to be able to see all that can be seen with our human eyes, hearts, and minds. People with vision are able to see and experience a future that may not ever be theirs to some degree as though it already is. They have, as well, developed their spiritual capacities to see all that can be seen with the eyes of our hearts. And they have developed their spiritual acuity to the point of being able to "see" those things that are coming in the future that may be foreshadowed to us on occasion by God. And such is true vision.

A Prayer:

Make me a person of vision, Lord,
Help me to see though blind,
Take away all veils that overshadow me,
Help me your Way to find.

Father, show me the path to follow,
Reveal what lies ahead,
Make me keen to see and understand,
Awaken my heart from the dead.

Teach me your light to follow, God,
Strengthen my eyes to see,
That I may behold your glory,
And in your presence forever be!

97
Wisdom

Wisdom is the truth of God and this present world understood and applied correctly.

The fear of the L*ORD* *is the beginning of knowledge, but fools despise wisdom and instruction* (Prov. 1:7).

WISDOM IS THE ability to use knowledge and insight in godly, productive, and effective ways consistent with deeply held social and character standards. What we deem as wise is determined by what we believe to be true and just, and perhaps even more so by what, or whom, we believe *in*. Wisdom is the inner capacity to produce helpful opinions and outcomes consistent with strongly held convictions by effectively processing beliefs, knowledge, experiences, insights, good judgment, and so forth. Whether we see something as wise in the micro or the macro, in the short term or the long term, will be decided by the purposes and standards by which we measure it.

But just a wee bit of wisdom is worth a whole lot of knowledge. If a choice must be made between the two, and rarely should it, we must choose wisdom every time. Because of the original bad decision of humanity to eat of the fruit of the Tree of the Knowledge of Good and Evil, we have the knowledge of both *good* and *evil*. In our fallen state, we are capable of *creating* both good and evil opinions and outcomes—"For we are God's handiwork, created in Christ Jesus *to do good works*, which God prepared in advance for us to do" (Eph. 2:10, italics added), and "They *invent ways of doing evil*" (Rom. 1:30, Easy-to-Read Version, italics added).

Our knowledge can and is used for both good and bad purposes. It can easily be argued that nothing is more dangerous than a knowledgeable, intelligent person who, lacking the restraint of godly wisdom, is bent on evil. If intelligence is one's capacity for mentally processing information or knowledge, wisdom is the ability to process knowledge not just with the mind, but with our whole person—mind, heart, spirit, and body. And godly wisdom is, most of all, deeply spiritual.

The Bible argues that there is no real wisdom apart from the knowledge of God, and to deny God and his wisdom is the ultimate in foolishness—"The fear of the Lord is the beginning of knowledge, but fools despise wisdom and instruction" (Prov. 1:7). If God exists and is who the Bible claims him to be, then the denial of God is the greatest sin and failure of all—"The fool says in his heart, 'There is no God'" (Ps. 14:1). Even though it is quite humanly understandable, denying the existence of an intelligent designer and creator in our incredibly well-designed universe is even more absurd than denying that a lovely, beautifully decorated mansion had an actual architect and builder!

In addition to godly wisdom, there is also wisdom that is worldly. Worldly wisdom is, in fact, not really wisdom at all but rather is foolishness. But it is indeed the way the world processes information and knowledge. Such "wisdom" is humanistic and self-serving. In the end it will spell the doom of its users—"Although they claimed to be wise, they became fools" (Rom. 1:22). Worldly wisdom is the ability, in this present life, to use knowledge, intelligence, and so forth for selfish purposes and gain. Godly wisdom, on the other hand, is the ability to use all we possess rightly according to the plan and purposes of God.

Godly and worldly wisdom are generally best discerned and differentiated by their long-term outcomes and the standards by which they are measured—"But wisdom is proved right by her deeds" (Matt. 11:19), and "Who is wise and understanding among you? Let them show it by their good life, by deeds done in the humility that comes from wisdom" (James 3:13). Godly wisdom achieves the purposes of God; worldly wisdom seeks to accomplish the desires of those imposters among us who seek to act as if *we are* gods.

Worldly wisdom produces arrogance and ignorance, and it is most destructive—"But if you harbor bitter envy and selfish ambition in your hearts, do not boast about it or deny the truth. Such 'wisdom' does not come down from heaven but is earthly, unspiritual, demonic. For where you have envy and selfish ambition, there you find disorder and every evil practice" (James 3:14–16). Worldly wisdom is selfish, prideful, subjective, and impure.

On the other hand, godly wisdom is easily identifiable over time, seen by its true humility and godly purposes—"But the wisdom that comes from heaven is first of all pure; then peace-loving, considerate, submissive, full of mercy and good fruit, impartial and sincere. Peacemakers who sow in peace reap a harvest of righteousness" (James 3:17–18). Godly wisdom is unselfish, meek, objective, and pure. Such wisdom is otherworldly because it is not of this world; it is of God and the kingdom of God. It can only be had through God. It does not and cannot originate with humanity.

The universe is the temple of Yahweh, and all that exists is consecrated for his purposes—"For in him all things were created: things in heaven and on earth, visible and invisible, whether thrones or powers or rulers or authorities; all things have been created through him and for him" (Col. 1:16). Any other uses of this world than for God are desecrations of what he has designed and created. Even our bodies themselves are created for him to cohabitate with us—"Do you not know that your bodies are temples of the Holy Spirit, who is in you, whom you have received from God?" (1 Cor. 6:19).

To live aligned, then, with God's predetermined design and purposes for creation and for our role in it, we must above all seek out his wisdom—"Get wisdom, get understanding; do not forget my words or turn away from them. Do not forsake wisdom, and she will protect you; love her, and she will watch over you. The beginning of wisdom is this: Get wisdom. Though it cost all you have, get understanding. Cherish her, and she will exalt you; embrace her, and she will honor you. She will give you a garland to grace your head and present you with a glorious crown" (Prov. 4:5–9).

And godly wisdom can only be had from a trusting relationship with God—"If any of you lacks wisdom, you should ask God, who gives generously to all without finding fault, and it will be given to you. But when you ask, you must believe and not doubt, because the one who doubts is like a wave of the sea, blown and tossed by the wind. That person should not expect to receive anything from the Lord. Such a person is double-minded and unstable in all they do" (James 1:5–8).

The kingdom of God is inverted from the kingdom of this present dark world. It is in actuality the original right-side-up world God created. The kingdom of the world is what is upside down. Thus God's wisdom will generally be seen as upside down to those who see the worldly as the norm—"For the message of the cross is foolishness to those who are perishing, but to us who are being saved it is the power of God" (1 Cor. 1:18). But God's wisdom supersedes and reigns supreme over all that humanism can conjure—"For the foolishness of God is wiser than human wisdom, and the weakness of God is stronger than human strength" (1 Cor. 1:25).

From the shores of eternity, the wisdom of God beckons us, even calls us, in this present tumultuous world, as a lighthouse beckons the weary sailor out on a storm-tossed sea—"Now then, my children, listen to me; blessed are those who keep my ways. Listen to my instruction and be wise; do not disregard it. Blessed are those who listen to me, watching daily at my doors, waiting at my doorway. For those who find me find life and receive favor from the LORD. But those who fail to find me harm themselves; all who hate me love death" (Prov. 8:32–36).

To ignore wisdom's lighthouse beacon is to choose to he dashed on the rocks this side of eternity; to heed the light is to find eternal safe harbor.

A Prayer:

> Father, give us wisdom to use the knowledge that we have (Ott Hollis, Ratliff City Church of Christ, Ratliff City, Oklahoma, 1963).

98
Worldliness, Part 1

Sadly, the failure of Christians to grow is pandemic. In the name of numerical growth, and because of carelessness and laziness, the church and Christian families have masterfully produced an endemic lukewarm-ness and mediocrity among the Christian masses. Individual disciples have failed to truly follow Christ and take personal responsibility for growing spiritually.

We have much to say about this, but it is hard to make it clear to you because you no longer try to understand. In fact, though by this time you ought to be teachers, you need someone to teach you the elementary truths of God's word all over again. You need milk, not solid food! Anyone who lives on milk, being still an infant, is not acquainted with the teaching about righteousness. But solid food is for the mature, who by constant use have trained themselves to distinguish good from evil (Heb. 5:11–14).

WORLDLINESS IS THE opposite of holiness. Holiness is the state of being set apart for God's purposes alone. It is living by the Spirit of God—"Those who are led by the Spirit of God are the children of God" (Rom. 8:14). The Holy Spirit's work in us as Christians is to sanctify us or to make us holy—God's alone. To continue to live worldly or carnal lives, especially under the guise of actually serving God in it, is purely of Satan, the Deceiver. We deceive it is because we are ourselves deceived. We are indeed assigned to live in this world, but we must not be of the world, or else we simply are the world—"I do not ask You to take them out of the world, but to keep them from the evil *one*. They are not of the world, even as I am not of the world. Sanctify them in the truth; Your word is truth" (John 17:15–17).

It is our responsibility, collectively as churches and Christian families and individually as disciples, to carefully follow Jesus, ensuring growth in him, because of his transforming power in us—"Therefore, my brothers and sisters, make every effort to confirm your calling and election. For if you do these things, you will never stumble" (2 Pet. 1:10). We are in fact to "make every effort" available to ensure our growth and development in Christ. Growing in Christ means becoming increasingly and solely to God. Our roles in spiritual growth cannot be delegated and must not be relegated to anyone or any entity. Our growth is our responsibility. However, other individuals, parents, churches, and church leaders will all be held accountable now as well as later for their roles in individual and collective spiritual development—"Fire will test the quality of each person's work" (1 Cor. 3:13), and "Have confidence in your leaders and submit to their authority, because *they keep watch over you as those who must give an account*" (Heb. 13:17, italics added).

We must make sure that it is Jesus that we are making every effort to follow and that we are teaching others to make every effort to follow. All should be in accordance with Christ rather than slavishly aligned with the dictates of philosophical church views and mere human reasoning, devoid of biblical or spiritual substantiation, or the failing social and church traditions sometimes sloppily handed down to us—"See to it that no one takes you captive through hollow and deceptive philosophy, which depends on human tradition and the elemental spiritual forces of this world rather than on Christ" (Col. 2:8).

Complacency and apathy are, of course, not new human maladies. Ancient Israel was warned of impending judgment because of just that—"At that time I will search Jerusalem with lamps and punish those who are complacent, who are like wine left on its dregs, who think, 'The Lord will do nothing, either good or bad'" (Zeph. 1:12). On the contrary, scripture teaches us to be full of zeal for God and our service to him—"Never be lacking in zeal, but keep your spiritual fervor, serving the Lord" (Rom. 12:11). Jesus, our supreme role model, was noted for his fiery service to God—"Zeal for your house will consume me" (John 2:17, Ps. 69:9).

The early churches, too, battled worldliness and complacency—"I could not address you as people who live by the Spirit but as people who are still worldly—mere infants in Christ" (1 Cor. 3:1), and "I know your deeds, that you are neither cold nor hot. I wish you were either one or the other!" (Rev. 3:15). But such worldliness and complacency are repugnant to Christ—"Because you are lukewarm—neither hot nor cold—I am about to spit you out of my mouth" (Rev. 3:16). We must not settle for it.

All of us struggle with worldliness, sometimes more than other times. But just because our flesh is drawn to it, we must never succumb to it and let the exception become the rule. All of us are prone at times to use our Christian freedom to gratify the desire of our personal sinful natures, albeit often justifying it as a way to "help" or "reach" others—"You...were called to be free. But do not use your freedom to indulge the flesh" (Gal. 5:13). We must take prayerful care to not fool ourselves and certainly not to try to fool God. Worldliness is comfortable to our fleshly natures but uncomfortable to our spiritual one.

Modern "cool" Christianity—laid-back, often-intellectual, and complacent Christianity—is not really modern. Its spiritual tradition is as old as the Garden of Eden. The Spirit within us will fight against any regression of the one born again back to the old nature—"For the flesh desires what is contrary to the Spirit, and the Spirit what is contrary to the flesh. They are in conflict with each other, so that you are not to do whatever you want" (Gal. 5:17). And it is our responsibility to actively fight against this old nature of ours!

To be worldly is to oppose God.

A Prayer:

> Father, help me to be solely of you and for you.
> Defeat my fleshly, fallen nature within me that makes me wander.
> Rather, fill me with your Spirit that my focus might be laser sharp on you.
> I am sorry when I desire and enjoy worldly things that are against you.
> Transform me by your Holy Spirit that I can desire only that which is from you.
> Have mercy on me, and forgive me, that I can approach you with freedom and confidence.
> Have mercy on those I love and on all people, as none of us is worthy of you.
> Amen.

99
Worldliness, Part 2

Our salvation is by faith from beginning to end, not just in the beginning. We are not just expected to come to faith but also to *live* by faith. When we break faith with God and allow worldliness to encroach on our walk with him, it will literally choke the spiritual life right out of us.

Still others, like seed sown among thorns, hear the word; but the worries of this life, the deceitfulness of wealth and the desires for other things come in and choke the word, making it unfruitful (Mark 4:18–19).

SIN'S CORRUPTING INFLUENCE exempts no one; it excludes none. In coming to faith, we are made new again in Christ—"If anyone is in Christ, the new creation has come: The old has gone, the new is here!" (2 Cor. 5:17). It is God himself that remakes us in Christ and gives us a completely new life—"We were therefore buried with him through baptism into death in order that, *just as Christ was raised from the dead through the glory* [power] *of the Father, we too may live a new life*" (Rom. 6:4, italics and brackets added).

Our faith is in God's power to remake and renew us. Our confidence must not be in anything of this world, ourselves or anyone else—"Your whole self ruled by the flesh was put off when you were circumcised by Christ, having been buried with him in baptism, in which you were also raised with him through your faith in the working of God, who raised him from the dead" (Col. 2:11–12). Faith is not a standalone virtue though; faith is *in* something or someone. For the believer that someone is God!

According to his own divine right and ability, God predetermined to see us in Christ as completely without sin or blame! It was his plan from the beginning of creation—"For he chose us in him before the creation of the world to be holy and blameless in his sight" (Eph. 1:4). It is God and God alone who can enable us to become his children; no one else, nor any institution, has a say—"To all who did receive him, to those who believed in his name, he gave the right to become children of God—children born not of natural descent, nor of human decision or a husband's will, but born of God" (John 1:12–13). Since each is given by God this exquisite personal right to have a relationship with him in Christ, each must accept the commensurate gravity of the accompanying personal responsibility. On a much greater scale and to a deeper degree, our relationship to God is as with marriage. We come into the faith relationship of marriage by saying "I do," but that doesn't *make* the relationship; it only *begins* the marriage. A good relationship takes daily effort and care.

As fallen creatures we have no "right" to salvation on our own apart from God. It is by God's choice and election alone that we may be saved. It is by his exclusive calling and selection of us that we are, by an act of his grace, given the right to come to him—"No one can come to me unless the Father who sent me draws them" (John 6:44).

How God does all this, no one knows and none can fully understand, no matter how smart we seem or make ourselves sound—"Oh, the depth of the riches of the wisdom and knowledge of God!

How unsearchable his judgments, and his paths beyond tracing out! 'Who has known the mind of the Lord? Or who has been his counselor?'" (Rom. 11:33–34).

Further, our subsequent growth in Christ is also of God's own doing—"We all, who with unveiled faces contemplate the Lord's glory, are being transformed into his image with ever-increasing glory, which comes from the Lord, who is the Spirit" (2 Cor. 3:18). Just as it is by an act of grace that we are given the right to come to Christ, it is by God's grace and his continuing work that we are also being transformed to become more and more like Jesus.

It is God, then, who first justifies us, or declares us as right before him—"We have been justified through faith, we have peace with God through our Lord Jesus Christ, through whom we have gained access by faith into this grace in which we now stand" (Rom. 5:1–2). And it is God working through the Holy Spirit who transforms us or sanctifies us. Sanctification is God making us holy—set apart for his purposes.

However, we have been, by God's eternal plan, given certain rights and choices, along with the associated inherent responsibilities—"Choose for yourselves this day whom you will serve" (Josh. 24:15), and "Seek the Lord while he may be found; call on him while he is near" (Isa. 55:6). These are granted to us only by acts of God's grace (his gifting) toward us; we have no actual rights to them separate and apart from him. They can only be gotten through his gifting them to us—not by our attainment but by his atonement!

We will be judged for the choices we make and how we exercise these God-given rights. God's wants all to come to him—"[God] wants all people to be saved and to come to a knowledge of the truth" (1 Tim. 2:4), and "He [God] is patient with you, not wanting anyone to perish, but everyone to come to repentance" (2 Pet. 3:9). However, sadly, by Christ's own admission, few will actually do so—"Small is the gate and narrow the road that leads to life, and only a few find it" (Matt. 7:14).

As we can choose not to receive Christ and thus not be chosen because our hearts indict and convict us, we can also impede his work in us after receiving him—"Do not quench the Spirit" (1 Thess. 5:19). We are given continuing faith responsibilities regarding our own salvation in order to continue to access his work in us—"Continue to work out your salvation with fear and trembling, for it is God who works in you to will and to act in order to fulfill his good purpose" (Phil. 2:12–13).

But our carnal, fleshly nature will continue to haunt us and to want what it wants. However we, by the power of Christ's Spirit living in us, must contend against it—"Walk by the Spirit, and you will not gratify the desires of the flesh" (Gal. 5:16). And, his Spirit is far greater than the spirit that seeks to influence our flesh—"The one who is in you is greater than the one who is in the world" (1 John 4:4).

We can only eschew worldliness by choosing godliness.

A Prayer:

Father, my heart desires what's worldly,
My flesh delights in sin,
Strengthen me to be like you, Lord,
Transform me completely within.

I praise you for your grace, God,
I am desperate for what is of you,
As I kneel before you, renew me,
That your will for me I can do.

100
Worldliness, Part 3

The Christian's drift back toward worldliness can be ever so subtle and, in the near term, easily unnoticed. Decadence, egotism, contentiousness, complacency, laziness, selfishness, and self-justification are some of its red danger flags. Every single one of us must search the Spirit's scrutiny of us to see ourselves as God sees us.

Brothers and sisters, I could not address you as people who live by the Spirit but as people who are still worldly—mere infants in Christ (1 Cor. 3:1).

SCRIPTURE TELLS US that the fruit of the worldly, carnal nature, even among Christians, is obvious—"The acts of the flesh are obvious: sexual immorality, impurity and debauchery; idolatry and witchcraft; hatred, discord, jealousy, fits of rage, selfish ambition, dissensions, factions and envy; drunkenness, orgies, and the like. I warn you, as I did before, that those who live like this will not inherit the kingdom of God" (Gal. 5:19–22). It is impossible to draw a line, logically, as to when any of these sins become to us "how we live" rather than sin exceptions in an otherwise holy life. But alarm bells should go off within us when we see the creep of any desire for or aspect of anyone of them into our daily lives. Hints of their presence should drive us to our knees in humility before him and never into the "bushes" in shame away from him. No matter what, always run to God not away from him!

Before worldliness is to be seen outwardly in us, it will exist first inwardly—"Each person is tempted when they are dragged away by their own evil desire and enticed. Then, after desire has conceived, it gives birth to sin; and sin, when it is full-grown, gives birth to death" (James 1:14–15). What makes certain things sin in the first place is determined by the inner motives. And most any behavior can be sinful if what drives it is not godly—"Everything that does not come from faith is sin" (Rom. 14:23).

Evil thoughts and motives come from the heart, and they defile us—"Out of the heart come evil thoughts—murder, adultery, sexual immorality, theft, false testimony, slander. These are what defile a person" (Matt. 15:19–20). Sadly, we can regurgitate on ourselves, and then, even worse than that, wallow in it. In sin, we ultimately vomit what is toxic within us on all around us.

Why do I do what I do; that is, what are the motives of my carnal nature? The reality is it is impossible to fully determine all the motives of the flesh—"I do not understand what I do. For what I want to do I do not do, but what I hate I do" (Rom. 7:15). But be certain, the motives of the carnal nature are counterproductive and destructive. Christ is the one good and godly motive for all right, spiritual behavior—"For to me, to live is Christ" (Phil. 1:21), and "Whatever you do, work at it with all your heart, as working for the Lord" (Col. 3:23). All else is of the flesh.

And there is nothing static about the Christian life. Either we are moving forward or we are moving backward. Either we are growing or we are dying. To live by faith in God is to remain faithful in learning, growing, and loving him. A failure to maintain faithfulness in adherence to Christ's word causes faith to be useless—"By this gospel you are saved, if you hold firmly to the word I preached to you. Otherwise, you have believed in vain" (1 Cor. 15:2). There is a vain, useless faith that the Christian can fall into. But we must not, for it is to us a new, worse kind of deadly—"If they have escaped the corruption of the world by knowing our Lord and Savior Jesus Christ and are again entangled in it and are overcome, they are worse off at the end than they were at the beginning" (2 Pet. 2:20). What could actually be worse than the hellish prospects of the original unbeliever? We should never hope to find out!

Doing the will of Christ, and thus receiving his final promises, requires a lifelong perseverance of wholehearted effort—"You need to persevere so that when you have done the will of God, you will receive what he has promised" (Heb. 10:36). Faith must be our lifestyle; faith must be "kept" in order for it to matter at all—"'But my righteous one will live by faith. And I take no pleasure in the one who shrinks back.' But we do not belong to those who shrink back and are destroyed, but to those who have faith and are saved" (Hab. 2:4, Heb. 10:38–39), and "I have fought the good fight, I have finished the race, *I have kept the faith*" (2 Tim. 4:7, italics added).

Just as a once-promising, fulfilling marriage can become passionless and apathetic over time, so can our individual and collective relationships to God—"I know your deeds, your hard work and your perseverance. I know that you cannot tolerate wicked people, that you have tested those who claim to be apostles but are not, and have found them false. You have persevered and have endured hardships for my name, and have not grown weary. Yet I hold this against you: *You have forsaken the love you had at first*" (Rev. 2:2–4, italics added). As with the loveless marriage, individuals and churches can walk down life's path, perhaps holding hands with God, but experiencing minimal real intimacy him—"Yet I hold this against you: You have forsaken the love you had at first" (Rev. 2:4).

Often, it is because an old lover—the world—has come calling and likely over time has wooed the unsuspecting back into an old deadly courtship. Infatuated by the world's charms, we can too easily fall victim to its unrelenting and deceptive "pickup lines." The world feeds our prideful egos. The world appeals to our baser instincts. It wraps its stifling cloak around us, and we can begin again to even proudly strut our worldliness, even our "Christian-worldliness." The world lures us through our worldly, carnal natures with its ultimate, original, and oldest line of all, if we will but come back to it—"Your eyes will be opened, and you will be like God" (Gen. 3:5). It's all a lie though!

We must not eat of the world's delicacies. We are to be in the world but not of the world. Rather, ours is to remember the truth and promises of the only real lover and savior of our souls, Jesus Christ, renewing our passions for him daily. Christ alone must be our only spiritual sustenance—"I am the living bread that came down from heaven. Whoever eats this bread will live forever" (John 6:51).

A Prayer:

> Remove from me, O Lord, all that is not of you.
> Conform me to your original design for me—to be like you.
> Give me an open heart that I might hear you.
> Grant me a trusting spirit that I might believe you.
> Produce within me a teachable mind that I might learn from you.
> Grow within me an ever-increasing desire that I might grow in you.
> Glorify yourself in me, Lord, whether in my pleasure or pain, whether in my honor or humiliation, whether in my prosperity or poverty.
> And grant me the only real life, the life that is eternal, found only in Jesus Christ my Lord.
> Amen.

Conclusion

I have long felt called, driven really, to think and write. I have been told variously that I don't need to think so much or talk so much. But I feel somewhat the spirit of Jeremiah within me that when I don't think, speak up, and write—"But if I say, 'I will not mention his word or speak anymore in his name,' his word is in my heart like a fire, a fire shut up in my bones. I am weary of holding it in; indeed, I cannot" (Jer. 20:9). It often burns inside of me. About sharing these inner thoughts, I feel similarly to our hero, the apostle Paul, as he shared how he felt about sharing the gospel with the world—"For when I preach the gospel, I cannot boast, since I am compelled to preach. Woe to me if I do not preach the gospel!" (1 Cor. 9:16). Woe to me as well if I don't share what is within me concerning God and his word.

For some it may appear as mere drivel. Perhaps to the deeper, more spiritual, or more learned, it is. To some I may appear an old fool merely rephrasing the great old truths into lesser expressions. Or even butchering them. But to me, these are my "God thoughts," those things I believe God has taught me, expressing the spiritual truths in the spiritual words that I've learned, as the Holy Spirit leads me to see (1 Cor. 2:13). I wake up early and think of them. I go to sleep thinking of them. I think of them as I drive down the road and go on long walks. Most of this book was written in the darkness and stillness of the early morning.

Intertwining so many scriptures into what I have written has come to be the way I think, as Paul said, "The word of Christ must live in you richly" (Col. 3:16, Common English Bible). Or, as Peter commanded, "If anyone speaks, they should do so as one who speaks the very words of God" (1 Pet. 4:11). I share so many scriptures because my thoughts now mostly flow from them and back to them. I believe anything not of God is at least useless or even worse, sinful. The words from God captivate me; I am enchanted by them. I marvel at their wisdom. So I love sharing them, letting them flow out of me as they have flowed into me.

I pray that more than just expressing my own God thoughts, they provoke within each reader their own musings on God. For these thoughts to have any positive effect on the reader, it is not enough for them to just remain as the thoughts of another; they must become owned by and personalized to each of us in order for them to mean anything at all.

A Closing Personal Poetic Rendering of Psalm 119:1–18

I wish my ways were blameless,
That I walked always according to your law,
I wish I kept your statutes,
Always held you in awe.

I wish I'd do no wrong, Lord,
Follow always in your ways,
Heard clearly all your precepts,
Was one who always obeys.

I wish my ways were steadfast,
In obeying all your decrees,
That I'd never feel the shame I feel,
When your commands I fail to heed.

I praise you with a sincere heart,
As your righteous laws I learn,
I seek to obey all your decrees,
So please do not me spurn.

How can young and old stay the way of purity?
By living according to your word.
I seek you, Lord, with all my heart,
May not one command be not heard.

I have hidden your word in my heart,
That I might not live in sin against you,
Praise be to you, O Lord, my God,
Lead me all your will to do!

With my lips I evermore recall,
All the laws that come from your mouth,
I rejoice to strive for them, everyone,
As for all riches, north to south!

I meditate on all your truths, my God,
Ever consider all that you are,
I delight in each and every command,
From my heart they are never far.

Be good to me while on earth I live,
Help me obey without one flaw,
Open my eyes to see all that is of you,
The beauty of all your law.

Other Books by Ronnie Worsham

Fighting and Beating Depression

Forty Days on the Mountain with God

Discovering Jesus

Reflections on Faith

A Funny Little Cow Ponders Pain (with Kristen Wilemon)